IN THE
FIFTIES

D1477317

IN THE
FIFTIES

PETER VANSITTART

JOHN MURRAY
Albemarle Street, London

To Moyra Fraser and Roger Lubbock

7594

© Peter Vansittart 1995

First published in 1995
by John Murray (Publishers) Ltd.,
50 Albemarle Street, London W1X 4BD

A catalogue record for this book is available from the British Library

ISBN 0–7195–5300 8

Typeset in 12½/13 Bembo by Colset Private Limited, Singapore
Printed and bound in Great Britain by
The University Press, Cambridge

Contents

Illustrations

All pictures are reproduced courtesy of the
Hulton Deutsch Collection and first appeared in
Picture Post.

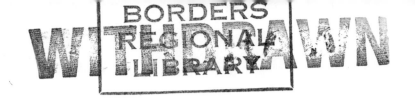

Introduction

THIS IS NOT autobiography, though autobiography intrudes, nor an anthology, nor an academic survey, but rather an impression of how life seemed to me in the Fifties, somewhat influenced by how it seems to me now. It is far from conclusive. My mind is unanalytical and is generally rated narrow and self-absorbed; my interest in sartorial fashions, Pop Art, smart restaurants, passing celebrities, wild singers, is minimal and C. P. Snow's definition of the Two Cultures found me wanting. My memory, of course, has lapses, but I have no obvious axe to grind, save to provide readable entertainment. At the start of the Fifties I was 30. I had spoken to Nijinsky and received no reply; had known a saint, Wilfrid Israel; as far as I knew, had met but one murderer, Leslie Hylton, Test Match cricketer, to be hanged in 1955; and had taught one future Cabinet minister, Henry Brooke. Today, the young are inclined to respect me, not for my personality, which they do not notice, or for my work, which they do not know, but for my longevity. 'You were there. In the Sixties. You saw History being made.' Actually I did not, and the Sixties recall for me little save huge coiffures, pretentious idleness, much noise, a drizzle of slogans, some curiously named Adult Cinema, gaily tinted and over-priced clothes, skirts rising rapidly, prices rising more slowly.

Probably because I was younger and, if not purer, at least not very worldly wise, I enjoyed the Fifties, often laughing immoderately. If sometimes melancholy, I was seldom wretched; certainly not, like Hamlet, wretched in a dramatic way. These feelings make me wish to recall the decade, itself often dismissed as a mere prelude to the Sixties, without remorse or rancour and, I hope, without nostalgia. In 1950,

1

with a meagre income from teaching and book-reviewing, I was striving to establish myself as a writer, an ambition based more on desire than on substantial equipment. Blandly educated at enjoyable but conventional schools, I had managed to remain sensitive to human oddity and keep an eye open for the bizarre. A very early memory was of being taken to see Father Christmas at a department store but, alas for innocence, we found two red-gowned, white-bearded toughs, sodden and reeking with beer, quarrelling with much obscenity about rights of pitch, a conflict that safeguarded me forever against surprise and disappointment, making me wary of adult institutions and reputations. I thought it very appropriate when I read, years later, that Hitler's skull lay in bits, one with a bullet hole in it, inside a box marked 'Blue Ink for Pens', in Moscow.

As a child I had some mistaken awe for the diction of the Prime Minister, Ramsay MacDonald, whose grave reminder that it was impossible to clip the wings of the rising tide made politics appear a constant fight to the last ditch with one's back to the wall. My imagination was further fostered by indiscriminate reading: the lighter works of 'Sapper' and Wodehouse – ' "They?" said Bingo, surprised that the butler should have spoken of his employer, stout though she was, in the plural' – Richard Jefferies' *Bevis*, Carlyle's history of *The French Revolution* or sections of it, *Little Women, Just William, Jew Süss*, biographies of such fellows as W. G. Grace, Napoleon III, Dr Crippen, Robespierre. These were all overlaid by Hollywood melodramas, romantic speculations and the cricketing extravagances of Don Bradman. Overheard conversations could interest, if not enthral. 'Shall I compare thee to a summer's day?' 'No.'

By the Fifties, I had learnt that prayers are often answered, but ironically or sardonically, so that the longed-for gift arrives years too late; the first book gets published, to tumultuous jeers; the beautiful girl, at last acquiescent, proves a major crook; the cheque bounces so high that it scars the ceiling.

I had published three novels. The first, about an imaginary dictator, was greeted rather tepidly in *John O'London's Weekly* – 'This must be the worst book ever published' – the second concerned a French and a German family during the Franco-Prussian War, the third traced Nazi elements in a German provincial town, in 1922. None of them sold, indeed the first was the only book left unread during the book-hungry wartime years. Nevertheless, I now had a platform, however rickety.

Certain decades attract labels – Naughty Nineties, Roaring Twenties, Swinging Sixties – but I find none for my period, despite Hannah

Arendt's contempt for 'the disgusting, posturing Fifties'. I was very conscious in 1950 of much that remained from the Thirties; ageing celebrities, ancient rituals – the Chelsea Flower Show, the Lord Mayor's Show, the Cup Final, the Promenade Concerts. The Gentlemen still met the Players at Lord's, Neville Cardus remained on the *Manchester Guardian*, writing on cricket and music in prose that suggested the former was an adjunct of the latter. Trams still ran to Greenwich. *Picture Post* showed a live Mexican soldier who had been one of the firing-squad at the execution of the Emperor Maximilian, depicted in Manet's painting of the event. He died in 1952, aged 101. Still working and honoured in Yugoslavia were two of the murderers of Archduke Franz Ferdinand whose death precipitated the Great War. For this they felt no remorse, for had not the conflict produced Yugoslavia itself?

Elsewhere, echoes of the past reverberated. France was grappling with her Fourth Republic – how many Frenchmen, I wondered priggishly, could readily identify the other three? De Gaulle was in eclipse, awaiting his triumphant day of return in the 1958 Algerian crisis. Grandly ignoring television, the telephone and journalists, he was writing memoirs in classical French, but seldom speaking. 'Nothing', he wrote, 'more enhances authority than silence: it is the crowning virtue of the strong.' He might not have relished comparison with the Jacobin terrorist Saint-Just, who had remarked that power belongs to the impassive, to the laconic. Pétain, hero of Verdun, and leader of Vichy, was incarcerated on the Île d'Yeu in the Bay of Biscay on a charge of treason, dying in 1951.

In Japan, divested of godhead and unofficially considered a war criminal, Hirohito remained Emperor. His reign was formally designated 'Enlightened Peace'. Announcing surrender, he had mentioned that the war was 'not necessarily to Japan's advantage', adding that Japan had waged war 'as part of the process of striving for the coming prosperity of all nations'. China's last Son of Heaven, Pu-yi, Japan's puppet ruler of Manchuria, was currently in a Russian jail, before being promoted in 1959 to assist the Chinese economy as a gardener.

And from Germany, a powerful film – *The Murderers are Amongst Us* – was a grim reminder that the past was still with us, for many Nazis had clawed or slid back into influence. Not so the gifted, intelligent, morally irresponsible architect and Hitler's favourite, Albert Speer, imprisoned in Spandau alongside Deputy Führer Rudolf Hess. There he had seen what he could never have forgotten: eleven Allied soldiers staring into the eleven condemned cells where Göring, Ribbentrop, Streicher and other leaders of the Master Race awaited the rope: 'As the rules demanded, most are lying on their backs on the blanket, heads turned to the inside of the cell. A ghostly sight, all of them in their immobility as though already laid in their biers.'

Such matters and images were jostling in my head, around 1950, and from these I yearned to become, at some distant date, a serious writer.

1

Literary Survivors

'I AM DETERMINED to get into the literary world,' a woman in a red skirt, with wooden earrings, told me, 'but where is it?' I could not tell her then and I could not tell her now. My own title deeds were very obscure and, in 1950, I knew few writers. Once I had joined others for tea with Lord Alfred Douglas, when querulous, high-pitched, he told us, in monologues evidently of long standing, about Wilde, *The Yellow Book* and Churchill's iniquities, but I remember little else of what should have been an occasion of some moment. Douglas was always indigent. His lost libel actions could not have helped, and I had been warned to leave five shillings on departure. This worried me and I could think of little else. I could not envisage the procedure; I could not very cheerfully imagine slipping it into that gaunt hand. I had read, somewhere in Compton Mackenzie, that you left a tart's hard cash on the mantelpiece, but this recollection was discouraging. I think I left two half-crowns on my chair, where perhaps they slipped down beside the deep, shabby cushion. I do remember Douglas clutching the *Oxford Mail*, reading aloud some article, then demanding: 'Can any of you tell any difference between this and the so-called poetry of T. S. Eliot?' One of us could, and began to do so, which precipitated a rather hasty departure.

I had played cricket with another literary character antipathetic to Eliot – J. C. Squire, former literary editor of the *New Statesman*, anti-modernist, who dismissed *The Waste Land* as double Dutch and was apt to boast that he had never finished *War and Peace*. As a cricketer, he was enthusiastic, myopic, very inexpert, beery, prone to accidents. He once stalked out grandly to bat, unaware of the dead bird which had dropped from the sky on to his cap.

At school, I had much admired Stephen Spender. His poem 'Vienna' and his play, *Trial of a Judge*, for me wrenched poetry away from busy hedgerows, bosky solitudes and 'songsters', into the urgencies of unemployment, moral and physical courage, crucial personal choices. After school, I lived for a while with Wilfrid Israel, Anglo-German-Jewish businessman, sculptor, philanthropist, anti-Nazi, a mixture of Gandhi and the Scarlet Pimpernel, to whom Leslie Howard, Hollywood's Scarlet Pimpernel, compared him until they were shot down together, by the Germans, over the Bay of Biscay. Reticent, gifted, Wilfrid exemplified Camus's definition of charm, as a way of getting the answer 'yes', without having asked any definite question. In Isherwood's *Goodbye to Berlin*, he appears as Bernard Landauer.

To foster my self-confidence, Wilfrid affected ignorance of English literature. How, he diffidently asked, should he rate Robert Southey? Southey was no good. My opinion of Wordsworth? Over-valued, not least by himself. Tennyson? Elegant rot . . . As Eliot explains, as Auden says . . . But Stephen Spender? Ah! At Wilfrid's respectful curiosity, I quoted freely. I would pause to commend, compare, interpret, instruct, while Wilfrid, patient as a Buddha, nodded gratefully. Encouraged, I quoted further lines, implying that I had gathered them from Spender himself on long, intimate country walks or over cosy suppers. Then, one Sunday afternoon, during the interval at a Cambridge Theatre concert, a tall, glistening young man, a Viking on sabbatical, approached Wilfrid speaking in low, even conspiratorial tones, of such names as Adam von Trott. Wilfrid thought it unnecessary to introduce me. Afterwards, faintly aggrieved, I turned to him. 'Wilfrid . . . who was that?' Courteously enigmatic, he paused, though not for long. 'Stephen Spender.'

In 1950, my third novel won praise from a writer I had enjoyed, and whose critical stature I now redoubled – Pamela Hansford Johnson. She was a friend and briefly fiancée of Dylan Thomas, and her novel *This Bed thy Centre*, on a young virgin's physical terror of marriage, was a moving treatment of a theme not then much discussed. Tosco Fyvel, Orwell's successor on *Tribune*, advised me that to meet her would do me no harm. Actually it did. I sent her a card, thanking her, too fulsomely, for the review. She invited me for a drink. Cocoa. Never mind. I sat with her in her flat; she was dark, slender, friendly, informative, recommending, with some emphasis, the opening of Bram Stoker's *Dracula*. 'Mysteriously powerful atmosphere . . .' I had not read it and, feeling at a disadvantage, looked for a chance to retrieve myself. I muttered something about new writers . . . Francis King, Jocelyn Brooke, Denton Welch. But no. She refilled my cup with now-tepid cocoa, lavishly poured in cold milk, then shook her head. The coming novelist was C. P. Snow. 'There lies the future. I am convinced . . . you wait.' Unwilling to wait, chary of confessing total ignorance of this paragon, I replied, imitating her own tone, that he wrote irredeemable trash. 'Up and coming? I think not. They say he's a rocket already falling. A pity! Certain personal weaknesses, of course . . .'. She froze with the cocoa. She was Medea, she was Clytemnestra, I was back in the dark night, not until next week reading of her engagement to C. P. Snow.

Snow, from the Fifties, had large sales, though not unanimous critical esteem, as 'the modern Trollope'. He later aroused some discussion when, as a junior Labour minister, he sent a son to Eton, explaining that he would be more likely to meet his social equals there. Once, at a dinner, during a chance silence which quickly deepened, his voice was heard at the senior end of the table: 'I have to admit, though without more than a modicum of shame, that I am only in the Second Eleven . . . along, I suppose, with Trollope, Virginia Woolf, Forster, Turgenev, and we might include that man Bellow.' Frances Partridge, who had known Bloomsbury in its prime, met Lord and Lady Snow and recorded in her diary that the evening had been dull: 'Once people have become public figures, they seem to be pretty well doomed. All they want to do on social occasions is to show off and to secure to themselves admiration which is hardly necessary in view of their tremendous opinion of themselves.'

My youthful novel had given me more self-esteem than I had earned. In 1951 I was sitting opposite a fat man who talked, talked well, talked copiously. When at last he paused for breath, I leaned forward. 'You know so much about so many things . . . I wonder if you have ever thought of writing any of it down? I might perhaps . . .'

The eyes, small, within small bulges of flesh, were unamused: 'My name is Priestley.'

J. B. Priestley, for years a best-seller in fiction, journalism and the theatre, had written one of the best though least-known accounts of the Great War, in which he had served throughout and in which he was once blown up by a shell: *Margin Released*. His *English Journey* was one of the most vivid portrayals of 1930s England. His recent play, *An Inspector Calls*, attacking bourgeois smugness, greed and callousness, with Ralph Richardson as star, had been hugely acclaimed, not least in Russia. He was as 'committed', *engagé*, as the Thirties poets and current French writers. Arthur Koestler had mocked 'the French flu', British intellectual awe of moderately gifted Continentals – Brecht, Sartre, Camus and Anouilh, and from North America Marshall

McLuhan and Arthur Miller. Priestley's indignation matched that of the fierce young British dramatists, but he also had insights into dreams and fantasy which, if they possessed them, they kept concealed. He had never needed Camus to know that to write is to choose.

'I have no genius but I have one hell of a lot of talent,' he would rumble, often followed by 'I'm not quite as good as most of my readers think I am, but a damned sight better than the remainder imagines.' For years he had raged at pollution, the shoddy, the fraudulent and the hypocritical. Always vigorously independent, he had refused to broadcast accounts of merchant seamen's wartime heroism unless he was allowed to promise them post-war escape from vile conditions. In the Fifties, his energies were unabated. Amongst his delights, listed in 1951, were: teasing bureaucrats; orchestras tuning up; home music; being recognized in public, especially by head waiters; London streets resembling stage sets; cooking at picnics; watching old-style actor laddies swaying into pubs, with loud checks, loud voices; fountains. By the late Fifties he was becoming a traditional man of letters, big-hatted and cloaked, banging away about Jung, democracy, Falstaff, atomic policies, using words like 'magic', 'wonder', 'ecstasy', not current among the élite. These condescended to him as bustling, quirky, over-hearty Jolly Jack, more craftsman than artist, aggressively insular in his approach: 'The Mediterranean is too classical and cut-and-dried; too many damned olives.' Theatre of the Absurd, of Cruelty, of Anger made him caustic, though he had experimented in them, together with his own Theatre of Time. Complaining of intellectual disrespect, he did much to invite it. Grossly philistine, new audiences and readers declared, remembering childhood hatred of his pre-war blockbuster, *The Good Companions*.

He was indomitably pessimistic, writing in *World Review* (1949), 'I am sure the novel is a decaying literary form, capable, of course, of still offering us much distinguished and sensitive work, but no longer the form that absorbs some of the mightiest energies of our time.' Almost daily, from somewhere, his running commentary continued, as telling as Orwell's, and, despite his misgivings, he produced a row of contemporary novels: satirical, nostalgic, or combative.

The death in 1950 of George Bernard Shaw was the passing of a great personality but not the death of an era, for the best of Shaw had died years before, though books, plays, letters to *The Times* continued almost to the end, his *Buoyant Billions* being performed in London in 1949. After a slow start, he had been a world celebrity for over fifty years. On his death, a savage obituary appeared signed by his old friend and opponent H. G. Wells, which had lain like a time bomb since 1945, with accusations of conceited mendacity, emotional coldness, dishonest thinking and much else. It was the splutter of a great but deeply flawed and physically unimpressive man against a public charmer. Wells, a poor speaker, always resented Shaw's platform fluency, his unfailing good humour on which Wells's attacks melted like snowflakes, his adroitness in getting laughs, with an actor's flair dodging serious questions with a quip, witty, dismissive, but often barely relevant.

A generous man, he had tried to help the ruined Wilde, whom he had not much liked. In this he was exceptional. Vyvyan Holland remembered that one who angrily refused was the Pre-Raphaelite painter Holman Hunt, famous for *The Light of the World*. Behind the pirouetting, entertaining GBS was probably the more essential Shaw, shy, awkward, lonely, ill-schooled, who had known poverty and neglect, in London having to calculate the cost of a bus fare against that of shoe leather, developing wit and comedy to use against a world badly organized, philistine, cruel. Unlike many artists and writers, he spent much time speaking on public issues, working hard on committees and as a local councillor – he established women's lavatories in Camden Town – ridiculing some sacred cows, while remaining devoted to others. He had written to Henry James in 1907, 'There is absolutely no other sense in life than the work of changing it.'

For most of our lives he had been issuing lay encyclicals, as 'an unofficial Bishop of Everywhere', on politics, war, Russia, zoology, biology, the iniquities of doctors and meat eaters – he and Hitler were the most famous vegetarians of the age, after Tolstoy's death – economics, sex, education, H. G., the theatre, socialism . . .

'The capitalist economy of rent, idleness and waste is uneconomic and therefore unfavourable to virtue. The capitalist idea is to get more than you receive. The socialist idea, the economic idea, the gentlemanly idea, to give more than you can get.' He enjoyed making such statements as 'Liberty under the British Parliamentary system means slavery for nine-tenths of the people, and slave-exploitation or parasitic idolatry and snobbery for the rest.' On his visit to Russia, he must have seen but yet not observed actual slavery on roads, canals, railways. He was always a discouraging and slippery presence for those progressives who assumed his support. He had made mocking dissent at the Great War, but responded to a proposed No More War mass rally in 1922 in terms probably identical to those he would have made about CND marches in the Fifties: 'I grieve to say that I don't believe in these demonstrations. People who get so excited about peace are precisely the people who get emotionally excited about war.' They would do better to remain at home and read GBS. 'I write so well that it is a pleasure to read what I have to say on any subject for the few people who read anything at all; but the world goes on just as it did before.' In 1919, Shaw supported proposals for prison reform, while adding that incurable criminals should be gassed. In the first month of the war he praised Hitler and, like Lloyd George, supported acceptance of his peace terms.

Stories about him are manifold, usually agreeable. Colin Smythe tells of Shaw, before the Great War, playing cricket at Lady Gregory's Coole Park in Ireland, 'in a most civilized manner', an unlikely vision, but made more convincing by the addition that, when fielding, he employed a servant to chase the ball, so that he himself could then return it to the bowler.

Leonard Woolf, however, remembered that, 'If one met him anywhere, he would come up and greet one with what seemed to be warmth and pleasure and he would start straight away with a fountain of words, scintillating with wit and humour. You might easily flatter yourself that you were the one person in Europe to whom at that moment the famous George Bernard Shaw wanted to talk, but if you happened to look into that slightly fishy, ice-blue eye of his, you got a shock. It was not looking at you; you were nowhere in its orbit; it was looking through you or over you into a distant world or universe inhabited almost entirely by G.B.S.'

Gordon Craig thought Shaw was extremely charming with one person, fidgety with two, and stood on his head with four. Concerned for humanity at large, Shaw was thoughtless with his domestic staff. After his wife's death, and so many years of marriage, he said that only after reading her correspondence with T. E. Lawrence had he realized that she was deeply religious.

No determinist, uninterested in the Freudian unconscious, he was a natural existentialist long before Sartre, believing in the endless trial-and-error processes of Life Force, which required ample assistance from human will, its passions, courage and, above all, hard work. He invited one to feel 'part of a mighty purpose . . . instead of a feverish, selfish little clod of ailments and grievances'. Socialism he defined as a movement in which each man or woman is a hero. For socialists like Shaw and Wells, as much as for T. S. Eliot and Ezra Pound, the Century of the Common Man was unwelcome: they wanted the Uncommon Man and a high culture. Loathing poverty, Shaw wanted the poor not to be contented pigs but discontented Socrateses. His Seven Deadly Sins were 'Food, clothing, firing, rent, taxes, respectability and children. Nothing can lift those seven millstones from man's neck but money; and the spirit cannot soar until the millstones are lifted.'

In his plays he was a constant off-stage presence; perverse, teasing, irresponsible, mischievous, covering intellectual lacunae with ingenious exposition, rapid-fire eloquence, amiable raillery. He seldom probed very deep. That some of Mrs Warren's girls were not driven to prostitution by poverty, but by complex relations with fathers, siblings, teachers, pimps, by suppressed lesbianism, by actual enjoyment of the game, he ignored.

Considerable anarchism underlay his logic and orderliness. He was once asked to 'do something' for a local school: 'I offered a handsome prize for the worst-behaved boy and girl, on condition that a record should be kept of their subsequent careers and compared with the records of the best behaved, in order to ascertain whether the school criterion of good conduct was valid out of school. My offer was refused because it would not have the effect of encouraging the children to give as little trouble as possible which is, of course, the real object of conduct prizes in schools.'

He relied always on being forgiven as the friendly comedian, which prevented him from being seriously regarded even by those who laughed the loudest. After the Great War he conducted a love affair with the world with panache and goodwill, in the spirited process of getting almost everything wrong. He and the Webbs were as much appeasers as Chamberlain, Hoare and Simon. He vigorously supported the Ribbentrop-Molotov Pact and scorned those who did not, applauding 'the joyful news that Hitler is now under the thumb of Stalin.'

Incapable of cruelty even to a walnut, Shaw was increasingly ruthless in his opinions which, by the Fifties, still in the aftermath of war, debarred him from much serious consideration. 'If', Shaw wrote, in whatever tone of voice, 'we desire a certain type of civilization and culture we must exterminate the sort of people who do not fit into it.' One seldom discerned where the teasing ended. In old age he said to Stephen Winsten: 'All this talk of sacredness of human life seems piffle to me. As soon as lives become a burden to the community, the State must be unsentimental and dispose of its lunatics, its criminals and its misfits. The means, however, must be humane.' He compared Hitler to a stage Bolshevik but thought Stalin 'an English gentleman'.

In a radio series, his old friend Bertrand Russell told a story of a foreign woman begging Shaw to help rescue her husband from an Eastern European concentration camp. Shaw replied, in effect, that no such camps existed, and even if they did, her husband probably very much deserved to be in one, or very probably was trying to escape from her. Russell was outraged, attributing this to Shaw's inescapable vanity which always prevented him admitting any mistakes, or disowning previously stated beliefs. 'I never spoke to the man again.'

In childhood I continually heard of 'GBS', which I identified as a circus clown or a patent medicine. Later, I owed him much. He made literacy fun, while making fun of much that respectable adults most respected. He inferred a gay sense of getting on with the job, making work not only a job but a delight. To young unknown writers he was friendly, with advice and offers. Listening to St John Ervine's radio tribute on the night of Shaw's death – 'For I loved the man . . .' – I wept.

The years themselves added a postscript, inimitably Shavian. In 1956, I attended a Shaw Centenary Lunch. Attlee spoke, laconic, informative, about Shaw and the early Labour movement: Sybil Thorndike, Shaw's original Joan, then aged about 70, in a rapid, passionate, bravura outburst, movingly praised his unflagging labours for the theatre, for authors, for mankind, his generosity and style. Then, before Lewis Casson could get up, there arose from a side table an American academic, very loud, very drunk, who, mistaking the occasion for the centenary of Sybil Thorndike, felt himself called: 'A hundred years ago a little lady was born, came amongst us . . . does not look a day over eighty-five . . . I cherish this day . . .' Attlee stared like an astonished hare, Casson, Sybil Thorndike's husband, glared stagily from under bushy eyebrows, until willing hands dragged the speaker down, like Don Giovanni at his last supper.

The death of George Orwell, like Shaw also in 1950, was a loss now more relevant. Like Karl Kraus in pre-Hitler Vienna, he had thrust a moral spotlight on party hypocrisies, national injustices, false beliefs about the Spanish Civil War, the weaknesses of writers whom he personally much admired – Dickens, Shaw, Wells. Like Ezra Pound, but from a more acceptable podium, he denounced the political corruption of language, the squalid menace of Political Correctness. No poet himself, he earned respect from poets for his honesty and clarity, and once showed me Kraus's remark: 'The function of poetry is to upset the simple platitudes by which men live, to reveal the essential chaos in which human life must be led.'

His letter to Sir Richard Rees was more useful than anything from the later Shaw: 'I always disagree when people end by saying that we can only combat communism, fascism or what not if we develop an equal fanaticism. It appears to me that one defeats the fanatic precisely by *not* being a fanatic oneself, but, on the contrary, by using one's intelligence. In the same way, a man can kill a tiger because he is *not* a tiger, and uses his brain to invent the rifle, which no tiger will ever do.'

Orwell was kind to me, giving me a few books to review for *Tribune* and, occasionally, his column, *As I Please*, but I felt uneasy with him, not much liking him. I had read too little of his work, only later encountering, then often re-reading, his essays. I found him abrupt, of a dry, not always comprehensible humour, and was altogether too inexperienced to appreciate his complex virtues. In a pub he once told me that I would never be accepted as working-class if I spoke like I did, wore what I did. This irritated me, wishing to be accepted as no more than *me*. He too was irritated when the barman, impeccably working-class, called me 'Peter', and Orwell, 'sir'.

Bertrand Russell, world-renowned as mathematician and philosopher, was inescapable in the Fifties. He had published his first book back in 1894, his guardian and grandfather had been Lord John Russell, Victoria's Prime Minister, harking back to the Crimean War, to Garibaldi; he remembered Gladstone at the family table, commenting about the port. He had met and disliked Lenin: 'His guffaw at the thought of those massacred made my blood run cold . . . my most vivid memories were of bigotry and Mongolian cruelty.'

Fortified by mathematical precision, he had rescued philosophy from Teutonic metaphysical mystifications, verbal abstractions, restoring logic and common sense in language clear and reasoned, though he may at least have agreed with Nietzsche's belief that fixed convictions were straitjackets. His intellectual odyssey had not been one of a closed mind, though atheism and dislike of priestcraft remained constant. A. J. Ayer, in his own flat, once heard him talking to a pretty, convent-bred girl, who had been supplied by the nuns with questions to ask the famous sceptic: 'Lord Russell, why don't you like the Pope?' 'The Pope! He is paid his salary for telling lies.'

His politics he continually tested against current events. The Boer War, British rule in Africa, he first supported, holding that civilization and law were more important than local injustices and must be preserved at any price; British civilization, he thought superior to African. Later, his opinions altered. In 1914, he publicly rejected Britain's engagement in the War. Like Churchill, he had admired Rupert Brooke, on whose death in 1915 he wrote to a lover, Ottoline Morrell: 'There will be other generations – yet I keep fearing that something of civilization will be lost for good, as something was lost when Greece perished in just this way. Strange how one values civilization – more than all one's friends or anything – the slow achievement of men emerging from the brute – it seems the ultimate thing one lives for. I don't live for human happiness, but for some kind of struggling emergence of mind. And here, at most times, that is being helped on – and what has been done is given to new generations, who travel on from where we have stopped. And now it is all arrested, and no one knows if it will start again at anything like the point where it stopped. And all the elderly apostates are overjoyed.'

His pacificism was pragmatic; constant between the world wars, he rejected it in 1940, unlike Gandhi recognizing that good will, good sense, pleasant greetings, would not avail against irrational, obsessed Nazis. He must, however, have winced at General George Patton's 'Patriotism does not mean dying for your country; it's making some poor dumb bastard die for his.'

His admirers were startled when, in 1948, in 'the gaunt, roofless, bombed-out shell of the main hall of Westminster School', he urged threatening Stalin's Russia with the atomic bomb if she did not change her hostility to the West. Churchill was alleged to have thought the same. In 1954, however, on BBC radio, Russell proposed nuclear disarmament as the only chance of salvation from universal death. During the Fifties, the leader of CND and the Committee of 100, he joined demonstrations and sit-ins, again submitting to a brief imprisonment. In extreme old age, he became influenced, surely over-influenced, by a fanatical American youth employed as his secretary, eventually, without his old analytical cogency, telling the world: 'Kennedy and Macmillan are much more wicked than Hitler . . . they are abominable, they are the wickedest people who have ever lived in the history of man.'

The Fifties Poet Laureate, appointed in 1930, was John Masefield. Since youth, his poetic style had remained virtually unaltered, easy to parody, shot through with devotion to Chaucer, Villon, the Ballads, Keats, Rossetti, Morris, Yeats. His *Salt-Water Ballads* had saluted the ordinary seaman as Kipling, ten years earlier, had the common soldier in his *Barrack-Room Ballads*, and his sales before 1914 had rivalled those of Tennyson, Swinburne, Kipling, Housman. His narrative verse helped demolish the cosiness and gentility prominent during the early century, preceding Modernism, and the brutal and murderous in his rural poems rescued the countryside from certain Georgian sentimentalities. As a dramatist he had been praised by Shaw, and been included in the Vedrenne–Granville-Barker seasons at the Royal Court. Later, he attempted a fusion of Greek Tragedy with Japanese *Noh*, Scandinavian atmospherics with English village horrors, Shakespeare and the Bible; he dramatized Blake's *The Ghost of Abel*, and part of *Jerusalem*.

His adventure novels rivalled Conan Doyle's and his children's stories, notably *A Box of Delights*, those of Kipling.

He was a workmanlike Laureate, establishing poetry festivals and verse-speaking competitions, encouraging verse-drama, advising King George V to found the King's Medal for Poetry, awarding it to Robert Graves, Laurence Whistler and 'a man of genius', W. H. Auden. His own most substantial official writing was *The Nine Days Wonder*, a prose tribute to the Dunkirk evacuation. His official verses, conscientious but lifeless, he regularly despatched to *The Times*, prudently enclosing a stamped addressed envelope.

By 1950, his poetic nerve flickered only occasionally, and his reputation had long been superseded by the allusive fragmentations of the Modernists, Ezra Pound and T. S. Eliot, and the left-wing sociological period of Auden and his friends. In 1953, a young novelist, Muriel Spark, published a short critical book on him, balanced, just, favourable, republished in 1992; Betjeman later issued a Masefield anthology; Philip Larkin praised his strength and simplicity.

He had known the mail coach and the crying horn, and life on the roads and canals, had talked with old men who had fought at Waterloo, who had spoken to Napoleon, to Wellington; as a boy he had believed that only singers could enter heaven; as a man he had watched Lenin in the British Museum Library, had been friends with Hardy, Yeats, Synge, Lady Gregory, Tagore, and landlord of Graves, and had trained robins to take sultanas from his mouth. Though winning renown in two continents for sea poems, and joining a windjammer in his teens, he hated the life, and in New York had deserted, becoming a tramp, barman in a brothel, gardener, dynamiter of rocks, farm hand, carpet factory dogsbody alongside men with vicious knives, one Yonkers colleague assuring him that he knew ten murderers.

Through the Fifties and early Sixties he was writing on Shakespeare and Cervantes, Voltaire, Gerard Manley Hopkins and, with lifelong indignation, on the execution of Admiral Byng. He wrote on the deficiencies of Stevenson as a nautical observer, and on a Brueghel painting, 'I cannot imagine what they were doing on board to leave the foresail as they do.' He wrote on the shape of mice's feet, Texan seamanship, Rabelais, Napoleon, Harun-al-Rashid, Jesse James, Apuleius, Greek poetry, Henry Irving, reincarnation, fear of spiders, old family circuses, the eighteenth-century scholar Richard Porson drinking ink, a dying Spanish grandee murmuring that his killer had been a gentleman. He wrote on music-hall songs, Babylonian ziggurats, Victor Hugo's 'tommyrot' about Waterloo, Wagner in cloth-of-gold trousers, nightmarish ports and cut-throat occasions, vanished

New York landscapes and Lily Langtry. Four times he had seen a fox surreptitiously turn, then safely mingle with the hounds in headlong pursuit of nothing. To the violinist Audrey Napier-Smith, he wrote of the Zulu King Tchaka, 'who made up poems to sing, and also practised divination to find out if people should be killed. One of his best poems, which he could listen to all day, ran like this (the whole poem),

> "What nations have I scattered!
> Who next shall be battered?"

'His divination was more subtle. He used to ask women "Do you like cats?" And whether they said yes or no he killed them, by some spiritual prompting which died with him and cannot now be surmised.'

In 1954, reading his *New Chum*, I realized that almost an entire vocabulary had swiftly become obsolete. 'I had noticed and remembered, some little points of rigging, as signs of age; single top-sails on mizzen-masts; dead-eyes and laniards (sometimes with most excellent paunch mattings covering the laniards), and the big, rigged-in jibboons and flying jibboons, the sailor killers, which mates would have to rig out with four boys and a drunken boatswain, on the way down river, outward bound.'

In Poets' Corner, Westminster Abbey, Masefield's stone carries no epitaph, but he had long ago written it in his novel *Odtaa*:

> I have seen flowers come in stony places
> And kind things done by men with ugly faces,
> And the gold cup won by the worst horse at the races,
> So I trust too.

Fifties aesthetic appetites had largely swung away from literary Modernism. Its leading entrepreneur, Ezra Pound, wayward, generous, tirelessly helpful to other poets, musicians, sculptors, painters, was currently in St Elizabeth's Hospital for the Criminally Insane, Washington, DC, consigned there to avoid an embarrassing capital treason charge. He remained there until released in 1958, helped by the appeals of T. S. Eliot, Archibald MacLeish, Hemingway, Robert Frost and Dag Hammarskjöld, Secretary-General of the United Nations.

Pound had always insisted that shallow thought, rootless verbiage, corrupt concepts had rotted classical Rome and the Renaissance, undermined modern civilization. 'The one thing you should not do is to suppose that when something is wrong with the arts, it is wrong with the *arts only*.'

Allen Tate, who had supported the award of the Bollingen Prize in 1949 for Pound's *Pisan Cantos*, argued that treason scarcely invalidated society's debt to Pound for his concern for language. An old friend, William Carlos Williams, had reflected: 'He is the essence of optimism and has a cast-iron faith that is something to admire . . . but not one person in a thousand likes him and a great many people detest him, and why? Because he is so full of conceits and affectation.' Even his English publishers, one of them his admirer T. S. Eliot, had to expurgate from the *Pisan Cantos* such anti-Semitic lines as 'Pétain defended Verdun while Blum was defending a violet.'

Pound's wartime broadcasts from Mussolini's Rome had betrayed his concern for language. Fervid admirers – myself among them – had to pause before his tirades against 'Mr Jewsevelt', 'Franklin Finkelstein Roosevelt', 'Stinkie Roosenstein', before his sneers at 'kikes, sheenies, and the oily people'. He preached 'It is a choice between Europe and Jewry', reiterating the archaic nonsense of International Conspiracy. On radio and in Fascist journals he wrote that Hitler and Mussolini were, through their magnificent intuition, maintaining the doctrines of Confucius, and related them to Thomas Jefferson; he shouted that not even the BBC could hold Germany responsible for the war; that *Mein Kampf* was 'keenly analysed history', and Hitler was a saint and martyr, comparable to Joan of Arc, who had 'taught the Germans manners'. Freudian analysis he dismissed as 'Viennese poison . . . pewk of kiketry.' America should start a pogrom at the top: 'The United States has been invaded by vermin.'

His old friend and colleague Wyndham Lewis lamented in 1950 'a great American in eclipse'. Debate continued as to whether fine art excused disgusting politics. That Pound's work was fine art was roundly disputed. F. R. Leavis had thought Pound's *Hugh Selwyn Mauberley* a masterpiece, with 'impersonality, substance and depth of great poetry,' but found the *Cantos* 'boring, boring with the emptiness of the egotism thrust upon us, lacking creative theme, with bullying assertions, uncreative blatancy'. Actually, creative themes were obvious enough: heroic avatars, returns from the underworld, Light against Darkness, the iniquity of Usury, shallow language and indifference, within the ebb and flow of high culture, though much else of Leavis's strictures was undeniable.

In 1950, writing in *Nine*, Roy Campbell had asserted that English then possessed at least three poets who had not suffered 'nuclear fissure of gender' – T. S. Eliot, Edith Sitwell, Wyndham Lewis. These, in his matador way, he upheld as 'the triple literary armour of our race against the real eastern invasion, conquest and colonisation of England, from which Hitler's diversionary theatricals diverted our attention'. Of the 'orientals', Campbell thought Marx and Freud the most significant.

'There's Wyndham Lewis fuming out of sight/That lonely old volcano of the Right', Auden had written, in *Letter to Lord Byron*. Lewis was the author of a pre-war book extolling Hitler, and co-founded *Blast* with Pound in 1914: he was also founder of Vorticist painting, critic, polemicist, novelist, poet, Great War soldier, author of *Blasting and Bombardiering*, and, in the Fifties, still a powerful baleful presence in Notting Hill, beginning to go blind but, as art critic of *The Listener*, issuing weekly manifestos. His portraits of T. S. Eliot and Edith Sitwell hung in the Tate, the latter, after a row, claiming to send Lewis a mocking telegram every day. Vorticism, with its fierce, upthrusting strokes and metallic sheen, the painter explained – 'You think at once of a whirlpool. At the heart of the whirlpool is a great silent place where all the energy is concentrated. And there, at the point of concentration, is the Vorticist.'

He had always been poised to bait all comers, particularly celebrated middlebrows, Communists, left-wing pacifists, 'the Bloomsberries', and self-advertising millionaires, and frequently did so. He was not readily envisaged on his knees before Betjeman, Augustus John, Vaughan Williams. At the start, he and Pound had proclaimed: 'We want to make in England not a popular art, not a renewal of a lost folk art, or a romantic fostering of such unnatural conditions, but to make individuals, wherever found.' Lewis, self-styled 'the Enemy', could be brutal – 'Killing somebody must be the greatest pleasure in existence,' he had written in *Blast*, before his own arrival on the Western Front. He was suspicious, alert for the bogus, prickly – a mild insult from him could denote affection – working as if from behind a drawbridge with a wife, seldom seen, lurking in secret interior regions. For him, an explosive heap amongst the Academy portraits, the bored witticisms, the sherry, satire was essential. His autobiography, *Rude Assignment*, published in 1950, showed the old drive had survived wars, rebuffs, disabilities.

Julian Symons thought that of all modern writers, Lewis had most in common with Orwell, sharing intellectual independence when many drifted into conformity; a concern for politics; sharing too an infor-mality and lack of literary or social affectation. 'Yet although he was so easy to talk to, Lewis was inhuman, in a way that Orwell was not; he was a man devoured by a passion for ideas, which he wished to put at the service of art ... He was poor or very poor most of his life, he fathered five illegitimate children by three different women, he got clap and did not treat it properly, so that in the Thirties he had four operations in five years.' Finally, altogether blind, he continued to write, blast, bombard, with obdurate courage and disrespect.

Another writer who romanticized power alongside Oswald Mosley and T. E. Lawrence, was Henry Williamson, whose *Tarka the Otter* (1927) had made him famous amongst readers of all ages. During the Fifties he was writing his massive *A Chronicle of Ancient Sunlight*, extending from late Victorian Britain to after the Second World War, and of which his friend Daniel Farson writes that, because of its range, 'It has been compared to Tolstoy, Proust and Dickens. But the image that occurs to me is that of a Brueghel painting, which shows us a landscape alive in detail in which every person, going about their business or their play is granted an equal importance.' About landscape Williamson, a marvellous nature writer, once complained that the countryside was too open. 'It's like living in a salad.'

Also included are Williamson's internationalist, anti-war, anti-democratic sentiments, left from the scalding horrors of the Great War, in which he had fought. Quarrelsome, self-destructive, yet with a charm which fluctuated like a barometer, Williamson had one experience which channelled his spirit until death. During the 1914 Christmas fraternization, he had talked with a young German soldier near the Bois-de-Ploegsteert, had been greatly moved, and became convinced that his confidant had been Adolf Hitler. As a schoolboy I had loved his four-volume *The Flax of Dreams*, heavily scented with sensitive childhood, adolescent tatters and passions, rich but acutely observed English skies and landscapes, though was perplexed by his foreword: 'I salute the great man across the Rhine, whose life symbol is a happy child.' He believed that the Nazi SA 'possessed the spirit of English gentlemen who had transcended class-consciousness', and that the Führer possessed not only 'spiritual grace' but also 'the truest eyes ever seen in a man's face'.

Unrepentant, Williamson too underwent wartime imprisonment, and remained unpopular, embittered, solitary, despite some devoted women and literary admirers. Farson recollects him, approaching 80, vainly awaiting some honour from Buckingham Palace in recognition of his genius.

The Modernism of T. S. Eliot throbbed with 'inner life'. He was sometimes accused of teaching negation, unjustly, for the 'Give, Sympathise, Control' of *The Waste Land* was a most positive injunction, and the *Four Quartets* are an effective guide down moral pathways towards conceptions of right action. Herbert Read once heard Eliot say, rather surprisingly, that above all writers he respected Johnson – his Christian faith and his fear of death giving him unmovable staying power. In poetry, and the verse plays, he moved within time and myth, history and cultures, mysticism and everyday life, he revived the Furies, coalesced religions, was affected not only by Virgil, Dante and fashionable French writers but also by Kipling and Conan Doyle and the music hall. Such Modernists as Eliot, Pound and Lewis were acutely aware of the coeval discoveries and techniques in Post-Impressionism, physics and cinema, and drew them into literature. A new sensibility seemed to have emerged, an enlarged world. By the Fifties, the effect had diminished, and by 1959 Philip Larkin, in *Listen*, could write that Modernism was an aberration that blighted all the arts.

Something of a Grand Cham himself, Eliot possessed a sly, teasing side at the expense of the pretentious. At the Wednesday Club in 1956, Paul Bloomfield reported Eliot flummoxing some high-minded intellectuals. Asked for his favourite passage of English prose, the great poet at once replied, assisting his performance with appropriate gestures:

'Well,' cried Boss McGinty at last, 'is he here? Is Birdy Edwards here?'

'Yes,' McMurdo answered slowly, 'Birdy Edwards is here. I am Birdy Edwards.'

After a bemused silence, in which none knew or, snobbishly, cared to admit the source, Eliot pleasantly revealed it: Conon Doyle's *The Valley of Fear*.

Younger readers in the Fifties could feel Eliot something of an anachronism, despite his vast prestige. Stephen Spender, later, noticed his 'either-or' attitude: society for Eliot was either Christian or Pagan, with liberalism, possibly shared by most of us, only an ineffective shallowness, inorganic, materialistic, vulgar. Eliot's religion had been unshaken by Virginia Woolf's sneer, after a session with him, that there was something obscene in a living person sitting by the fire and believing in God.

Eliot believed in God. Also in intellectualism, issuing a ukase in 1951: 'Poets, in our civilization as it exists at present, must be difficult', because 'our civilization comprehends great variety and complexity', and 'playing on a refined sensibility, must produce various and complex results.' This was a slap at those of us who, with sensibilities less refined, appreciated MacNeice, Betjeman, Alex Comfort, Cecil Day-Lewis, John Heath-Stubbs and, from America, Robinson Jeffers, Louis Simpson, Robert Lowell, Richard Wilbur. I was not ashamed at enjoying Wilbur's 'Mind':

Mind in its purest play is like some bat
That beats about in caverns all alone
Contriving by a kind of senseless wit
Not to conclude against a wall of stone.

Like Karl Kraus, like Pound, Eliot had in *The Rock* urged the refinement of language:

Out of the sea of sound the life of music,
Out of the slimy mud of words, out of the sleet and hail of
    verbal impressions,
Approximate thoughts and feelings, words that have taken
    the place of thoughts and feelings,
There spring the perfect order of speech, and the beauty of
    incantation.

Well enough, though by now, in the post-war democratic hubbub, accusations of élitism, High Tory politics and obscurantism were louder. 'I have no objections', he himself allowed, 'to being called a bigot.' His classicism, Anglicanism, moral rectitude, implied that most of us were spiritually inert, emotionally shallow, intellectually torpid, and this, having observed those afflicted by wartime grief and sufferings, and their reactions, I rejected. If we were the damned, at least our subscriptions supported his publishing house, our reading bolstered his royalties, our military and civilian war efforts had saved his bacon, and I was disinclined to accept participants in the last as Hollow Men, like too many Beats, Angries, Great White Hunters, Flying Saucermen or Victims of the System. Two passages from *Four Quartets* – poems which have haunted me for forty years – I thought outrageous in the Fifties:

... when an underground train, in the tube, stops too long
    between stations
And the conversation rises and slowly fades into silence
And you see behind every face the mental emptiness deepen
    leaving only the growing terror of nothing to think about.
                                        (from *East Coker*)

And in *Burnt Norton*, still on the train, he condescended to our

strained time-ridden faces
Distracted from distraction by distraction
Filled with fancies and empty of meaning
Tumid apathy with no concentration.

Riding the tube myself, I was angry, suspecting, wrongly that Eliot travelled by taxi and that his own face was as much time-ridden as mine and those of my fellow passengers. We were not

terrified of nothing to think about. We were reading *Forever Amber*,
or *Lolita*, or E. V. Rieu's Penguin translation of *The Odyssey*, or *Burnt
Norton*. We were comforting children, reassuring dogs, arguing about
Tottenham Hotspur or the Duke of Windsor. On what evidence did
the clever poet mount his attack on the vacuum behind all our faces?
Look, man, we are speculating on each other and undressing the girl
opposite, planning an epic story. We are dreaming of the marvellous
telegram, 'You've won.' We are lamenting the magic mirror, 'Others
are better.' We are remembering a walk on the Quantocks, bad
behaviour at Corfu, a dropped catch at Chalfont St Giles and a sight
of Denis Compton; we are inventing rapscallion pasts, counting our
bank balances, reading of Stafford Cripps' sermon in St Paul's, calculating the cost of earldoms, making mental cut-outs of hula hoops,
Danny Kaye, the Whisky a Go-Go, and Sir Bernard and Lady Docker's
gold Daimler.

I have already mentioned Roy Campbell, South African poet, translator of Baudelaire and St John of the Cross, Francoist soldier in the
Civil War, author of the Francoist epic, *Flowering Rifle*, and *The
Georgiad*, a scathing satire on 'The Squirearchy' poets and critics
around, or close to, J. C. Squire, and baiter of his left-wing contemporaries, Auden, Day-Lewis, Spender, MacNeice, lumped together as
'Macspaunday'. He regarded Fascism as 'religious, not fanatical, human
and not mechanical'. Latterly he had sought work at the BBC, pre-
ferably as a commissionaire with a uniform, but accepted a post as a
Literary Talks Producer. In his 1951 autobiography, *Light on a Dark
Horse*, he recounted a Riviera episode. Walking, he saw a broad figure
ahead, back towards him, seated at an easel under a large hat. Always
impulsive, he immediately assumed that this was an art critic whom
he particularly despised, so he stole up, as stealthily as a war-wound
permitted, and pinched the wide-acred buttocks.
  Campbell had played South Africa rugby, appeared with some
panache in the bull-ring, fought in Spain – allegedly firing an arrow at
George Orwell – and against the Axis, but now was at last abashed at
a slow turnabout of the hat, exposing a pudgy face, enquiring but not
enthusiastic, an expensive cigar, then a methodical and soundless return
to the easel: Winston Churchill.

Hilaire Belloc – Catholic polemicist, incautious historian, poet, wit,
novelist, essayist, ex-MP, scorner of parliamentary plutocracy, inter-

national Jewry, the British Empire, Modernism, Russia, supporter of trade unions against bosses, and much else, not all of it disreputable – lived until 1953. He had been a friend of Chesterton's, incessant debater with Shaw and Wells, vigorous traveller. Exhorting readers to 'stay rooted in one steadfast piece of land', he himself, disregarding jobs, family and social obligations, seemed absent for long months abroad or at lordly country seats. In France, he could sometimes be addressed as 'M. Bloch' which, as an anti-Semite, he rejected, doubtless with some asperity.

His most popular medium, the Essay, was now vanishing from the daily press. I myself had earlier enjoyed turning from cricket scores and murder trials for the customary ration of Chesterton, Arthur Bryant, Robert Lynd, Ian Mackay, Belloc himself: 'No one has written verses to ropes ... yet the rope has one very important place in literature which is not yet recognised. It is this: that ropes more than any other subject are, I think, a test of man's power of exposition in prose ... I find over and over again in the passages of those special books which talk of ropes, such language as: – "a bight is taken in the standing apart and then is run over right-handedly, that is, with the sun, or again, the hands of the watch (only backward), and then under the running part and so through both times and hauled tight to the free end." But if any man should seek to save his life on a dark night in a sudden gust of wind by this description, he would fail: he would drown.'

Certain lines of Belloc would unexpectedly and agreeably drift into me. From *More Peers* came this: 'After the execution (which/is something rare among the Rich)', but his appeal in the Fifties was limited. Just before the fall of Barcelona he had interviewed General-issimo Franco in the Ebro Valley: 'When I entered Franco's presence, I entered the presence of one who had fought that same battle which Roland in the legend had died fighting and which Godfrey in sober history had won when the battered remnant, the mere surviving tenth of the first crusaders entered Jerusalem – on foot, refusing to ride where the Lord of Christendom had offered Himself up in Sacrifice. I had been in the air of what has always been the Salvation of Europe – I mean the Spanish Crusade. Worse luck for those who do not understand these things.' Belloc always appeared to prefer Franco and Mussolini to Jesus. 'I revere him because I am instructed to by the Church but personally I find him repellent. The fellow was a milksop.'

Franco, metallic, credulous, vainglorious, unprepossessing, was scarcely that. Even Himmler was shocked by his peacetime cruelties. Though the claim is thought exaggerated by some, he may have saved Spain from the World War, despite blandishments from Hitler who, after their interview, told Ribbentrop that he would prefer to have all his teeth extracted than repeat it. He did save Sephardic Jews from the Gestapo in occupied Greece. He lacked magnanimity and was now, in 1950, erecting a grandiose monument to the Fascist dead, overworking thousands of Republican prisoners as virtual slaves who had preferred this to the executions which long continued. Norman Mailer, already famed for *The Naked and the Dead*, had contrived the escape of two Republicans from a Franco prison, less publicized than Hemingway's liberation of the Ritz Bar in Paris. Throughout the Fifties, Franco was successfully angling for international acceptance, American support, access to the IMF.

Another Catholic writer, and an admirer of Belloc, who had said that had he been Spanish he would have fought for Franco, was Evelyn Waugh, whose satires had delighted the Thirties, particularly his victims. He was totally immune from fashion, rating the later Joyce and Pound demented, and without reverence for Picasso. When critics strangely praised Le Corbusier's description of his houses as 'machines for living in', Waugh retorted that they hailed him merely for being avant-garde, rather than for providing logical solutions to practical problems. He was infuriated by the Communist Tito being received at Buckingham Palace. In his *Sword of Honour* trilogy, surely the best Second World War novels, the disillusioned romantic Guy Crouchback utters one of the most quoted passages in military fiction. After witnessing betrayals, hypocrisies, cynical jiggery-pokeries, murder, high comedy and low farce, he ends in Yugoslavia, with Tito victorious, listening to a Jewish-Hungarian fugitive. ' "Is there any place that is free from evil? It is too simple to say that only the Nazis wanted war. These communists wanted it too. It was the only way in which they could come to power. Many of my people wanted it, to be revenged on the Germans, to hasten the creation of the national state. It seems to me there was a will to war, a death wish, everywhere. Even good men thought their private honour would be satisfied by war. They could assert their manhood by killing and being killed. They would accept hardships in recompense for having been selfish and lazy. Danger justified privilege. I knew Italians – not very many perhaps – who felt this. Were there none in England?"

' "God forgive me," said Guy. "I was one of them." '

Guy Crouchback, believing in honour and decency, might have applauded Göring at Nuremberg, objecting to his Russian judges, representatives of the Katyn murderers. To Julian Jebb, Belloc's grandson, Waugh said: 'An artist must be a reactionary. He has to stand out against the tenor of his age and not go flopping along; he must offer some little opposition.' No more than Graham Greene did he find the Fifties scene attractive. Vatican policy grieved him, such institutions as the United Nations invited scepticism. Eastern Europe was abandoned to atheist collectivism, Britain herself was rejecting traditional values, beliefs, leaders, on behalf of the lower-middle-class Hooper, a character in *Brideshead Revisited*. 'These men must die to make a world for Hooper; they were the aborigines, vermin by right of law, to be shot off at leisure, so that things might be safe for the travelling salesman with his polygonal pince-nez, his fat, wet handshake, his grinning dentures.' The Century of the Common Man was proving very common indeed.

'Vermin' echoed Aneurin Bevan's declaration that Conservatives were 'lower than vermin', which had him literally booted out of White's Club. In France, Sartre and de Beauvoir were saying much the same, finding virtue only in the Left, unwilling to admit that de Gaulle was an upright man, that his contribution against Fascism was overwhelming compared to theirs.

Waugh could be observed as clubman, country squire, in red-brown checked tweeds. Perhaps ironically, for he lacked the customary quarterings, he liked to assume aristocratic trimmings, which he imagined included hauteur. Christopher Sykes would tell, then publish, a story that would have repelled most dukes and not a few earls. At a dinner table, a woman had praised *Brideshead Revisited*. Waugh apparently replied that he himself thought it good 'but now that I know that a vulgar common American woman like yourself admires it, I am not so sure'. Stories of his arrogance towards private soldiers, club servants, also a commanding officer, suggested some fourth-century Roman patrician of suspect pedigree, bemoaning the upstart freedmen, hired barbarians, parvenu cosmopolitan jobbers, all busy rigging the Empire. 'Which of the Yids', he demanded at a party, 'is Freddie Ayer?'

George Woodcock, critic, biographer, admirer of Blake and anarchist friend of Orwell, felt that by 1949 Waugh had become dominated by his nostalgia at the expense of his satire, and particularly deprecated *Brideshead Revisited*. Disclosures of Waugh's psychological disorder in *The Ordeal of Gilbert Pinfold* (1957) evoked much amateur though sympathetic psychoanalysis of the novelist. Graham Greene had long detected this conflict in Waugh, his friend, between the satirical and the romantic, his disappointment with England, Europe and Catholicism surely accounting for many of his bilious remarks and much of his boorishness. To have written a row of novels still fresh years after their appearance, to have achieved mastery of a clear, supple, pointed prose, to have maintained the devotion of gifted men and women – Harold Acton, Nancy Mitford, Christopher Sykes, Diana Cooper, John Betjeman – and to be possessed of a family, he somehow found insufficient. I heard of him weekly attending, alone, some scrappy cinema irrespective of the programme which could seldom have satisfied his wit and intelligence. This venture, if true, suggested a loneliness, perhaps desolation; gave me fellow-feeling which he would have contemptuously rejected. I never met him, thankfully, but was grateful for him allowing me, an unknown, to share a Chapman and Hall advertisement panel for our latest novels. To the historical novelist Alfred Duggan, he was always generous, rescuing him as a writer and from the bottle. To read him always made me rejoice in the adroit economy of his effects, and unlaboured wit. 'Mrs Ape had no beard to speak of . . .'. In 1955 he delineated his own literary style, for me as effective as any in Europe: 'Properly understood, style is not a seductive decoration added to a functional structure; it is the essence of a work of art. The necessary elements of style are lucidity, elegance and individuality; these three qualities combine to form a preservative which ensures the nearest approximation to permanence in the fugitive art of letters.'

As a man, Waugh seemed adolescent, though the greater artist, beside the calm austerity of Aldous Huxley. He too had been a pre-war satirist, viewing much of society with Swiftian disgust – its need for instant gratification, its trivial fashions and cults, its sexual vulgarity, its absurdity in taking affection for folksongs to be love of music, its lack of visual discrimination. He was increasingly 'committed': to ecology and population control, to educational and ethical reform, to philosophical debate, to pacifism, to 'non-attachment'. By the Fifties he was attempting to reconcile science with the paranormal, rationalism and mysticism, art and morality, believing that man could recover mental and physical elements long neglected in the mechanical age. He felt that a scientific poet could be a man of the future.

Huxley knew so much. He had now abandoned verse, but from him I could learn about Piranesi; about the most exquisite buttocks perhaps yet painted; about the domestic habits of an Earl of Shaftesbury, drinking with a sprig of rosemary in his pot of ale; about the scheming Father Joseph, the original *Eminence Grise*, and his Ends and Means corruption; about the political influence of armament firms on peace conferences; about Mayan language and Aztec religion; about the Devils of Loudon and the non-necessity of glasses for better eyesight. He discoursed on the after-life – Pagan 'squeak and gibber' versus Christian harps of the blessed and screams of the damned – on El Greco, on Bach, Andalusian ethics, Buddhist *ahimsa*, cosmetics, magic in poetry (Tennyson's superbly unnecessary swan gliding in after many a summer) and Foreheads Villainously Low. Despite his own defective, often painful eyesight, he had a range of thought denied to most of us through laziness, lack of curiosity, and self-satisfaction.

Didactic, he was never frantic or shrill like his friend D. H. Lawrence. Though a prolific author, he had a voice, a demeanour, a literary tone, that recalled St Bernard's remark: 'In the forests you will find more than in books. The trees and the rocks will teach you things that no master will tell you.' He told much and suggested more, and was never over-awed by his contemporaries, by old age, by youth. 'Fénélon and La Rochefoucauld knew all about the surface rationalisation of deep, discreditable motives of the subconscious, and were fully aware that sexuality and the will to power were all too often the effective forces at work under the polite mask of the *persona*.'

His pupil, friend and biographer, Sybille Bedford, who, resolutely anti-Fascist, demurred only at his pacifism, reports his reaction to the novel *The Roman Spring of Mrs Stone* (1950) by a Fifties idol, Tennessee Williams: 'Mindlessness and horror are all right provided that they are shown in relationship with the mind and the good that will keep the world from collapsing. Constant mindlessness, such as one gets in Tennessee Williams's plays, becomes a great bore and is also completely untrue to life.'

Huxley's occasional appearances on television suggested a grave and humane embodiment of the civilization that Russell, whom he satirized in *Crome Yellow*, so cherished, a luminous mind, of grace, irony and humour, which treated the world of nature and society as one. Isaiah Berlin met the Huxleys at a conference in India: 'He was very simple, very serene, very easy to talk with. The fact that, a few weeks before, his house and all his books had been destroyed by fire seemed hardly to trouble him at all, nor did he by the slightest allusion reveal the fact that he knew he was suffering from a mortal disease; he complained of his eyesight – his old, familiar infirmity – but said nothing about the cancer that was ultimately to end his life.'

In India, Sybille Bedford had a glimpse of the fastidious Aldous and Maria being offered a meal of ice cream, chocolates and curried mice.

In the Thirties, for youths like myself, W. H. Auden was an anti-Fascist cheerleader, a revivalist calling, in Richard Hoggart's words,

'Repent, Unite, Fight'. He combined the magic of that Tennyson swan with fairytale and urban desolation; enchanted forests and dangerous ravines with abandoned mines and railways; public school cliques and secret agents knowing about the control of passes, bridges mined and trouble coming. A world of nursery-rhyme allusion and psychological reference, Marx and Freud and personal confession gave delicious sensations of recognition, a reassurance that I was not alone in my melodramatic griefs and hopes.

> The glacier knocks in the cupboard,
> The desert sighs in the bed,
> And the crack in the tea-cup opens,
> A lane to the land of the dead.
> (from 'As I Walked out
> One Evening')

Never totally understanding, and glad of it – I loved the half-glimpsed, the oblique, the rumour of a white glimmer hidden in the maze – I murmured to myself behind the armoury, lines from Auden's *May*.

> The real world lies before us,
> Brave motions of the young,
> Abundant wish for death,
> The pleasing, pleasured, haunted:
> A dying Master sinks tormented
> In his admirers' ring,
> The unjust walk the earth.
> And Love that makes impatient
> Tortoise and roe, that lays
> The blonde beside the dark,
> Urges upon our blood,
> Before the evil and the good
> How insufficient is
> Touch, endearment, look.

Still inexperienced with literary society, I assumed his ascendancy was complete. Not so. Like Kipling, Auden lectured and moralized, never a recipe for critical immunity. In 1940, Orwell castigated a phrase, 'the necessary murder', from Auden's 1937 'Spain', one of my most cherished poems: 'The Hitlers and Stalins find murder necessary, but they don't advertise their callousness, and they don't speak of it as murder; it is "liquidation", "elimination", or some other soothing phrase. Mr Auden's brand of amoralism is only possible if you are the kind of person who is always somewhere else when the trigger is pulled. So much of left-wing thought is a kind of playing with fire by people who don't even know that the fire is hot.'

Orwell could have added that 'necessary murder' echoed the Webbs' justification of Stalin's slaughter of Ukrainian kulaks in 1932-3, which they pronounced 'necessary to be faced' in the interest of increased agricultural output, a brutal thesis unsupported by results. A quarter of a century later, Russian agriculture had not recovered.

In 1938, a mildewed colonel, about whom we gibed that he had lost one leg at Mons, another at Ypres, a third on the Marne, and the last of his wits on the Somme, had barked at me: 'Your Mr Auden's no great lover of Herr Hitler, but will he be joining me to fight the bugger?' Many whom Auden derided – colonels, retarded public schoolboys, suburban golfers, trite-tongued mediocrities, romantic but goofy stuffed shirts – saved Western civilization. My vision of Auden as anti-Fascist commando could not be maintained when, with the barbarians at the gate, he departed to America.

Roy Campbell wrote in 1950, in *Nine*, in typical manner that Auden 'has always been attracted by safety and the most violent action he ever saw was when he was playing table tennis at Tossa del Mar on behalf of the Spanish Republicans – apart from the violent exercise he got with his knife and fork'.

Cyril Connolly, whose journal *Horizon* closed down in 1950, much regretted, explained that Auden's departure had been an acknowledgement of the aesthetic failure of social realism. Auden himself disconcerted some aesthetes by remarking that artists and politicians would get along better together if the former would only realize that the political history of the world would have been the same if not a poem had been written, a picture painted, or a bar of music composed.

Criticism was not always personal. D. S. Savage in 1944 had seen a decline in Auden's vitality and seriousness. 'Morbidly sensitive to the Zeitgeist, orientated towards an entirely fictitious Future, Auden has been caught up along with the flow of events, the real poetic integrity he had to begin with dispersed, his moral standpoint confused and obliterated, his meaning, both as a poet and as a focus of thought and feeling for his time, rendered merely negative and symptomatic.'

Having spent most of the war in America, Auden returned to England as an American major, assigned to the Morale Division of the US Strategic Bombing Survey, Vladimir Nabokov having assured him that a telephone call for an interview would guarantee him this. There were unpleasant reports of him telling Spender and John Lehmann that London had suffered only light bombing, and that for a civilized visitor, conditions were harsh and the rationed food unacceptable.

In the Fifties, my own devotion had waned, not because of war records, or Auden's reversion to Anglicanism, but through no longer feeling an electric thrill from his work, though periodically, in such poems as 'Streams', 'The Shield of Achilles' and 'In Praise of Limestone', it returned.

Robert Graves, like Sassoon, Blunden and Priestley, had survived the Great War, also the experience of having been reported dead. In 1950, with his usual contemptuous vigour, he was assaulting the psychoanalytical interpretation of mythology, in the wake of his controversial *The White Goddess* (1948), writing in *Nine*: 'Once one has tracked down all the relevant historical and physical facts of any particular mythic problem, there is no need to run to Papa Freud for his opinion on it.' In 1955, he tracked down further historical and physical facts, in *Greek Myths*, to his own satisfaction if not to that of all classicists, but certainly transforming the subject for thousands of readers, for whom old stories were given origins and meanings hitherto unsuspected. His life's output of poetry, unaffected by Eliot and Pound, found many readers, who were particularly appreciative of the lyrical matched by precision, the passionate tempered by irony, if at times bemused by his own much-evoked Muse, the White Goddess. In his Clark lectures, delivered at Cambridge in 1954–5, he called Pound a barbaric and self-important charlatan, his *Cantos* ignorant, indecent, unmelodious. Eliot, he allowed, had once been, 'however briefly', a poet, but one who, during the Battle of the Somme – in which Graves had fought – allowed himself too many London tea parties given by boring hostesses. Auden, with his 'zinc-bright influence' which exceeded that of Yeats, Pound and Eliot, was a borrower, even a plagiarist, though saluted as 'the Picasso of English poetry', sufficient to damn him for Graves. Dylan Thomas 'never pretended to be anything more than a young dog – witty, naughty, charming, irresponsible and impenitent. But he did give his radio audience what they wanted.'

Academics, assiduously instructing us, in bad prose, how to write, were doubtless aggrieved when Connolly and V. S. Pritchett occasionally reminded them of the existence of W. Somerset Maugham. There was one stratum of Maugham then almost forgotten by 1950. He had been a secret agent in the Great War, briefed to prevent the Kerensky government from making peace with Germany after the February 1917 revolution in Russia, and maintained that had he been

sent out six months earlier, he could have altered history by preventing Lenin's October 1917 coup. In their *Spy Fiction* (1990), Donald
McCormick and Katy Fletcher wrote of his *Ashenden* tales that they
were the first exposure of what espionage really means: 'long periods
of boredom, fear, human weakness, callowness and deceit'. For myself,
Ashenden alone rescued me from the boredom of espionage fiction,
which always made me agree with A. J. P. Taylor that if men were
sane, there would be no history.

In the Fifties, Maugham, living easily in his South of France villa, was
writing no plays and little fiction, retaining his scepticism and apparent
objectivity. He was generous to the young and, believing travel and lack
of worry essential to their talents, endowed a literary prize to assist this,
also leaving his prodigious literary estate to the Royal Literary Fund,
to benefit indigent authors. Yet Richard Buckle thought him 'surely the
most unpleasant man since Caligula'. Noël Coward knew him for
almost fifty years, grateful for kindness and hospitality. He said that
Maugham always maintained he had no illusions about people; actually,
Coward insisted, he possessed a major illusion – that they were no good.
His own affection lapsed after reading Maugham's vindictive outburst
against his ex-wife in *Looking Back* (1962).

Frederic Prokosch thought that Maugham had amply fulfilled, without ever transcending, his particular gifts of rigorous honesty, perception, craftsmanship and unpretentious narrative. He once gave the old
man a moonlit picnic on the Via Appia, amongst cypresses and ancient
tombs, round which *carabinieri* lurked in the shadows, suspecting that
Maugham was corrupting youth. They had to be bribed away, while
the novelist sat in tranquillity, 'like a big spotted toad with razor-sharp
eyes'. Prokosch, who may not have met Arnold Toynbee, Benedict
Nicolson, or C. E. M. Joad, thought him the stingiest man he had ever
known. He was by then complaining of having been denied a
knighthood, also the Nobel Prize and satisfactory love. Life, he concluded, is long, sad and horrid, and one takes refuge in unfulfilment.

Prokosch was an elegant American from Wisconsin, long-legged,
broad-shouldered, with a squarish, high-boned, outdoor, rather hard
face, a chin cut as if by a laser, decisive as a Teutonic Knight's, and,
Walter de la Mare told him, ears like a vixen's, eyes like a magpie's;
thick brows, a dark, sometimes arrogant presence. He was a novelist,
poet, Chaucerian scholar, translator of Euripides and Hölderlin,
lepidopterist, tennis star, squash champion of France and Sweden, with
drop-shots that plummeted 'like rotten apples'.

I was puzzled by hearing the more sophisticated refer to him as Fred
Prick. Apparently, before reaching pre-war England, he had, as entice-
ment or warning, sent a photograph of himself, naked, to Auden,
MacNeice, Spender ... perhaps to Maugham and Hugh Walpole,
almost certainly not to Eliot, Virginia Woolf, Ivy Compton-Burnett,
Elizabeth Bowen, Russell, Shaw and H. G. His Austrian father, an
academic, had written a history of Indo-European languages, and
Frederic was early accustomed to the great. 'One day my father told
me that Thomas Mann was coming to lunch' and indeed he did,
his talk spreading from his head like antlers. Prokosch remembered
sitting in a fig tree, secretly listening as Mann walked in the garden
exchanging consonants and diphthongs with the Professor. 'These
little fragments of vanished dialects traced in the air, like the call of
birds, the mysterious journey of the human tongue from the depths of
the jungle into its modern complexities.' Pavlova visited, talk abounded
about Mary Pickford, Douglas Fairbanks, the Fatty Arbuckle scandal.

To a newcomer, Prokosch glittered with success. Wilfrid Israel had
given me his *The Asiatics*, a novel which T. S. Eliot of Faber had lost
to Harold Raymond of Chatto & Windus. Mann was 'unable to tear
myself away from this astonishing, picaresque romance, flashing
with talent and an audacious, adventurous spirit'. Not then a world
traveller, Prokosch had concocted 'Asia' from travel books, articles and
brochures, like V. S. Pritchett claiming to have invented a South
America for his novel *Dead Man Leading* from the Kew Gardens hot
house. Prokosch excelled in luxuriant descriptions, as the narrator
wanders from the Mediterranean to India and beyond, in a meandering
quest for a golden fleece of self-fulfilment, some Fortunate Island of
love and success, a pattern for several more novels.

He mingled his talents with audacious brashness, accosting Marianne
Moore, Mario Praz, Malraux, Karen Blixen, Frost, Thomas Wolfe,
Wallace Stevens and Housman, who called *The Asiatics* 'a little masterpiece' and *The Waste Land* 'perfunctory, though I liked his little song
about the drowned Phoenicean Sailor'. He strode into Virginia Woolf's
workroom: 'Mrs Woolf, what are your thoughts about *Ulysses*?' 'A
veritable collapse of the critical faculties.' 'How do you feel about
Dostoevsky?' 'Today I have no feelings about Dostoevsky.' She kept
referring to 'buggers', apparently convinced that this included all men.

Prokosch talked music with Beecham, who thought Beethoven's last
quartets over-done, over-reached, under-controlled, and that Gertrude
Stein wrote 'pure drivel'. He talked butterflies with Nabokov, met
Granville-Barker, de Chirico and Alexandra Kollontai, the only woman
Lenin invited into his first cabinet. (Incidentally, she refutes the

character in a Koestler novel who pronounces that one can judge the deficiencies of the Left by the ugliness of its women.) He was privileged to watch a shrimp, dipped in mayonnaise, dive from Edmund Wilson's toothpick on to the elaborately built hair of Edith Sitwell, without disturbing her dissertation on the incantatory element in Milton, and the dominant murmuration of the cryptomagical in *The Rime of the Ancient Mariner*, while Wilson still peered at the shrimp with scrupulous curiosity. As a teenager, Prokosch had met Joyce, looking like an embittered provincial surgeon with green fingers, as he talked of éclairs and constipation; and, at the boy's mention of the stream of consciousness, begged him not to talk drivel, and began talking of wine. All this was dazzling to beginners.

Prokosch was like a machine: you dropped in a name and instantly received a verdict, a story, a description. Cyril Connolly 'used literature not as a source of illumination but as a decor for his misanthropy, and his impeccable sense of vogue'. Brecht resembled a playful and malevolent abbot; Auden condemned Verlaine and Rimbaud as 'songsters', from a face suddenly resembling a quick shaft of lightning on a war-shattered landscape. On Ezra Pound: 'I could see that his *Cantos* had something in common with his tennis: a convoluted rage pierced with moments of half-mad splendour and flecked with a certain flamboyant incoherence.'

In a Cambridge college, a Nepalese snow-pit, an Alpine village, a Tuscan farm, Indian crossroads . . . there, as if waiting, was Prokosch. He drove T. S. Eliot to Nemi, and they found a hollow, dilapidated oak, wispy and commonplace. 'I was sick with disappointment, though thrilled to see it with Eliot who was so indebted to *The Golden Bough*.' At a fountain he saw Dylan Thomas and drove him to Ostia. *The Skies of Europe* was an apt title for another novel. At Cambridge, he had called on the formidable F. R. and Q. D. Leavis. For them, literature was a serious matter involving discrimination, puritan dedication, moral integrity. F. R. Leavis said that only two poets in pre-war England deserved scrutiny. Eliot 'with certain rigorous reservations. I shall never forgive him for *The Rock*, to put the matter charitably. To have written it was ignominious but to go and publish it was, how shall I phrase it . . .'

'Irrelevant', said Queenie rapidly. She also supplied the name of the second: 'not that Sitwell woman' but Ronald Bottrall. Of novelists, Joyce, Lawrence and Forster were, that afternoon, accepted, also two more.

'How do we feel about Virginia, dear?'

'We have accepted Virginia Woolf.'

Queenie had, too, accepted T. F. Powys, though with an air of self-reproach. 'He is of his own effects repetitive, but he has integrity and that is what matters.' Prokosch demanded the sixth. Leavis peered at him.

'Is there a sixth? Who knows? Quite possible. Do we accept a sixth, Queenie?'

'We have considered L. M. Myers, dear.'

'To be sure, *The Root and the Flower*. I had almost forgotten Myers. There is indubitably a concern for the moralities. There are moments of frivolity but the basic gravity is unquestionable. He has a moral amplitude. We have accepted L. M. Myers.'

Leavis added that they had learnt to live with Dostoevsky.

Throughout the Fifties, and for another thirty years, Prokosch published regularly: criticism, poems, novels, still ready to talk of the famous and of his own plans. He remained vivid, even exotic, elegiac, then, increasingly, melancholic. Some friendships, notably with Auden, were somehow blighted, and Auden, critics were saying, had far too emphatically influenced his own poetry.

Within the polished façades and the high-flavoured chatter, there must have been lurking a sadness as death overcame the great, and new champions bounded on to the courts. He sought rare love, but less successfully than he did rare butterflies. By 1960, the masterpiece already seemed out of sight: not 'a slim little masterpiece like *Billy Budd* or *Death in Venice*, but a big fat masterpiece like *Don Quixote* or *Anna Karenina*'. In his novels, the décor remained: fretted mountains, seashores, lakeside villages, Bangkok cafés, seedy Indian palaces, Malaysian brothels and jungles, empty railway stations – landscapes scented, heavily flowered, steamy with drugs. But little developed from it, or the chatty strangers, perhaps spies, unpublished poets, inscrutable gurus with well-filled pockets disdaining materialism, that peopled it.

From about 1952, he annually issued, from Paris, or Florence, Venice, Bangkok, Singapore, Naples, Barcelona, Stuttgart, Zurich, Antwerp, Vienna . . . a tiny edition of a single poem, bound in mauve, or vermilion, or violet, with labels of chromium, oak and ambergris, inscribed to his various friends 'to remind them that I still existed'.

All these writers had reputations established during or before the war. Younger men and women would soon be competing with them in talent, though most of them were content to produce fewer works. The role of the Book itself was being modified, though not seriously undermined, by the advance of television which, for all its energy, often revealed itself as lacking the depth, allusiveness and range of print.

2

Home Preserves

THE EARLY FIFTIES were enlivened or encumbered by some Victorian notables, born in an age that had not known electronic media, aeroplanes, tanks, Freud, female suffrage or Keynes, and who would not have thought their absence an irredeemable loss. Chesterton had written that it takes an age that has nothing to say to invent the loudspeaker.

The foremost Victorian, an outstanding collector's item, was Winston Churchill, who returned to power in 1951. In 1897 he had been called the youngest man in Europe. Next year he had charged, with the 21st Lancers, at Omdurman. He had early become the highest paid journalist in London, and later had escaped from a Boer jail with a price on his head which he thought insufficient. He had been savaged by Labour for despatching troops during a Welsh miners' strike, at the request of a socialist mayor, had mobilized the Fleet in 1914, had vigorously opposed the 1926 General Strike, and had supported Mussolini and praised the early Hitler, though he had been foremost in landing forces against the young Bolshevik republic. He was an early subscriber for Joyce's *Ulysses*. E. M. Forster had sneered at him for his responsibility for the Gallipoli fiasco. In 1951, at a Royal Academy dinner, he suggested that Picasso should be kicked up the backside, though before the Great War he had supported him.

Churchill relished controversy and never lacked it. The military experts Basil Liddell Hart and General J. F. C. Fuller deplored his refusal to discuss Hitler's peace terms and accept the Führer's promise to maintain the British Empire, arguing that to fight would certainly lose the Empire. He had mocked Gandhi, at Yalta had connived at the betrayal of Poland to Stalin and, when safely dead, was to be accused in Rolf Hochhuth's play, *Soldiers*, of having engineered the murder of the anti-Communist Polish commander, General Sikorski, in 1943. In 1945 he had forecast that a Labour government would introduce Gestapo rule.

Philip Larkin's father, City Treasurer of Coventry, thought Churchill's face that of a criminal in the dock. After meeting Niels Bohr who, along with Einstein, was the supreme theorist of atomic physics and quantum processes, Churchill had scoffed at 'this blithering idiot'. He was intolerant of 'this damned psychological nonsense' and thought military psychiatry a shirker's charter. He was cheered or blamed for fox-hunting at 74 and buying a race horse, Colonist II. Sentimental, he wept at Harrow School songs and would say that his own favourite tune was 'Makin' Whoopee'. Throughout, he had been accused of war-mongering, of helping to partition Ireland, of never having used public transport. He had suggested killing the captured Nazi leaders without trial, by an archaic but simple Act of Attainder. A royalist, he maintained that the retention of the German monarchy would have prevented Hitler. Vehemently anti-socialist, he was pro-trades unions, seeing them as tenaciously conservative. He had been sufficiently insensitive to attempt to badger George V into naming a warship *Oliver Cromwell*. Proud of his American mother, and of possessing one-sixteenth Red Indian blood, he must have chuckled when Adolf Hitler in his glory denounced him as a 'yid-ridden, half-American drunk'.

Like his Victorian contemporaries, Kipling, Joseph Chamberlain, Cecil Rhodes, Rider Haggard, he cherished the Anglo-Saxon moral and administrative virtues. Jews he much admired but not Arabs, and in 1952 wrote to Anthony Eden that Egyptians were 'lower than the most degraded savages now known'. 'Blackamoors' he respected little more than he did Indians, 'the beastliest people in the world, next to the Germans'. In 1955, readers of *Tribune* and the *New Statesman* were shocked at his opposition to mass immigration. Many Conservatives still derided him as an adventurer, mysteriously, for art, literature, science, even politics, depend on adventurers rather than on conformists. The socialist Emanuel Shinwell mocked 'his ignorance of all social trends'.

Much of this was as unattractive to Fifties youth as it had been to their grandparents. That he was arrogant, bumptious and unscrupulous was generally agreed, though in crisis these might come in handy. 'Winston', rumbled Bob Boothby, 'was a shit, but we needed a shit to defeat Hitler.'

In 1954, rather speciously, we thought, he was awarded the Nobel Prize for Literature, but critics rebuked his dilution of deep convictions with romantic ideas, or his lack of any ideas at all. His histories, they added, were mere narrative, ignoring genetics, climate, class, myth, the unconscious. He disregarded urban guilts and frustrations, still used words like 'wicked', even 'evil'. He was only, like Gladstone, a politician who wrote, not the genuine article, like Disraeli, a writer who entered politics. Though Auden conceded 'the old monster knows how to write', Evelyn Waugh condemned his prose style, 'sham-Augustan, the metaphors violent', and his war speeches continued to agitate fastidious nerves. To call Hitler a 'bloodthirsty guttersnipe' lacked decorum, let alone Modernist principles.

During the War, Dr Alex Comfort, poet and novelist, physician, anarchist and pacifist, more recently the author of the hugely successful *Joy of Sex*, had lambasted 'The Baron' in *Tribune*, then edited by Aneurin Bevan and Michael Foot, with George Orwell the literary editor:

> You've heard the Baron's bloody-minded speeches
> (Each worth a fresh Division to our foes)
> That smell so strong of murder that the crows
> Perch on the Foreign Office roof and caw
> For German corpses laid in endless rows.
>   (from 'Letter to an American Visitor')

Orwell himself responded in 'As One Non-Combatant to Another':

> But you don't hoot at Stalin – that's 'not done' –
> Only at Churchill; I've no wish to praise him,
> I'd gladly shoot him when the war is won,
> Or now, if there was someone to replace him.
> But unlike some, I'll pay him what I owe him;
> There was a time when empires crashed like houses,
> And many a pink who'd titter at your poem
> Was glad enough clinging to Churchill's trousers.
> Christ! How they huddled up to one another
> Like day-old chicks about their foster-mother.
> I'm not a fan for 'fighting on the beaches',
> And still less of the 'breezy uplands' stuff,
> I seldom listen to Churchill's speeches,
> But I'd far sooner hear that kind of guff
> Than your remark a year or so ago
> That if the Nazi came you'd knuckle under
> And peaceably 'accept the status quo'.
> Maybe you would! But I've a right to wonder
> Which will sound better in the days to come,
> 'Blood, toil and sweat,' or 'Kiss the Nazi's bum.'

Bevan, revered by the militant Left, to Churchill 'a squalid nuisance', had remarked, when conscription was introduced, 'We have lost, and Hitler has won'; scarcely the fighting spirit of a resolute anti-Fascist.

In 1950, stepfather of a girl half-Jewish, though admiring Comfort's poetry, I sided with Orwell. As for Churchill's writing, I found more of it in my commonplace book than I had expected, the work of a dramatist with himself as hero, containing a streak of the joker, a Coriolanus with relish for fun, always addressing a large audience. His prose, like his paintings, sought colour, flourished on contrasts. Had he written verse, it might have imitated Macaulay's *Lays*. He would have agreed with Wilde, that he for whom the present is the only thing that is present knows nothing of the world in which he lives.

On Lord Curzon: 'The morning had been golden, the noontide was bronze, and the evening lead; but all were solid and each was polished till it shone after its fashion.'

On the débâcle of the Singapore defences: 'I ought to have known. My advisers ought to have known, and I ought to have been told, and I myself ought to have asked.'

On his Cabinet role: 'All I wanted was compliance with my wishes after reasonable discussion.'

In his *History of the English-speaking Peoples*, appearing throughout the Fifties, he mentioned that Bishop Beaufort opened the parliamentary session of 1414 'with a sermon on "Strive for the Truth unto Death", and with an exhortation, "While we have time, let us do good unto all men." This was understood to mean the speedy invasion of France.'

On Dictators: 'Dictators ride to and fro upon tigers from which they dare not dismount.'

On China: 'Punishing China is like flogging a jelly fish.'

He had some instinct for everyday joys and troubles. With W. G. Grace he had vigorously attacked the closing of the Empire Music Hall on moral grounds. Kipling had rebuked him for helping start old age pensions, John Galsworthy's play *Justice* induced him to initiate prison reforms, and, by starting wage councils, labour exchanges and unemployment relief, he and Lloyd George had moved towards the Welfare State.

Legend, the Empress Eugénie said feelingly, always overcomes history, but anecdotes and sayings, however apocryphal, are seldom totally misleading. Churchill grew them like bright feathers. I enjoyed the one of his offering an Arab diplomat a drink, peremptorily refused on religious grounds. Churchill stared. 'My God ... I mean, Christ! That is ... Allah!'

Having used gaudy invective against Treasury and Foreign Office, he was asked which of these he more resented. 'The War Office!' When out of office he lived by his public utterances 'from mouth to hand'.

I myself was then collecting historical details: Paris executioners during the Terror, working with a rose in their mouths; Peter the Great's shyness; Beau Brummell's snuff-box, more exclusive than most clubs; Robespierre's quiet but chilling stare; Churchill's top hat on the end of his stick as he toured ravaged streets. A. J. P. Taylor supplied another: Hugh Dowding, head of Fighter Command, was, Taylor claimed, the only officer to appeal against Churchill to the War Cabinet, and win: 'When argument failed, Dowding laid down his pencil on the Cabinet table. This gentle gesture was a warning of immeasurable significance. The War Cabinet cringed, and Dowding's pencil won the Battle of Britain.'

By 1955, I was hearing that Winston Churchill was a mouldy dinosaur; his world had vanished in disrepute, the new world was clean contrary to his hopes, that he had left no message. The last is surely mistaken. He had shown that personal courage and initiative and lack of theory can carry as much punch as the big battalions, bigotry and cruelty; that power can be exercised with humour and restraint even in crisis; and that a politician concerned only with politics will usually leave little by way of a message. He had added to what Boswell called the juiciness of the English imagination. I was interested to read, in 1962, some words by Milovan Djilas, Tito's delegate to Stalin. Molotov told Djilas that during the war, Churchill, drinking as copiously as his Moscow hosts, joked that, having taught the Red Army to fight so well by his 1919 intervention at Archangel, he deserved the highest Russian honour. Djilas recorded: 'One realised that Churchill had left a generally deep impression on the Soviet leaders as a far-sighted and dangerous "bourgeois statesman", though they did not like him.' A. J. P. Taylor, writing *English History, 1914-1945*, during the Fifties, considered Churchill 'made some great mistakes and many small ones. The wonder is that he did not make more. No other man could have done what he did, and with a zest that rarely flagged.'

I never met Churchill but did, so to speak, collide with his rumbustious, heavy-drinking son, Randolph, former MP, journalist, clubman, fellow-officer with Waugh in wartime Yugoslavia, who possessed a flair for ringing friends and ex-friends at four a. m. with 'What's the news?' He produced the first two volumes of his father's official biography very competently, but then died.

My episode occurred around 1954 and cannot be entirely fantastical, despite my recalling it through a haze which seemed inseparable from this alarming man. I was in a country house near where he was staying. After dinner, lateish, he wandered in, sufficiently drunk to imagine himself in some hotel, an illusion reinforced by the sight of us unknowns sipping our drinks. Brusquely he ordered a double brandy, which our hostess, handsome, talented, and at this moment perplexed, swiftly supplied, while not recognizing him. Matters seemed well. Churchill settled himself down like an ill-designed galleon on a yellow sandbag, until a woman, a painter of some merit, resumed the conversation: 'The Queen does perfectly well, even considering her salary.'

The last word struck the gate-crasher like a pogo-stick. He staggered up, he swayed, pudgy, glistening, outraged, he drew breath, then bellowed, 'I will not have my monarch insulted,' and banged her in one eye.

All looked at her husband. Of considerable literary achievement, he was physically small. Eyes ranged the company, eventually accosting the youngest and tallest present. Myself. I had boasted at dinner of my physical fitness and was now, silently but emphatically, being invited to prove it. Churchill was showing signs of improving his feat, on the remaining eye, as though dissatisfied with his first attempt.

I thought, I thought fast, snatching the brandy bottle and, dangling it before him like an amateur matador, drew him towards the door, across the hall, past the front door, into the cold, cold night where I finally halted, yielding the bottle. He emptied it, spun, unexpectedly patted my shoulder and, with considerable dignity, tipping me half a crown, shouldered his way through an imaginary multitude towards wherever he had come from: Mecca, Jerusalem, or Downing Street.

In contrast, Clement Attlee was a 'grey man', not in itself a handicap. Exciting government is usually bad government. From a moderately imperialist public school, Haileybury, whose original function had been to issue civil servants to the East India Company, Attlee had joined the Independent Labour Party in 1907, mentioning in his rather tepid autobiography, *As it Happened*, that he found there 'a characteristically British interpretation of socialism.' William Morris, Robert Blatchford, Ramsay MacDonald and the Fabians, as against Marx and Lenin. Rule by the Elect, the Saints, the One-Party Mafia was not for him. He wanted not the Perfect State but better government. Another Victorian, Mayor of impoverished Stepney and social worker, a Great War veteran, dedicated to peaceful reform, unhedonistic humanism, fairness in distribution, he preferred not to lay down the law but, sometimes tartly, sought reasonable conditions to enable Law to be maintained. His socialism was tempered by his public-school loyalties. He had limitations. In government, he was more concerned with leaving India than entering Europe, which briefly could have been achieved virtually on Britain's own terms. In 1950, he listened without visible interest to a newcomer, Edward Heath, speaking of the Schuman Plan for a common market in coal, iron and steel: 'By standing aside from the discussions, we may be taking a very great risk with our economy – a very great risk indeed.' His alleged objection, 'foreigners don't play cricket', might have been somewhat more than a joke.

He was tough, trouncing the great over-rhetorical Winston in the 'Gestapo' debate, and later resisting Truman over the proposed use of the atomic bomb in Korea. Kindly to the young and unpompous, and to Aneurin Bevan who was so frequently at odds with his patient reform policies, he distrusted the 'too clever by half': Harold Laski and Richard Crossman. His most substantial biographer, Kenneth Harris, tells how Crossman, anxious to convince the Premier about the determination of refugee Jews to reach Palestine, asked to see him: 'Attlee agreed ... Crossman went to his room in the House, sat down opposite him at his desk, and waited. "Go ahead", said Attlee. Highly nervous – "It's now or never, I thought" – Crossman launched into his argument and, spurred on by his nervousness, spoke nonstop for about twenty minutes. There was a pause, then "How's your father, Dick?"'

I learnt from a personal mentor, T. R. Fyvel, that having established a remarkable Welfare State, Attlee confessed in the mid-Fifties that, when he contemplated the new social services existing alongside mass demands 'for tabloid newspapers, Hollywood films, television, racing, betting pools, he felt he no longer knew what people wanted'. His list sounded fairly comprehensive.

My relations with Attlee were fruitful but remote. In 1950, I heard from a source undeniably disreputable of an obscure literary fund in the gift of the Monarch, on advice from Downing Street. My letter to Attlee necessitated more care than a short story – which, in a way, it was – and I worded it cunningly. Carefully casual, I mentioned my sojourn at Haileybury. Having read his views on current English cricket, I reproduced them as my own. I referred, decorously and with but slight manipulation, to encouragement that I had received from eminent personages, safely dead, including H. G. Wells. I added a judicious comment on post-war Stepney, implying I was worthily treading in his footsteps. Eventually, a cheque arrived, with an injunction not to repeat the request. I enjoyed thinking of Clem Attlee and HM, pacing the Palace gardens discussing me. 'I would suggest ...' 'But I don't ...' 'Ah, but have you read ... ?'

Around 1957, I attended an Old Boys' gathering at which Attlee was present. All was pleasant enough, until a busybody intervened – a busybody in 1937, as then. 'Gentlemen, please be upstanding, for a toast to the greatest Haileyburian.' Attlee went scarlet and remained seated. 'Gentlemen, I give you, Field Marshal Lord Allenby.'

Attlee seemed all of a piece, but that race and religion, like sex and sport, revoke Party lines remained true, whatever the official claims. Hugh Dalton, once a friend of Rupert Brooke, Labour Chancellor until thoughtlessly disclosing a minor Budget secret, was disgusted when Attlee offered him the Colonial Office in 1950. 'I had a horrid vision of pullulating, poverty-stricken diseased nigger communities for whom one can do nothing in the short run, and who, the more one tries to help them, are querulous and unhelpful.'

Sir Oswald Mosley, once a Conservative, later a Labour Minister, then the British Fascist leader, now lived in Paris, returning to fight unsuccessful by-elections. London walls were periodically plastered with apocalyptic posters, 'He is Coming', surmounted by a black-uniformed, ironclad figure striding towards infinity or a bunker, in an abandoned universe. Fascist street meetings, dominated by ex-boxers and ex-Service bullies, seemed unchanged since 1937: anti-Jewish, anti-Black, anti-Parliament and anti-unions.

I believe that in 1950 some twenty Fascist organizations had revived or started, scrawling PJ – Perish Judah – on walls, yelling patriotic slogans, shaking collecting boxes under Jewish faces, many flaunting Mosley's 'Flash in the Pan' insignia. To counter them, Morris Beckman, ex-Navy, founded the 43 Group, which disrupted Fascist meetings, stole anti-Semitic literature from shops and warehouses, and produced a news sheet, with considerable success.

In 1954, Desmond Stewart, novelist, Arabist, biographer of Jesus and T. E. Lawrence, forced me to take cover in a pub by loudly remarking: 'We can at least agree about this. Mosley got it just about right. After all, Churchill betrayed the country, Tom Mosley was brave enough to try and rescue it from Jews, nigs, the scum of history,' adding, when I cautiously emerged, 'whenever he looks at me, I feel brave enough to march against Mongols'. Desmond, a pacifist, had passed much of the war in front of a Buckinghamshire fire, in a large overcoat, writing poems, many of them about the beauties of winter, a season he particularly detested, and in which he had to be offered money even to open the front door.

Mosley could dominate a meeting with his powerful, convinced voice, jeering, strident, reminiscent, like that of Hitler, more of vulgar music than of reason. He was smart with hecklers:

A heckler: 'But in *Kapital*, Marx says . . .'

Mosley, with theatrical incredulity: 'You have read *Kapital*?'

Heckler, with brazen confidence: 'Yes.'

Mosley, smiling politely: 'All ten volumes?'

Heckler, defiantly: 'Of course.'

Mosley, after a telling pause: 'You have at least accomplished the impossible. There are only three volumes.'

Oswald Mosley had been six months on the Western Front, and was convinced that Britain should never again risk another such war. He had opposed the Second World War, pleading that it would sacrifice the Empire to American big business and to Stalin's Russia, where there was no business at all save factional barbarity in high places. He would have resisted a German invasion: 'We will fight for Britain, yes, but a million Britons shall never die in your Jews' quarrel.'

Mosley was interned during the war, released, against Labour opposition, by the intercession of an opponent, Churchill. Fifties Britain must have seemed to him propitious. Victory had gained Russia 182,400 square miles of new territory and 24 million non-Russian citizens; her hegemony in Eastern Europe embraced a further 92 million people and 400,000 square miles of land. Less blatantly, through monopolies and the CIA, America was interfering in Nicaragua, Haiti, Venezuela, Cuba, Panama . . . while Britain was relinquishing control over 500 million. Here was a demagogue's chance. He was advocating authoritarian European unity, to counter Russian imperialism. Britain's increasing racial tensions could also be exploited, yet his efforts to obtain power failed ludicrously, even in places like Notting Hill where anti-Black feelings were strong.

Another veteran, Lord Chief Justice Goddard, was in the tradition of R. L. Stevenson's Weir of Hermiston, the no-nonsense type – 'I've never seen a man yet whom hanging has done any harm to.' In 1952 the Craig-Bentley trial gave him an opportunity to back his convictions. Christopher Craig, teenage son of a bank official, received a life sentence, later reduced, for shooting a policeman. His unarmed associate, Derek Bentley, of sub-normal intelligence, illiterate and epileptic, was hanged. This execution inspired a 'folk song' from Ewan MacColl, ever alert for topical outrages, as he was for past seditions and angers. It also forced a remark – 'He had to die sometime. He was of no conceivable value to the world.' – from Walter de la Mare, poet of dreams and moonbeams, elfin wiles and dusky, rather sinister fantasies. Left and Right, abroad, agreed on hangings, shootings, gassings, electrocutions, though in Britain most of the

Left supported the tireless Sydney Silverman's ultimately successful Abolition Bill.

A Scotland Yard eminence, Commander Hatherill, declared in the early Fifties of murderers: 'Not all are serious, some are just husbands killing their wives.' Serious or not, they ran the risk of meeting Albert Pierrepoint, landlord of the North Country *Help the Poor Struggler* pub, and Public Hangman. In 1945, he hanged thirteen of the Belsen staff in one morning and, at his peak, seventeen in one day. After the atrocious Rillington Place murders, in 1949, he recalled: 'I hanged John Reginald Christie in less time than it took the ash to fall off a cigar I had left half-smoked in my room at Pentonville.' He resigned in 1956, after a Home Office dispute over expenses. Later, he too opposed capital punishment, asserting that all his professional efforts had deterred no one.

Abolition was hastened by the hanging, in 1954, of Ruth Ellis, a young, blonde night-club hostess, which evoked popular agitation, though this was absent when a middle-aged Cypriot, Mrs Cristoff, suffered the same penalty.

At 88, Goddard presided over a libel case which would have amused Wells and Shaw but not more austere socialists. Three Labour leaders, Aneurin Bevan, Richard Crossman and Morgan Phillips, attended a socialist conference in Venice in 1957, subsequently called the Venetian Blind. Robert Graves's daughter, Jenny Nicholson, a young journalist, saw the three drinking deep and published her sightings in the *Spectator*, mentioning that the Italian socialists were puzzled by their British comrades' capacity to fill themselves like tanks with whisky and water. The virtuous trio sued her, emptying her pockets and wrecking her career, though later jovially admitting that they, particularly Phillips, had indeed been drunk. Even Bevan's biographer, John Campbell, admitted that their reaction was over-sensitive, rash and irresponsible, not to say vindictive.

C. B. Fry was an early Fifties personality unaddicted to wife-murder, though he might occasionally have contemplated it, for Mrs Fry was masterful, some thought sadistic, as his partner in running a naval training ship, *Mercury*. In youth an Oxford classicist, a lover of Herodotus, and rated the foremost scholar of his year, he had been a triple Blue, had been in the English soccer eleven in 1901, and played in the 1902 Cup Final. He captained England at cricket, and played in twenty-six Tests between 1895 and 1912. In a university contest he rather casually broke the world long jump record. After the Great War he worked in Geneva and helped his old friend and Sussex and England cricketing partner, Ranjitsinhji, Jam Saheb of Nawanagar, in his work as Indian representative to the League of Nations, and with a green pencil 'thick as a walking stick', wrote a speech for Ranji to deliver which, Fry claimed, ejected Mussolini from Corfu.

Two Englishmen during the first decades of the century were offered the throne of Albania. One was Aubrey Herbert, inspirer of John Buchan's *Greenmantle*, who once dropped from a plum tree onto a tea party 'because I was ripe', the other was C. B. Fry. The post demanded courage and resourcefulness, which Fry possessed, but also £10,000, which he did not. Ranji, unwilling to lose him, did not come up with the money.

Fry's concern with youth training led him elsewhere. He wanted liaison between Boy Scouts and the Hitler Youth, and found Hitler himself quiet, courteous and simple. 'That the Führer is hasty, over-emphatic and even noisy I cannot well imagine,' he wrote in 1939, and never withdrew it.

Inwardly complex and neurotic, outwardly he remained, in the early Fifties, the striding, upright *Boys' Own Paper* hero, a link with W. G. and a great sporting age. Before his death in 1956, he could be seen in the Long Room at Lord's, monocled, brightly waistcoated, quoting Greek, querying umpires' decisions and with his cane demonstrating how particular strokes should be played.

Another much-loved sporting survivor was the dynamic West Indian cricketer, Learie Constantine. Born very poor in Trinidad, as a child he had had to play with orange and branch instead of ball and bat, his father training him to catch by throwing cutlery and the best crockery at him. He became one of the most electric fielders in history. After the war, all Britain was roused when a northern hotel refused him admission, on racialist grounds. Called to the English Bar, he accepted public office in the Caribbean, became High Commissioner for Trinidad and Tobago, and eventually entered the House of Lords.

Football and its supporters had not yet reverted to what, in the sixteenth century, Sir Thomas Elyot had deprecated as 'nothing but beastlie furie and extreme violence'. Stanley Matthews, of Stoke, gave the title for a poem by Alan Ross, its central verse running

> Head of a Perugino, with faint flare
> of the nostrils, as though Lipizzaner-like
> he sniffed at the air,
> Finding it good beneath him, he draws
> Defenders towards him, the ball a bait

They refuse like a poisoned chocolate,
retreating, till he slows his gait
To a walk, inviting the tackle, inciting it.

The volumes of Arnold Toynbee's *Study of History* were still appearing
in the Fifties. Here, striving for clues to man's past and future,
he examined his twenty-six 'civilizations', extinct, suspended or
surviving, offering reasons for their collapse, ossification or success.
This approach, magisterial, theorizing, quasi-scientific, seeming to
teach colleagues their job, was often queried or resented, not least by
those who recalled his meeting Hitler and returning convinced of the
sincerity of that dismal man's love of peace. He would explain that
Jung's studies in mythology supplied him with clues to the rise and fall
of civilizations additional to one he had originally found in Goethe's
Faust: that of Challenge and Response. Also, the historian Lewis
Namier had shown him Spengler's *Decline of the West* which, though
suggestive and challenging, remained unsatisfactory, its thesis needing
amendments to make it less deterministic. Race or environment were
insufficient explanations. Most races had contributed to civilization,
similar environments did not axiomatically produce similar societies.
He held that 'civilisations are the handmaids of religion'; though,
while ending one volume with a plea for the restoration of Papal
authority, he generally treated the four higher religions as variations
on a common attitude, with no creed unique. Without spiritual
awareness, people perish. He detested nationalism, believing, like
H. G. Wells, in world unification, and was denounced as anti-Semitic
for treating Israeli evictions of Arabs in 1948 as the equivalent of Nazi
behaviour to Jews. Such new states as Israel and Jordan could be slotted
into such glum definitions as 'the stimulus of archaism'.

With Marx, he regarded history, like physics and biology, as susceptible to certain laws and rhythms, invisible to others who saw it
more as a muddle. He specified these laws in neat, suspiciously neat,
formulae: Challenge and Response, Stimulus of Penalization, Stimulus
of New Ground, Virtues of Adversity, Withdrawal and Return,
Nemesis of Creativity, Self-transcendence of Futurism, Schism and
Palingenesia, with alternating rhythms beneath symbolized by more
ancient concepts: God and Devil, *yin* and *yang*, male and female. Venice
was an example of stagnation and decline, the Idealization of a Dead
Self, living on past glories and succumbing to man's greatest temptation, idolatry.

His sales were mountainous, chiefly in America. America, like youth, applauds the big statement, the prophetic stance, the complete, vastly researched explanation with a flash of the apocalyptic. I myself was fascinated by Toynbee, as I had been by Wells. Wells had traced history from slime to the League of Nations, a linear progression periodically checked by ruffianly kings and scheming priests: Toynbee showed a row of mountains, some desolate and abandoned, some with climbers left helpless beneath the summit, some with climbers still struggling. Such an approach could make a Tiglath Pilesar comparable to Charlemagne, Peter the Great, Hitler; Jesus to have affinities with the Gracchi, Agis IV, Kleomones III. Like Reinach, and before Graves, he deconstructed myths – of Hercules, Jason, Perseus – as permanent symbols of human development, often originating in misinterpretations of iconographic symbols, or as shorthand for a communal swamp draining or the retreat of plague. Vast, interconnected spaces were visible under migrations, revolutions, the rise of a belief, the decay of a forest. Reading *A Study of History* was like seeing the earth from the moon, or Britain from Tibet, where, perhaps, our history could be reduced to a failure to cultivate the yak. Athens and Rome, London, Paris, New York, shared history with Guptic India, the Ottoman Ascendancy, Han China, with Bactrians, Hittites and Mayans.

Reading in Toynbee that Jesus could be docketed with Emile Ollivier, a scapegoat for the Franco-Prussian War, as an example of Withdrawal and Return, I felt snobbishly in the know. Like Graham Greene and John Buchan, Toynbee demonstrated the flimsiness of the grounds we inhabit: his description of tree and swamp overcoming a Mayan city was as powerful, as poignant, as Kipling's 'Letting in the Jungle'. His schema, if tendentious, allowed stimulating suggestions about the teeming lunacy of human enterprise. It challenged one to present further suggestions. J. L. Austen had said that importance is not important, truth is. This seemed relevant.

By the Fifties, British appreciation was decidedly mute. Universal historical explanations smacked of the last century. Tangye Lean noted Toynbee's pretentious omniscience, quoting what he called a typical assertion: 'if Austerlitz was Austria's Cynosephale, Wagram was her Pydna'. Critics maintained that, unlike G. M. Trevelyan or G. M. Young, Toynbee contaminated history by valuing it not for its own sake, but as a field for prophecy. Worse, from the viewpoint of a civil servant; T. R. Fyvel indeed castigated the Study as 'the perfect Foreign Office brief'. True, Toynbee did have at least one ulterior purpose: he had seen the desolate faces of mothers searching the daily casualty lists of the Great War, and resolved to help enlighten people so as to prevent war itself. 'For the unification of the world must come ... [But] the

Brotherhood of Man is, I am convinced, an utterly impossible ideal, unless men are bound together by belief in a transcendent God.' This suggested an inorganic deity, like the French Revolution's Goddess of Reason, or Serapis, a healing god combining Osiris and Apis, invented to unite the Alexandrine and Syrian factions of the Ptolemaic Empire. Spiritual awareness begged many questions, and I sometimes remembered Robert Frost writing about the Islands of the Blessed, and admitting that he had never met a blessed one.

I recognized Arnold's meanness, unendearing, rooted in some childhood distresses. On longish country walks round his son Philip's Suffolk home, near where I lived, he was benign, his grey-green eyes under short white hair in a head long and bony, always friendly, sometimes ironic, like his frequent, 'You know more about this than I do . . . but . . .', doubtless discussing the Schism of Palingenesia. He was as vulnerable as most of us, visibly affronted when his junior, the historian C. V. Wedgwood, received the OM, withheld from himself.

Montgomery and Mountbatten both deemed themselves essential to any study of history. Field Marshal Bernard Law Montgomery was Deputy Supreme Commander of Nato in 1951. He had enjoyed a rapport with his fighting men as successful as Cromwell and 'Old Nosey', and was the reverse of Napoleon III who, commanding at Magenta, exclaimed: 'A victory, is it? And I was about to order retreat!' He was noted for his trenchant, barking verbal style. Allegedly, about to be painted by Augustus John, he demanded: 'Who is this fellow? He is very dirty, and I'm sure there are women about.' Of his Supreme Commander, Eisenhower, installed as President in 1953, he was dismissive – 'Completely and utterly useless . . . He held conferences to collect ideas. I held conferences too – to give orders.' Himself a teetotaller, he was unattracted by A. V. Alexander, First Lord of the Admiralty – 'a mobile whisky and soda'. His prose style, indeed, would never have qualified for one of William Empson's seven types of ambiguity. 'I believe that one of the first duties of a commander is to create what I call "atmosphere",' he told his officers, on arriving in North Africa. 'I do not like the atmosphere I find here.' He listed doubts, a disposition to plan retreat, and ended, 'All that must now cease.' It did. Also: 'The task of the infantry is to find the enemy and kill him.' Revealingly, he particularly enjoyed Mrs L. M. Willis's hymn:

>   Father, hear the prayer we offer,
>   Not for ease our lives should be,

> But for strength that we may always
> Live our lives courageously.

Cromwell would have agreed. Monty, at home, after the early death of a beloved wife, allowed no flowers indoors: they had proclivities towards 'mess'.

While exemplifying the cool, managerial qualities of the modern hero the last Viceroy of India, Lord Louis Mountbatten, was also born royal and was not inclined to let you forget it. 'A relation of mine, who happened to be Queen of Spain . . .' He had manipulated Hindu and Muslim politicians with charm, adroitness and courage, exacting respect from Gandhi, despite the subsequent massacres at the time of Indian Independence, and affection from Nehru, an affection famously developed by Lady Edwina Mountbatten. Lord Moran, Churchill's doctor, called him a 'horrid, pushing go-getter'. Lord Beaverbrook agreed, doubtless resenting a fellow spirit. Moran, however, had a tongue incessantly acerbic. Of the royal physician Lord Dawson, he had written:

> Lord Dawson of Penn
> Killed so many men;
> That's why we sing
> God save the King.

I once had an encounter with Dawson, unpleasantly informal. He was coming to lunch, had demanded tennis, and I was ordered to mark out a court which, like opening a deck-chair, can be more tricky than it appears. Nervously, I confused the measurements and, by using yards instead of feet, produced a court, gleaming indeed, but appearing only slightly smaller than the average county cricket ground. In the light of Moran's revelations, I escaped lightly.

Heroism of a style perhaps more prophetic than that of Montgomery and Mountbatten emerged from Leonard Cheshire, VC, OM. At Oxford, his pre-war persona sounds unattractive, arrogant: 'I had little aim in life other than my own pleasure and profit – both of which I pursued with relentless determination.' Andrew Boyle, his biographer, contributed an Oxford story, absent in Cheshire's obituaries: 'Cheshire and Charles Ashton were dining together in a restaurant. A vast youth entered, with a small attractive girl. Two women soon followed, one horsey and tweeded, the other flashy, thickly made-up. Ashton swiftly promised Cheshire a bottle of champagne if he dared inquire which lady was the lesbian.

'Unhesitatingly, Cheshire rose, but, instead of accosting the female pair, halted before the fourteen stone youth and his clearly cherished companion. "I apologise for this intrusion, but my friend wants to know whether your friend is a lesbian."

'In the instantaneous fracas, Ashton was jerked from his chair, marched to the exit, where waiters and managers joined in the scrimmage, from which he ultimately escaped, and, returning, found Cheshire smugly contemplating a champagne bottle, already opened.'

As a wartime commander he showed flair and bravery. He was chosen as UK observer for the atomizing of Nagasaki, and observed that the pilots were two miles off course. This affected him more than the moral and historical significance of the explosion. He was never to yell 'Ban the Bomb', and indeed always supported Deterrence. After the war, until his death in 1992, he devoted himself to the sick and the unwanted, starting with daily care of an old man dying of cancer.

Very much in the Fifties, Leonard Woolf, at 14, had seen Gladstone – GOM, Grand Old Man, or God's Only Mistake – denouncing Bulgarian massacres. He had married Virginia Stephen in 1912, the year of the *Titanic*, recording in his biography: 'Our wedding ceremony was provided with an element of comic relief (quite unintentional), characteristic of the Stephens. In the middle of the proceedings, Vanessa interrupted the Registrar, saying: "Excuse me interrupting; I have just remembered: we registered my son – he is two years old – in the name of Clement and we now want to change his name to Quentin – can you tell me what I have to do?" There was a moment of astonished silence in the room as we all looked round sympathetically and saw the serious, slightly puzzled look on Vanessa's face. There was a pause while the Registrar stared at her with his mouth open. Then he said severely: "One thing at a time, please, madam."'

Woolf's detractors accused him and Virginia of anti-Semitism (he was a Jewish atheist); of unscrupulously dodging the Great War (he had a lifelong nervous affliction); and, refusing Virginia children (on medical advice), of precipitating her madness (which had begun years before). He survived her by nearly thirty years, and was probably underestimated. Novelist, short story writer, Fabian socialist, colonial civil servant, co-founder with Virginia of the Hogarth Press which published T. S. Eliot, Freud, Gorky, he was also a pioneer behind the foundation of the League of Nations.

Woolf was formidable. Professionally concerned with making the world healthier, better organized, less chaotic, to a stranger he could seem impatient, easily bored, in his own word, 'prickly'. Virginia's last letter to him belied much of this, repeated in her letter to Vanessa: 'All I want to say is that Leonard has been so astonishingly good, every day, always. I can't imagine that anyone could have done more for me than he has. We have been perfectly happy until the last few weeks, when this horror began. Will you assure him of this? I feel he has so much to do that he will go on better without me, and you will help him.'

In the Fifties he began his autobiography, often tart, displaying intellectual rigour, but touched with humour, never uproarious but dryly memorable. He mentions a dinner given by Rose Macaulay, at which Virginia misheard 'Holy Ghost' for 'The whole coast', and then he stooping, thinking to retrieve Sylvia Lynd's napkin, found he was raising her petticoat instead. When a civil servant in Ceylon in 1908, he had been asked by ex-Empress Eugénie, Napoleon III's widow, to arrange for her to inspect the most sacred relic, the Buddha's Tooth. Actually, it had been destroyed in 1560 by a Portuguese Archbishop in Goa, and what Woolf and Eugénie saw, keeping straight faces, was a dog's tooth. He resigned in 1912, his sense of ambivalence as an alien, regarding justice and law, a principal cause.

As caustic as Leonard Woolf, more realistic in her judgement than Shaw, witty, fiercely intelligent, emotionally vulnerable, bruised by tumultuous relationships with H. G. Wells and Lord Beaverbrook in the 1950s, Rebecca West was writing on British traitors, the Nuremberg trials, post-war murderers, on feminism, on Henry James, on Hamlet, Proust and Kafka, published in *The Court and the Castle* (1958). She was never an obsequious devotee of fashion ... 'I will declare to my last breath, that *War and Peace* is a stodgy pudding of events mixed by a loveless, restless, boring egotist who wanted to write a big big book.' Neither was age vitiating her asperities. Being embraced by Ford Madox Ford was like being the toast under a poached egg. Vera Brittain was 'a trumpeting ass'; Michael Arlen 'every other inch a gentleman'. For Beatrice Webb she reserved 'that silly, silly woman', perhaps overhearing Webb asserting that the Chinese were 'essentially unclean', and remembering that cycling through Normandy, in 1903, the Webbs had seemed not to enjoy cathedrals but merely to measure them.

She was travelling in Italy, Spain, France, lecturing at Yale, meeting Frieda Lawrence in Mexico, doubtless a resounding collision; and roundly attacking McCarthy in America. With memories of travels in pre-war Yugoslavia, she was passionately anti-Tito and berated his supporter, Churchill, for whom she had but a trifle more respect than for Tolstoy. She championed those who had failed, suffered, been overlooked.

She was always ready with the striking image or insight, on Dickens remarking: 'It is true that his books are sometimes so closely packed with characters of great liveliness but no significance that they recall the extreme but not exciting fertility of a cod's roe.' And on D. H. Lawrence's *The Plumed Serpent*: 'It represents not support of Hitler but hostility to Rousseau.' She once referred to that love of the disagreeable which is one of the most unpleasant characteristics of mankind. 'I had a radio brought into my room and for the first time realised how uninteresting life could be and how perverse human appetite.'

Winston Churchill wrote in the angry aftermath of the Great War, 'I am not a bit afraid of Siegfried Sassoon. That man can think. I am afraid only of the people who cannot think.' Solemn critics by 1950 had ceased to regard Sassoon but he remained, still captaining cricket elevens, and writing, mostly in prose. His *Collected Poems* (1957), included 'Doggerel About Old Days': verse written in 1939 which may explain his academic neglect and popular affection.

> Young people now – they don't know what the past was like.
> *Then* one could find the main roads museful on one's bike.
> Give me a moment and I'm back in Kent; I know
> How safe and sound life struck me thirty years ago . . .
>
> Kent was all sleepy villages through which I went
> Carrying my cricket bag. In wintertime, content
> To follow hounds across wet fields, I jogged home tired,
> In 1909 the future was a thing desired.

3

Foreign Survivors

TWO LONG-LIVING OLYMPIANS seemed to hover above the jangles of nation, race, fashion. Albert Einstein, refugee from the Nazis, still taught in America, now repented his part in preparing for the atomic bomb and was encouraging protests against Senator McCarthy's anti-Communist and blackmailing witch-hunt. A. J. Ayer commended Einstein's habit of discussing physics with unknown novices as though he could learn something from them.

The other, Albert Schweitzer, awarded the Nobel Prize for Peace in 1952, doctor, musicologist, organ-player, theologian – believing that Jesus was not *the* Son of God but, like all of us, *a* son of God, often very humanely mistaken, though of permanent relevance – remained master of his hospital at Lambaréné in French Equatorial Africa, though to Fifties progressives, he was not only an anachronism but worse, a paternalist. 'The African is my brother. But my younger brother': an attitude increasingly unpopular. His hospital was said to be virtually untouched by progress, his 'reverence for life' extending even to vermin, governed by Gandhi-like hostility to scientific research and development. Graham Greene, no less, was reported to have been shocked by it. The Africans were probably less so. And they might have recollected Schweitzer's savage indictment of the Europeans in Africa. 'Who can describe the injustices and cruelties that through the centuries, they have suffered through Europeans? Who can measure the misery produced among then by strong drink and hideous disease that we have taken to them?' He could have added more, though he might also have added the European virtues, of industry, common sense, know-how and irony.

In Europe, Germany posed a grave international cultural problem, so long morally and physically isolated, ignorant of world developments, and markedly divided between its Stalinist East and more liberal West, with the West still having to get used to new freedoms, arts, intellectual concepts.

For years, the chief cultural forces had been the Goebbels-controlled media and the Hitler Youth. Hesse was in Switzerland, Thomas and Heinrich Mann and Lion Feuchtwanger had fled the Nazis to America. The country abounded with equivocal figures. Ex-Crown Prince Wilhelm lived on, ex-Nazi, forgotten, with his women, debts and memories, none of them very wholesome. Emil Jannings, co-star of *The Blue Angel*, an assiduous worker for Goebbels in anti-Semitic films, would not be seen again. Heidegger kept some intellectual influence but not only Jews remembered his pre-war advice to German students: 'Your being is not governed by rules and theories. The Führer himself, and he alone, is the reality and the law of Germany now, Germany tomorrow.'

Not all were whole-hearted liberals and freedom-lovers. Ernst von Salomon had recently published his *Answers*, responses to an Allied questionnaire about his attitude to the war and Hitler. He had been a leading *condottiere* in the confused era of turmoil and civil war in north-eastern Germany following the end of the Great War and the collapse of the monarchy. His Freikorps fought pitilessly against the Communist Spartacists, most sensationally in Berlin in 1919, shooting dozens on the streets without trial. A passionate Prussian nationalist and writer, he had fought, freebooted, participated in political murders, including that of Walther Rathenau, the German Foreign Minister, a gifted economist, diplomat and philosopher, who had recently established a treaty with Lenin. Von Salomon's novel of the period fused Wagnerian anti-Semitism, myths of redemption and racial purity with the hankerings of the future SS: 'We saw red . . . we no longer possessed any human decency in our hearts. Where once peaceful villages had stood was now only soot, ashes, and burning embers, after our departure. We had lit a funeral pyre and more than dead goods burned on it – there burned our hopes, our longings: there burned the bourgeois commandments, laws, the values of the civilised world . . . and so we returned, swaggering, drunken, loaded with plunder . . .'

He had been contemporary with Wilhelm II, Franz Josef, Woodrow Wilson, as he now was with Clem Attlee, Dr Adenauer, Cary Grant and Brigitte Bardot. Whatever his reservations about the upstart Hitler, he remained one of the murderers amongst us. He was a friend of the novelist Ernst Jünger, whom Stephen Spender met in 1946 and called 'certainly the greatest German writer living in Germany'. When the

Englishman told him that he would not be attending the funeral of Jünger's friend, the pro-Nazi French writer Henri de Montherlant, to avoid ruffling supporters of the Resistance, Jünger complained of the stupidity of such people. 'It is really high time they became more mature.'

Jünger, still alive in 1994 aged 100, was a remarkable example of a riven European mind and experience. As a boy he had enlisted in the French Foreign Legion, then, gravely wounded in the Great War, had received the Kaiser's highest honour. His novel *In Shahlgewittern* (1929), praised by Gide as the greatest war book he had read, also profoundly moved Hitler. It showed his continuing belief in war, shared with Mussolini, as the sole opportunity for passion in action, for enlisting in a spiritual aristocracy of physical and mental endurance, replacing the effete and materialistic Empire with a state manned by selfless, technological, dedicated Platonic paladins, expert and merciless. He too had some dealings with the Freikorps and the early Nazis, and was reviled as 'the hangman' by Thomas Mann. Later, he courageously helped rescue some anti-Nazis and began opposition to the regime, though rejoining the army in 1939, the year of his fine, terrifying novel, *Auf den Marmorklippen*. An instant best-seller, it was swiftly banned by the furious Goebbels for its scalding forecasts of the Holocaust and nightmarish death camps, its anticipation of an officers' plot. In France, in 1940, he preserved Laon Cathedral from military hooligans and won his third Iron Cross for saving a wounded soldier.

Few conversions are complete, if indeed they ever actually happen. Jünger was no Montgomery or Alexander. Nigel Jones met him in his eighty-eighth year in 1982, and his *London Magazine* essay dispassionately evokes a personality rare in London literary parties of 1950: 'He found himself in Paris, where he acted as adjutant to the city's military governor, General von Stulpnagel ... At one moment he is rubbing shoulders with Cocteau, Céline, Picasso and Braque at fashionable afternoon salons, the next, he is supervising a firing squad at the execution of a deserter, and describing it in his usual clinical prose: the bullet holes appeared in the man's chest "like raindrops after a shower". One cannot resist speculating what fashionable salons would have appeared in London, had Hitler reached the Palace, and who would have attended. A visit to the Eastern Front, and some atrocity tales, and the influence of von Stulpnagel and other officers drew him towards the July conspirators, from whose débâcle he was apparently saved by Hitler himself. In 1950, immersed in travel, literature, conservationism and biology, he was 'one of the most renowned experts on the beetle'.

Likewise conspiratorial but less ambiguous, Axel von dem Bussche was a Fifties personality on the World Council of Churches. A former headmaster of Salem, from which Gordonstoun derived its ideas, as a young officer in occupied Ukraine he had resisted an order to massacre several thousand Jews, so that the job had to be given instead to Ukrainian deserters, who obeyed with alacrity, forcing their victims to dig mass graves over which, naked in a mile-long line, they were shot. After fighting before Leningrad, he joined a plot to assassinate Hitler in 1943, volunteering to greet him with grenades concealed within a newly designed military greatcoat which the Führer, connoisseur of appearances, wished to inspect. This was foiled, however, by the dictator's penchant for changing his programme, and by an inopportune Allied air-raid.

France retained many feuds and vendettas from Collaboration and Resistance. Cocteau, like Camille Desmoulins, was one of those to whom almost everything is forgiven, and his association with Germans in Paris was overlooked. Others, like Harry Bauer and Corinne Luchaire, theatrical stars, were hopelessly compromised. The latter was still beautiful, but her relations with Otto Abetz, Hitler's ambassador to Paris, had been flaunted too obviously. I once saw her in a night-club, glad to be asked to dance, acknowledging impassively that she could never work again in France, and disdaining Hollywood, or pretending to. Maurice Chevalier, Sacha Guitry and Jean Borotra, tennis champion and Pétain's Minister of Sport, were threatened, but survived. The American novelist and Paris-lover Kay Boyle, praising Samuel Beckett's work for the Resistance, was bitter against Gertrude Stein, now dead, and Alice B. Toklas. 'They had had German soldiers living in their home and had waited on them hand and foot. They were Jewish, they knew what people of their race were going through.'

I discerned another disagreeable image lurking beneath Fifties sunlight, learning more about Arletty, star of two of my favourite films: *Les Visiteurs du Soir* and *Les Enfants du Paradis*. She had had an affair with a Nazi officer in 1944. He was talented and artistic, but also sat on the bench, trying French partisans on capital charges. A Gaullist committee in Algiers condemned her to death for treason that year, though actually she suffered only house arrest and a shaven head. At a formal post-war arraignment, she declared that her loyalties were reserved for France, but that her arse was her own. When she was forgiven, and acting again, I learnt that she had kept her head permanently naked, and indeed did so until her death.

René Bousquet, admired by Laval, had been Pétain's Secretary-General of Police. As a youth of socialist beliefs, he had risked his life to rescue neighbours from flood. But at his trial as a war criminal in 1949, he had unimpressive explanations for the proven acclaim from Himmler and Heydrich for assisting them beyond the call of duty, over ruling Eichmann's initial hesitation in deporting French Jewish children for extermination. On his orders, 10,000 of these were rounded up, together with 66,000 adults, about 3,000 surviving. Mysteriously, though not untypically, he was released in 1951 and could thenceforward be seen, if not encountered, in Paris, living luxuriously as a banker until, very properly, he was murdered.

Charles de Gaulle attracted writers, some of them, like Jacques Soustelle, an authority on Mexico, and André Malraux, as political colleagues. Malraux was rousing more curiosity in Britain. No pro-Nazi suspicions touched him. He was in the line of Saint-Exupéry and T. E. Lawrence, the intellectual man of action, and indeed published *Lawrence and the Demon of the Absolute*. Art historian, administrator, critic, scholar, novelist, orientalist, soldier, archaeologist, anti-imperialist – who nevertheless stole Cambodian sculpture – resistance leader, he, I began to learn later from Jeffrey Meyers' *London Magazine* critique, partly manufactured and then believed his own legend. His professions were often very unreliable. His claim to have met T. E. Lawrence, to have flown over and photographed the Queen of Sheba's fabled capital, was romanticizing, and he probably exaggerated his revolutionary role in China and Indo-China after the Great War. Yet de Gaulle said of him that his presence gave him a sense of insurance against the commonplace. Spender called him the most brilliant and dynamic talker in his experience.

Talk aside, the truth remained considerable. Malraux, in the Spanish Civil War, collected volunteers and mercenaries and two obsolete planes, and attacked modern German tanks and artillery, while raising funds for the Republic. From Meyers I have learnt of his novel, *Days of Wrath*, which anticipated Silone and Orwell, as his film, *L'Espoir*, did De Sica and Rossellini, Meyers emphasizing the astonishing achievement of producing it during a civil war, without previous film experience, and focusing the significance of events within days of their occurrence. In the Second World War, he fought as a private, was captured, escaped, joined the Resistance in the victorious Alsace-Lorraine Brigade, heading a group that expelled the Germans from Strasbourg, was captured again and faced a mock firing squad. The war gave him his novel, *The Walnut Trees of Altenberg*, and I remember from the Fifties a tender and moving evocation of the delicious effect of the return of country sounds when the huge guns fell silent in 1918: the clink of milk pails, cattle lowing, an axe against wood.

Scandalizing the Left, from whom he had been alienated by the Stalinist purges, while supporting its anti-Fascist activities, he became de Gaulle's Minister of Information. Gaullism he called 'political passion in the service of France', and considered de Gaulle the only authentic anti-Communist. Minister of Culture on the General's return in 1958, he was the Jacques-Louis David of Gaullism; he organized its theatrical aspects, the rallies, processions, exhibitions and oratory; he cleaned the public buildings. He energetically worked in the decolonizing of five African states, most notably in Algeria.

In Britain he was far less known than Chevalier, Jean Gabin, Michelle Morgan, Borotra, François Mauriac, or that long-time denizen of Paris, Picasso. For many in Britain, modern art was summarized by the name, simultaneously hard and tender, sharp and caressing, clear as a sea-washed pebble, *Pablo Picasso*, though popular artistic appreciation had altered very little since before the Great War when, at Roger Fry's Post-Impressionist exhibition, Desmond MacCarthy had had to carry out a man so helpless with laughter that he seemed to be endangering his life. In 1945, a large Picasso-Matisse exhibition at the Victoria and Albert had been ferociously reviled. British insensitivity, however, was not unparalleled: an aristocratic lady, carrying her portrait by Picasso, was charged by Spanish customs officials with attempting to smuggle out a map of the fortifications of Madrid.

Throughout the Fifties, Picasso was in full flood, though some questioned his artistic depth. Moreover, his anti-capitalist, anti-American stance did not induce him to adjust his prices to the incomes of many Communists, nor inhibit him from collecting capital from fashionable New York galleries. His wartime support for left-wing victims of the Gestapo had been niggardly, though during the Cold War he designed a dove of peace which decorated many Communist-directed peace conferences. The dove had originated in a pigeon, a gift from Matisse; 'peace' appropriated by Marxists as if it were their discovery and monopoly. The late Allies were denounced as imperialists, while Russian imperialism in the Baltic states, Eastern Europe and the Balkans was justified as fulfilling the Will of the People, though elections to test this were forbidden.

Moscow attacked Picasso's work as élitist decadence, while vigorously exploiting his name on propaganda sheets. Their agent Anthony Blunt dismissed his *Guernica* as a private brainstorm lacking political relevance. In 1960, Kenneth Clark reckoned him midway between a naughty boy and an angry god. Whatever his final stature, he was a

vital hinge of Modernism, with its multiple vision, its kinetic fragmen-
tation of time and history, experience and imagination, its distortions
and grotesque montage, which he combined with his personal humour,
even fun, his malice and anger.

Picasso's innovations were not unanimously accepted by British
artists. Michael Ayrton, a young painter, sculptor, stage designer,
book illustrator – he designed a vivid cover for a paperback of Camus's
The Plague – art critic of the *Spectator* and novelist, whom Henry
Moore called a significant eccentric, admitted Picasso's genius and
technical mastery, and his influence on the applied arts and decoration,
though believing that this was largely to art's disadvantage, and that
his originality was less than it at first sight appeared. Indeed, he claimed
that much was a regurgitation of the ideas and formulae of others –
Ingres, Greek vases, African sculpture, Roman heads, Catalan murals,
Romanesque primitives, medieval pictorial glass, Van Gogh, Toulouse-
Lautrec, Grünewald, Vuillard, Denis, El Greco, de Chavannes,
Watteau, Cézanne, Seurat, Braque, Chinese and Persian styles, Matisse
himself – without coherent vision or organic conviction, more a perfunctory pastiche, an intellectual exercise, most of it artistic vampirism,
'a vast series of brilliant paraphrases on the history of art'. His were
superhuman talents striving to communicate the spurious, intriguing
the credulous with exciting trappings of bulls, women, guitars, blood,
cruelty, harlequins, circus performers. Ayrton rated Picasso an inexpert
and clumsy sculptor, and far superior as a draughtsman than as a
painter, his paintings usually faring better in reproductions. The
Spanish trappings were a menace to genuine art which derives from
genuine observation of nature and experience, from profound and
vital emotion.

Intellectuals mostly ignored this, or vilified Ayrton as iconoclast,
blasphemer, deicide, traitor or as merely jealous, though in an interview
published in 1951, Picasso told Giovanni Papini, perhaps jokingly,
that he was only a public entertainer exploiting his contemporaries'
imbecility, vanity and cupidity. 'Since Cubism, and indeed before it,
I have aimed to satisfy a public craving for novelty and scandal with
all the varying bits of nonsense that enter my head, and the less they
understand the greater their admiration for me.'

British writers could have found material in the fortunes of Charles
Tillon, a French Communist who, with his compatriot, André Marty,
both alive in 1954, had organized a French Black Sea naval mutiny
against the Allied anti-Red campaign in 1919. For his part in the
Spanish War, he landed in a Franco jail. A Resistance officer, he afterwards served in de Gaulle's first government. In 1952, we were reading

of Communist bosses accusing him of insufficient reverence for Stalin. On Moscow's orders, he was dismissed from all political assignments and expelled from the Party, with obedient Reds reviling him in the capitalist press.

Eastern Europe was showing no sign that any war had been fought against despotism and moral hooliganism. At the 1952 show trial in Prague of the Stalinist ex-dictators of Czechoslovakia, Slansky and Clementis, the language of the Public Prosecutor to the 'jury' telescoped the ages, could have been uttered by the ancient Assyrian, Ashur-bani-Pal, by Luther, by Fouquier-Tinville, or by Stalin's favourite pre-war prosecutor, Vyshinsky: 'May your sentence of death hit them like an iron fist, without any pity. May your sentence be a fire burning out this treacherous growth to its roots. Your sentence of death should ring like a bell through our Glorious Fatherland, a signal for new victories.'

4

Spectacles and Stages

ENGLISH INTELLECTUALS, ORWELL wrote, would rather steal from a church poor box than stand up when the National Anthem is played. Nevertheless, reinforced by the 1953 Coronation, Royalty continued as that section of live theatre the most continuously applauded. Cecil Beaton, at the Haymarket Theatre in 1952, watched the new Queen with her mother and sister attend Frederick Lonsdale's *Aren't We All?* for which he had designed the costumes: 'Throughout the performance the Royal Box was being surreptitiously watched by half the audience, so that the play received scant attention: but the general atmosphere was uncritical and good-natured, the display of manners and loyalty impressive. It was very interesting to note how the Royal Family seems to have acquired a communal manner of behaviour. They have developed an instinctive self-protection so that they should not bump into each other, or stumble down a step. They move in slow motion with care or a fluid grace; their technique is so perfected that it appears entirely natural.'

The Assistant Postmaster-General assured the House of Commons in 1954 that agreement had been reached with commercial television that, when a Royal Occasion was featured, the screen would be cleared of advertisements for two minutes before and after. Stories were seldom very malicious. The Queen Mother was reported to have confused *The Desert Song* with *The Waste Land* – reminding me of A. L. Rowse's anecdote of a Lady Salisbury with a flair for malapropism, regularly uttering, with unconscious aptness, 'Pea-green Insupportable' instead of 'Sea-green Incorruptible'. A Scottish socialist council sacked its secretary for shaking hands with Princess Margaret before the Lord

Provost had done so. I was told that, when the Royal Family was photographed, to suggest chatty relaxation each would in turn utter one letter of the alphabet, the Queen releasing *A*, the Duke *B*, and so on. The technique, however, fell down when it came to the Duke of Gloucester, to whom the alphabet was unknown.

Beneath the theatrical skills, human beings of course existed. Elizabeth Longford attended a Palace luncheon in 1958, and found the Queen herself could tell a story. She discussed her Christmas television broadcast and the complications of make-up. 'The first time, my white skin and broad jaw made my face come out like a huge, white plate with two dark cavities containing black boot buttons; my hair was parted in the middle and looked like a white line down a main road. It had to be blacked in and yellow paint daubed on my cheek and the top of my nose.'

Mention of Royalty at once prompts suggestions of religion. Prowling satirists did not neglect the Church of England which, while not inactive, did not greatly change; despite some challenging individuals – Michael Scott, Trevor Huddleston, John Collins, Bishop Bell, fierce opponent of Churchill's bombing policy – its middle-class hierarchy had little to say about war, capital punishment, nuclear power, immigration. Its livings were still rather haphazardly controlled: Trollope would have enjoyed knowing that their patrons included, as well as the Queen and Sir Osbert Sitwell, Cornish Manures Ltd and Smith's Potato Crisps.

Titles, a regular and malignant topic of conversation, continued unabashed, some 3,000 awarded annually, their attendant rituals catalogued by Michael De-la-Noy: 'Knights of the Garter and the Thistle (and Dames) grand cross, all of whom wear collars with their insignia, need to brush up on "collar days", the days on which the collar is worn: such galas are Christmas Day, various saints' days and the Duke of Edinburgh's birthday. It is also useful to know that collars can be worn at the introduction of a new member of the House of Lords – but only before sunset.'

Lord Melbourne once refused the Thistle to a Scottish peer on the grounds that he might eat it. Lord Northcliffe had said of an aspirant, 'If he wants a title, why doesn't he buy one, like any other honest man?' Bernard Shaw claimed to have refused the OM: 'People will think it means Old Man.'

Hollywood, synonym for glamour, romance and adventure, was also home to the bizarre, the extravagant, the gross and the corrupt. At

MGM studios, someone asked: 'Is it true, Mr Mayer, that your salary is double that of the President of the United States?' 'Yes, but look at my responsibilities!'

Louis B. Mayer paid two million dollars and forced a blameless subordinate to go to prison to cover up for Clark Gable, who had, while driving, killed a pedestrian. Harry Cohn of Columbia Pictures, dubbed 'White Fang' by Ben Hecht, had his office TV wired to a camera in a girls' changing-room, seduced aspirants, fired others as a Christmas present to favourites, and repeated, 'I don't get ulcers, I give them.' 'We must', ordered Darryl Zanuck, 'get out of this joint in twenty minutes.' He was speaking of the Louvre. Such tyrants had not yet surrendered to maverick producers, independent stars, East Coast corporations. George Raft apparently hired his call girls in pairs; Garbo maintained her stardom by never appearing, and, though a lesbian, underwent abortions. Marlene Dietrich was still active, her staring, impassive face apparently set for eternity. Her daughter, Maria Rivas, thought she actually disliked sex but craved unending romance.

In the early Fifties we queued, as we had for over a decade, for Astair's grin and cane, Barbara Stanwyck's voice, scraped with wire and soothed with straight gin, George Sanders's languid, caddish tones – 'The trouble was', Zsa Zsa Gabor said after their divorce, 'we were both in love with George' – Judy Garland's bouncy songs, Cagney's strut and mirthless smile, the quiet menace of Bogart, Charles Bickford's mighty head, Edward Everett Horton's turkey-cock expostulations, Bob Hope's double-look, Edgar Kennedy's slow burn. Jeanette Mac-Donald and Nelson Eddy had dwindled. Richard Tauber was dead: Auden had written in *Letter to Lord Byron*: 'Someone may think that Empire wines are nice/There may be people who hear Tauber twice.' There were. Over the radio, on *Housewives' Choice*, he sang 'Girls were made to Love and Kiss' almost daily, the Lehar song that did not then rouse wild laughter with its resounding line: 'I thank the Lord for having made me Gay'.

Probably my favourite was Charles Laughton, diffident, though a colossus in performance. His great screen roles were almost all behind him: in 1952 he had sunk into *Abbott and Costello meet Captain Kidd*. On stage he had collaborated with Brecht, in *Galileo* (1947), and appeared in London in 1958, with his wife, the gifted, zany Elsa Lanchester, in Jane Arden's *The Party*. At their marriage she was unaware of his unflashy homosexuality, but they remained close until his death. Increasingly religious, he left a card, 'To the World':

> I suppose all that you can gather, is
> that the Spirit goes on –
> to a great French painter –
> to an actor –
> Same thing, you know:
> And it'll go on from there.

I was moved by what must have been his last BBC radio broadcast: personal, ruminative and, despite Hollywood, not so very far from the overweight, clumsy tyro from Yorkshire. 'For someone with a face like the back-end of an elephant – I haven't done too badly.'

Yet Hollywood had been changing. McCarthy's anti-Communist inquisitors and those of the FBI were at large early in the decade, assisted by, amongst others, Walt Disney and Ronald Reagan. One threatened with proscription was the harmonicist, Larry Adler: he and John Huston, Ira Gershwin, and William Wyler helped form the Committee of the First Amendment, resisting, for free speech and livelihoods. Forty years later, a Hampstead newspaper printed Adler's disillusion with a screen idol believed to be toughly liberal: 'Bogart was a coward. The only reason he came with us to Washington was that he was a disciple of John Huston. When he suddenly realised that it was making him unpopular, he called his own press conference without telling us, apologised for going, and said he was sure his public would forgive him his one mistake.'

Hollywood periodically released intelligent movies – Westerns with existentialist heroes and serious moral issues, such as *High Noon* (1952), *Shane* (1955), and *Bad Day at Black Rock*, or dramas attacking anti-Semitism, *Cross-fire* and *Gentlemen's Agreement* – but despite the lasting appeal of Gene Kelly's *An American in Paris* (1951), economics and changing tastes were undermining the Hollywood musical, a singular genre with its joyous lack of restraint, massed human patterns, enduring tunes, dotty plots and inventive dance routines distinctly American.

In *Skirts Ahoy* (1953), the black jazz musician Billy Ekstein was forbidden to look at any white actress during his performance. By the mid-decade, however, new racial and sexual attitudes were in vogue, and television and faltering cinema attendances required new techniques, and new names – Burt Lancaster, Kirk Douglas, Jack Lemmon, Marilyn Monroe and Marlon Brando, one whose script-writers I did not envy.

In a mediocre London musical, *High Button Shoes* (1951), one could have glimpsed Edda Hepburn van Heemstra, 'Audrey Hepburn', who

that year also appeared briefly in *The Lavender Hill Mob*. Soon trans-
planted to Hollywood, she made a quiet but effective contrast to the
erratic and tiresome Monroe and the gifted but wilful Garland. Of
Fascistic parents, Hepburn had been a neighbour of Anne Frank, whose
diaries she was later to read from the stage, had endured near-starvation
in occupied Holland, privations less publicized than Monroe's, and had
risked herself for the Dutch Resistance.

If Hollywood was transforming itself, the music-hall was dying,
victim to television, its slow decline the theme of Priestley's novel, *Lost
Empires* (1965). It had been part of a popular culture: audience and
artiste, if not always at one, shared common prejudices, values, traditions, assumptions, reaching back to Chaucer, to jokes often older. The
conductor, frequently an amiable butt, had, so to speak, faced both
ways, mediating between the two. Foreign policy, political leaders, the
Empire, the rich, historical legends, all were applauded or reviled,
without delicate nuances but with gusty favouritism, forerunning
public opinion polls. Their humour recalls Anthony Kenny's assessment of Sir Thomas More: 'The first person to embody the peculiarly
English ideal that the good man meets adversity and crisis not with
silent resignation, nor with a sublime statement of principle, but with
a joke.' They were the last echo of the theatre of Shakespeare and
Burbage. There was complicity: all understood the comedian's leer,
wink, stare of shocked surprise at his own double-meanings; they
joined in raucous choruses, patriotic, sentimental, libellous, ribald,
some outliving the halls themselves. John Osborne, in *The Entertainer*,
(1957), gave their requiem: 'a significant part of England has gone,
something that once belonged to everyone, for this was truly a folk art'.

Along with the music-hall, the popular literary essay, trams and
tuppeny teas, the dance band was expiring. Since the Twenties, it had
produced sounds and personalities familiar throughout the country,
like a doctor dispensing mild opiates: tunes facile, sentimental, with
occasional clever twists, tricks of wit. Nightly, from West End hotels
and nightclubs, and over the radio, I heard the mooing saxophones,
muted trumpet, lulling piano, discreet drum, tactful clarinet, subdued
avuncular double-bass, the epicene 'vocal refrain', with its 'lyrics'
usually of pronounced vapidity: 'The things that rich folks go for, The
Rolls-Royce and the chauffeur'. Occasionally, all broke free into a 'hot'
outburst, before gently subsiding, for dancers to resume their polite,
somnambulist shuffle. By the mid-Fifties, Jack Payne, Jack Hylton,
Henry Hall, Geraldo, Sidney Lipton, Carroll Gibbons, Lew Stone,
Roy Fox, Maurice Winnick, Billy Cotton, all were dead or retired,
ousted by a wilder beat, a howling voice, leaving only Joe Loss and,

periodically, Harry Roy, who in a brave attempt to adapt, recorded his version of 'Rock Around the Clock'.

In the world of classical music, Reginald Goodall was under-employed in the Fifties, having to wait some twenty years before near-apotheosis. A conductor with profound understanding of Wagner, he had conducted the première of Britten's *Peter Grimes* in 1945, but managers were wary, not of his pacificism but of his sympathies with Nazi Germany. He tended to explain, with stubborn conviction, that the death camps were only a British propaganda stunt concocted at Denham film studios. Lord Harewood, a power in the opera world, considered he had genius but no talent.

Priestley asserted, around 1950, some years before the supposedly great sea-change initiated at the Royal Court Theatre: 'Unlike the novel, the drama as a form seems to me more important than it was, although it is certainly not as solidly rooted among us as it was among the later Elizabethans . . . Audiences in provincial towns especially seem to me to have improved wonderfully during the last ten years, and I prefer them now to the average West End audiences which still contain too large a proportion of playgoers who are having a vague sort of night out.'

Noël Coward was not on a peak in the Fifties, for all that his con-troversial play about drug addiction, *The Vortex*, had rattled well-bred nerves as far back as 1924. In *Relative Values* (1951), one character com-plains that the trouble with modern English life is that so many of one's friends have to work, and it closes with a toast from the butler to 'the final inglorious disintegration of the most unlikely dream that has ever troubled the foolish heart of man, social equality'. Coward's personality, however, was undimmed. He had become an institution, a curious blend of sophistication and romanticism, flippancy and sentimentality, snobbish affectations and generosity, the clipped under-statements covering powerful sentiments. Born when open homosex-uality was barely mentionable, let alone applauded, he bore his sexual pressures with dignity; 'dry, not like a desert, dry like a very good sherry, the adjective "unflappable" seemed designed for him'. To the young, however, his legend had dated, as Coward well knew: 'I am now an ageing playboy, still writing, still brittle and still sophisticated, although the sophistication is, alas, no longer up-to-date, no longer valid. It is a depressing thought, to be a shrill relic at the age of fifty-two, but there is still a little time left, and I may yet snap out of it.' To a friend, he had written that he had changed little. 'I love smoking, drinking, moderate sexual intercourse on a diminishing scale, reading and writing (not arithmetic). I have a selfish absorption in the well-being and achievement of Noël Coward.'

He rejected the role of Professor Higgins in *My Fair Lady*, that of the Colonel in *The Bridge on the River Kwai*, and of Humbert Humbert in *Lolita*. He conducted the New York Philharmonic in his own music at Carnegie Hall, performed Shaw's King Magnus in *The Apple Cart*, and more than held his own with Guinness, Richardson, Paul Rogers and Burl Ives in *Our Man in Havana*. He painted, 'Touch and Gauguin'. In cabaret he tamed Las Vegas. He knew his own worth. 'The world has treated me very well – but then I haven't treated it so badly either.'

John Osborne, so often set up as part of the reaction to him, reflected, 'Mr Coward, like Miss Dietrich, is his own invention and contributes to this century; anyone who cannot see that, should keep well away from the theatre.' His biographer, Sheridan Morley, refers to Coward's dramatic influence, his 'elliptical twin-level technique which he had first perfected and which Harold Pinter later adapted to his own darker purposes; the technique, illustrated in *Brief Encounter*, of having a character saying one thing while thinking and meaning something different.'

Coward had known my mother, and it was he who recommended to me an early Fifties production of *Antony and Cleopatra* at a London school. I saw the best Cleopatra I have known to this day, a 15-year-old boy, incisive, wilful, graceful, knowing, and was violently moved. Afterwards, in an exchange that Coward would have appreciated, I congratulated the boy, rather banally, on an excellent performance. He winked. 'Yes, yes. Good enough performance. Actually . . . first class. The trouble is . . . such a bloody bad play.'

To imagine a stage partnership between Coward and Donald Wolfit is to imagine Indian classical dancing performed to beebop, or directing the Marx Brothers: almost, if not quite, impossible. To call Wolfit a barnstorming actor-manager of the Edwardian type to whom understatement was unknown, is no major compliment, yet he had roots in the tradition not only of Tree and indeed Irving, but also of Kean, Burbage and another outsize performer, Dickens. Excluded from the exciting inner circle of Gielgud, Olivier and Ashcroft, he was jealous and resentful, mortified by intellectual derision, by an accusation of 'singing' Hamlet, unappeased by James Agate's salute to 'the best Lear I've ever seen, tearing down boundaries', a performance which did indeed reduce a world to ashes, he himself an angry chunk hacked from a stone age.

With his top hat jauntily askew, a vast red chrysanthemum looking like a stage prop, he appeared the strutting actor laddie out of Arnold Bennett and Priestley. His gait suggested he owned a mortgage on every house, every tree; at 'Good Morning, Sir Donald' he lifted a hand as if blessing a regiment while riding in triumph through Persepolis. In production, he had an uningratiating way of prowling around with a notebook to record his actors' faults. With unstoppable theatricality, at a curtain call he would stand, as if exhausted. This was no doubt justified after Lear, but scarcely convincing after brief bob-ups as Touchstone. He had small sense of irony or taste: having alarmed, shaken, wrung out an audience as, I think, the Master Builder, he spoilt it all with some curtain-call speech about the British Commonwealth and Empire.

Yet he was a considerable force. Under German bombs he had given lunchtime excerpts from Shakespeare for which Londoners were grateful. In his post-war *Tamburlaine*, a Storm Prince ranging the world, his 'Divine Zenocrate' rolled around the theatre like bits torn from a thundercloud and must have reached the streets. In *The Clandestine Marriage* he had to sneeze: he halted mid-stage, glared about him, quivered like a house perched on an earth-tremor; his face contorted like a window cracking in slow motion; then a wheeze, an impatient gesticulation, a stealthy glance behind, a low growl, a groundswell; another pause, incipient crisis, a gathering momentum splitting into a stamp, a switch, a grimace that threatened to remove an unsteady nose, a shudder of the torso, a recoil of the head as if from a thump, a convulsion from the lower depths, surging to an elaborate, even baroque whinny which subsided to a low hoot before, nature finally losing patience, he erupted, with a sneeze like the explosion of the petard by which a prisoner escapes his dungeon, almost knocking him off balance. While he recovered, the audience stood up and cheered.

He avoided competition from others in his company, though Richard Goolden as the Fool in *Lear* memorably hovered around Wolfit like a plaintive bird. In Montherlant's *The Strong are Lonely*, a courageous venture at the King's, Hammersmith, Wolfit and Ernest Milton grandly upstaged each other in a manic play-within-a-play for themselves alone. Comedy often broke through into the most chastening tragedy. Presenting an Oedipus double bill at Hammersmith, Wolfit staggered about the stage in a magnetic display of blindness, impaired when a young couple stood up to leave in mid-peroration; any pretence of blindness or even short sight at once fell like a flat-iron. Wolfit ordained a spotlight, to focus unremittingly on himself. Once, as Othello at the Bedford, Camden Town, he fell down in his epileptic fit, missing the spotlight, and then rolling about the stage in search of it. He was not a great man, fitfully a great actor, always a great phenomenon.

Reviewing Wolfit's autobiography in 1955, John Wain reckoned some of his performances perhaps the most profound that we shall see in our lifetime. For myself, this last could be allowed Alec Guinness, survivor from a wretched childhood which featured a stepfather menacing him with a loaded gun. In David Lean's *Oliver Twist*, his Fagin – agile eyes dodging about the huge curved nose, the acquisitive hands and purring charm – provoked Jewish uproar in Berlin and New York. In an idiotic irrelevance, Tynan asserted, 'he will never leave a school behind him'. Few actors were less concerned to do so. I saw him years later, in the film *Hitler: The Last Ten Days*, reducing a huge, very youthful audience to tears of sympathy, as he played the Führer dishing out poison to his glum birthday guests, while the Russian guns boomed round Berlin: an acting feat with disturbing implications. More happily, I remember him as Menenius, in *Coriolanus*. In one scene he had merely to cross the stage, nod at the two tribunes, and exit. But in that nod was concentrated the complexities of old age: wisdom and shrewdness, malice and humour, style without mannerism, which I shall relish for ever. At least two decades afterwards, in a ship crossing the Bay of Biscay, I was at a bar, empty but for myself and a grave, brooding, self-enclosed presence: Alec Guinness. I yearned to thank him for this memory, but had read that he much disliked being accosted by strangers, and I have never yet spoken to him.

5

London

'YOU WILL PROCEED with the utmost care and never forget that a capital city, a great metropolis, can hold danger, suspicions, and temptations of considerable gravity. Do not wear the same outfit twice, never repeat the same route. Always give the exact change, to avoid lingering. Never address a stranger, even a bus conductor. Especially a bus conductor.'

Mr Lupton waved a cigar. His accent was not quite English, like that of the spy in a British low-budget film, so obviously the villain that you feel he cannot be, though actually he is. I fancied I heard a key turning in the glass door behind me, and thought myself in a John Buchan novel: Sandy, deciding it is time for him to take a hand in the game.

The apartment was in clean, polished Fifties style: severe Scandinavian chairs and tables, edges and rims glittering in April light; stark angles, harshly abstract patterns stamped on rugs and curtains: a glass coffee table on which rough-cast bowls and goblets seemed to stand to attention in a monotony of pale blues. On a shiny desk were three telephones, black, green, red. Foreign books were ranked within padlocked white cases. Several paintings hung at different levels, all of steel moonlit bridges stretched across dark, glimmering houses. The silence seemed not expectant but chastened, before Mr Lupton resumed, not yet explaining the purpose for which I had been summoned, 'under conditions of extreme confidentiality'.

'You will', he told me, 'need to be observant, particularly around places named as of historical interest, whether fortified or not fortified.

You should take a stick, but . . .' the cigar traced an oval, the metalled eyes gleamed warningly, 'not a sword-stick. In this country they are forbidden. I should say, prohibited. Police regulations. Law of the Land, they call it. You must provide yourself with a notebook – in this I may be able to help. In regions like the Strand, and further East, you should keep close to the wall.'

Finally, he explained that a company of German students had arrived in London, on peaceful purposes, and that he was required to find them a guide to London. I, he decided, would do.

I had found Mr Lupton through his *New Statesman* advertisement for a young man of energy, discernment, resource. He managed some agency for foreigners; peaceful purposes, I soon suspected, might include currency speculation and black marketeering.

I had my own concerns about currency, and also about the students. Stephen Spender had written that pre-1945 German Youth had been glorified and flattered since 1919, but that Hitler's collapse had left them exhausted, ignorant, thoughtless. My little group in 1950 were not exhausted. They were healthy, opulent, friendly, loutish, following my lead round London with grunts of satisfaction or contempt. They knew of Jack the Ripper but not of Johnson or Dickens. They shied at the British Museum but not at the Chamber of Horrors and the endless frieze of enticing pub signs. The huge bomb craters, broken walls, exposed rooms, ominous gaps like entrances to Hell, the ruined acres of coarse, luscious weed-lustred rubble – evening primrose, ragwort, bindweed, dandelion, thistle, golden rod, poppy, purple strife, the motley yellows, scarlets, blues, off-whites – gave them animal pleasure. In these patches of jungle, wild cats could be half-seen, pythons imagined. They also showed some professional appreciation, informing me of the types of bomber and bomb employed, the unsatisfactory outcome. That thirty-nine City churches survived, that St Paul's still gleamed high aloft, aggrieved them. The wrecked House of Commons stirred no democratic lessons, merely an observation about amateurish aiming. They objected to Hitler in that he had been too loyal to such friends as the Reichsmarshal Göring, who had been technologically backward, making dire scientific and strategic mistakes. They were critical of his killings of Jews, which had united the world against him, influenced by 'Churchill's Jewish wife', thus forcing their fathers and uncles into alliance with Italians and Japanese, people of 'stale rot' that had ensured what had looked very much like failure.

The enterprise, however, incited me to saunter alone through London streets. While others hurried, I lingered, seeing myself a boulevardier, ready to pounce on the lost girl, observe a house on fire or, with far-fetched childhood memories, rescue a publisher's daughter from a runaway horse. Poetry, wrote Anna Akhmatova, grows from rubbish. Mr Lupton's notebook, hitherto empty, began to fill. In 1950 I was young enough to disregard the Belfast shipbuilder's warning to the young V.S. Pritchett: 'Writing poetry don't drive no rivets', or the Spanish proverb, 'Love is a furnace but it don't cook the stew'.

I wandered at random towards unknown regions through a London still visibly part of the war, anchored in the past, though the new architects – Basil Spence, Leslie Martin, Arne Jacobsen, Erno Goldfinger – promised a new and spacious city of glass, steel, aluminium, fresh shapes, clean air, an uncluttered future. Huge cranes swung across the sky, bulldozers heaved, thrust, grabbed: roofs crashed, blocks fell, pre-fab asbestos bungalows sprouted on razed acres. A few yards east, immune to rain and soot, Tilling lamps hissed and flared above crowded street markets and posters hung like stage directions in English and Yiddish, competing with ghostly history chalked on walls: 'Second Front Now', 'I Voted Labour and Got it – Hard', 'Wot, No Eggs!', 'Is there Life before Death?', 'Frank Sinatra for Pope', 'Hands off Guatemala', 'Korea Out', and, on a church wall, 'You don't drop catch with the Son of God'. Men still wore hats. Jaguar cars were beginning to be seen. In jocular market jargon, 'liberate' was replacing 'lift', 'nick', 'scrounge', as the synonym for theft. From pubs, in affluent Knightsbridge, decrepit Deptford, songs drifted, banal as the conversations between the married, yet with ripples of memory, emotion and threats:

> O, My
> I don't want to die,
> I just want to go home.

Sharp-faced children crouched in further bomb sites, their voices like knives: 'You bugger', 'you weed', 'you mystic', and their elders spoke of fixing a joint.

Church and burial common held their small griefs, forcing me out of the Fifties. (I remembered Whistler's description of Rome as 'an old ruin alongside a railway station where I saw Mrs Potter Palmer'.)

> To a Blackmore belonging to Mr John Davies deid in a White-chapele parishe, was laid in the Ground of the churchyard without any congregation present and without ceremonie because we knew not whether or no he was a Christian.

> To the memory of William Symington, 1763. He constructed the Charlotte Dundas, the first steamboat fitted for practical use. Dying in want he was buried in the adjacent churchyard.

humour appropriate to his long, mobile face, melancholy, teasing, profoundly thoughtful, suddenly acerbic. He had survived interrogation by the Gestapo, had in England found intolerable the slackness of fellow-performers and conductors and, renouncing orchestral playing, had now joined the BBC. Like Karl Kraus, he ridiculed psychoanalysis as the disease it was supposed to cure, and in fact cured no one. Infuriated by some words of Saul Bellow, to the effect that Mendelssohn's Violin Concerto was no good, he first wrote a crushing article, then a damning book.

I would pass the painter David Bomberg in a black hat who, with Isaac Rosenberg and Mark Gertler, had been 'the Whitechapel Boys' and, fragile but still working, was a link with Modigliani, Picasso, Hulme, Pound, Wyndham Lewis. Then another refugee, Erich Fried, poet and translator, his head, though enormous, at times seeming too small for the knowledge within. He admired E. E. Cummings and liked to intone:

> anyone lived in a pretty how town
> (with up so floating many bells down)
> spring summer autumn winter
> he sang his didn't he danced his did.

A mountain of heavy furniture on the pavement, as if filched from the Babylon set of D. W. Griffith's *Intolerance*, showed that Bernice Rubens and Rudolf Nassauer had been invaded by the itinerant Michael Fraenkel, co-author with Henry Miller of *The Hamlet Papers*. Beatrice Scott, a Russian married to the novelist Douglas Scott, herself a translator of Pasternak and Dostoevsky, always called Fraenkel 'Death', which was justified by his appearance. His reputation for generosity was meagre: a girl complained that he had rewarded her for typing a longish book with a sixpenny edition of Voltaire's *Candide*, then offering to double its value by signing it.

Oswell Blakeston was a familiar stroller, usually with the painter Max Chapman. A novelist, poet, travel-writer, joker, who had worked in films with Cocteau, stories flowed from him, never sensational, not often forgotten, which he called Essential Information. Thus, at treeless Peterhead, the minister built a wall with holes to make tree noises: after the murder of the Archbishop of St Andrew's, a little box opened and a bee flew out; a miller locked in a dungeon at Castle Jardine ate his own hands and feet; the last knight of Denmilne rode out on a dark horse on a black night and fell down a coalmine; hands sink deeply into the flesh of the ghost of Thirsk whose inner parts can be seen through the mouth and who forms his words through his entrails. Blakeston's name, 'Oswell', he contracted from 'Osbert Sitwell'.

In a Finchley Road café, I would meet Dannie Abse, doctor, who not only was a poet, but looked like one, pale, dark-haired, Byronic. His mother once told a shop assistant in Lear's Bookshop, Cardiff, that her son was the Welsh Dylan Thomas.

More voices fluttered around me, on buses, the tube, park benches and from open windows. 'What do you remember best about London? The Tower, the National Gallery . . .?'

'The Gargoyle, there isn't really anywhere else, is there!' The Gargoyle was a drinking club with a tiny dance floor, more expensive that most of the similar places popular throughout London, with its over-priced champagne and meals. Here, at the long dining-table, the painter Eleanor Bellingham-Smith, then married to Roderigo Moynihan, volunteered her party piece, to pull away the tablecloth so expertly that plates, glasses, bottles were left undisturbed. Her bill was considerable, and included our cleaners' bills. Years later, Janet Watters of *The Observer* remembered the Gargoyle: 'Not exactly a nightclub, it was open all day. It was a kind of hell, really. I saw quite a lot of Dylan Thomas at that time. It was very drunken and very bitchy, and everyone made passes at everyone else. I look back on all this in a very dismal way. Not because it was sinful, but it was a terrible wastage of the human spirit – from a literary point of view. We spent so much time talking in an idiotic way, and drinking too much: and there was very little – well, – love, really.'

Through the haze of such Soho ménages glimmered various reputations, seldom at their best, Philip Toynbee, Dylan Thomas, Nina Hamnett, the Roberts – MacBryde and Colquhoun – W. S. Graham, Maurice Richardson, George Barker, Francis Bacon with an arrogant and parasitical retinue, John Minton, of whom a popular story was told:

Policeman: 'Sir, I have to charge you . . .'

Minton: 'What? In that hat?'

Bars flourished: espresso bars, milk bars, potato bars, wine bars, salad bars, snack bars, and small grubby cafés within earshot of Leicester Square and the Circus, not yet grabbed by property sharks with a grievance against cheap living. One had no name, only a blackboard, announcing: 'No queues. No cigarettes. Customers are invited *Not* to bring their own food.' Portraits of Bardot adorned them, or a motorcycle or dustbin parked in a corner. Young tortured voices – Lonnie Donegan, Tommy Steele, Cliff Richard – strained above the clamour, preparing for the scatter and jitter, the more feverish pace of Elvis Presley. Some songs were reputed to contain codes, for the disposal of drugs. Class-bound hats and ties were forsworn, jeans, duffle-coats, wind-cheaters were obligatory, often as unconvincing as Churchill's boiler suit in Moscow, and at odds with the velvet collars and brocaded waistcoats of suspicious teddy boys, too contemptuous or hostile to join us. Hairstyles of both sexes were like curtains, like galleons, like daggers, like jungle clearings. At the Partisan Coffee Bar, the militant self-taught and the leftish public schoolboy – the distinction would be inexact – argued, persuaded, occasionally wept: 'But Schiff . . . I'm begging you on my hands and knees . . .' 'Filthy hands and, I dare say, disgusting knees.' 'Anyway, she's Virgo. This means that she's severely analytical and critically advanced. Yet she isn't.' 'Scott Fitzgerald called America the story of a moon that never rose. I could have written it myself.'

Here, Fifties characters swarmed in incessant flux: they flickered, said something, lingered a few weeks, then usually evaporated. A Spanish war veteran; an escaped prisoner, a vagabond grandson of a famous Victorian historian; a girl, very intelligent, very hideous, reputed to sleep with J.B.S. Haldane. Once a very thin apparition, antlered but two-legged, stalked through starlit Soho Square as for prey. 'That's Abdul-rajak,' Nicholas Moore said indifferently. One habitué of many pubs and cafés was a short young man, eyes slightly askew, known for some reason as the Dean. His pallid face was landscaped, pits here, channels there, leaving room for gingery undergrowth and patches of scrub. His allusions were numerous and varied, his activities vague, his beliefs unsound. Like the others, a considerable pack, he possessed much miscellaneous information and nowhere very significant in which to put it.

He knew that the three most powerful names of God were Agla, Tetragon-Maton and Om. Through him I learnt that, in 1940, invasion had been prevented by the activities of 400 naked Hampshire witches. He had powerfully assisted Mao Tse-tung, and was said to have acted a statue in Wolfit's *Oedipus the King*, but been sacked for over-acting. He was apt to refer to himself as an orphan, once within hearing of his mother at Richard Findlater's wedding. He never invited people to his home, explaining that it was bugged, though we sometimes met his Irish wife whom, impeccably Left, he referred to as 'The Dialectic', and on whose forehead he had implanted a constantly repainted red spot. A modest, soundless girl, she was always, as it were, between brackets, an echo of Wodehouse's line: ' "This", he said, with some disgust, "is my wife." ' The Dean, the Left notwithstanding, was apt to boast kinship with a Spanish nobleman, the Marquis Merry del Val. A writer like almost all of us, he had some reputation for a thesis, as yet unpublished, maintaining that History was masculine or feminine; the question 'which?' he left unanswered. A girl incautiously suggested 'Neuter', and received a slap and the removal of her name from the list of those to be allowed the book at cost price. Eventually published, it made a small stir, in that it was remaindered before it actually appeared. When I first met him he was at a street café, certainly writing, but no more than a letter to the Financial columnist of the *Spectator*, Nicholas Davenport, whom he had not met, requesting a loan of £500. Nicholas sent him a gift of £50, and the Dean threatened to sue, for defamation. Tapping his chest like a barometer, the Dean announced, 'The world is my spiritual centre', though behind him a disgruntled girl muttered that he was filling without satisfying.

A more tiresome sponger, a meagre Sinhalese, each smile a begging letter, each raising of an empty glass an operatic flourish, was 'Masar Macfarlane General', posing as Lieutenant-General Sir Frank Mason-Macfarlane, DSO, former Governor of Gibraltar, creator of the war-time 'MacForce', and subsequently a Labour MP. At the bar, the counterfeit always reminded you, rather pointedly, that as a royal governor he never carried money and was entitled to a royal salute which, in a way, he eventually received, dying from a pistol shot on Wimbledon Common.

A genuine retired General could be sighted in the underground Criterion Bar, Piccadilly Circus, where he would sit brooding before blurting out, irrespective of context, such remarks as 'Churchill talked guff', 'John Buchan hated Napoleon', 'Logical, but morally unsound'. He would hum, 'and the boys that were boys when I was a boy walking along with me', once adding that someone should put this into verse. 'You ask me (I had not done so) what is my hobby? I tell you, it is . . . life!' Pulling rank, he secured work with Robert Maxwell, publisher, currently socialist MP for Buckingham. Arriving for his first day's work, the General collected three months' advance salary then vanished, resurfacing precisely three months later, with a 200-page blueprint for the protection of Maxwell's private office under atomic attack. This silenced even his employer, though briefly.

I might pass on the street a bookstall, managed by a small, intense young man, Bernard Kops, an East Ender like his contemporaries Harold Pinter and Arnold Wesker; his family was mostly slaughtered in Holland by the Nazis, and he had lately received in recompense from West Germany, five pounds, which he presented to an indigent poet. Novelist, poet and dramatist, Bernard had graduated from Toynbee Hall evening classes. He was stubbornly independent, observant, painting, as he said, his dreams, like Chagall, and, forty years later, telling Michael Arditti about himself and his fellow dramatists: 'Jewish families all had the gift of the gab, look at market stalls and the way they use language, with everyone talking the whole time. We were a bit like the brat pack of Jewish painters, Bomberg, Rosenberg and Gertler, who sat in the Café Royal full of chutzpah, refusing to accept their position in life.'

First to arrive at the Wheatsheaf, Rathbone Place, in long camel-hair coat, with gloves and silver-topped cane, to hold court at the far left corner of the bar, was Julian Maclaren-Ross, high face with faint lids which deepened before closing time, under crisp dark hair. Offering snuff, accepting drinks, discoursing on his movie favourites, the latest novels, a new scandal, writing a story in small, exquisite letters, formal as print, he was apparently a model for 'X. Trapnell' in Anthony Powell's *Books Do Furnish A Room*, though his end was less dramatic. He would inveigle newcomers into a tiresome matchstick game, Spoof, which, living up to its name, allowed him a regular income until the landlord, Reg, finally forbade it before himself departing to prison.

Once, as Maclaren-Ross left, pulling on gloves, adjusting his coat, contemplating the stick, some plug-uglies – a word from childhood which up until now I have always resisted – accosted him. 'Say something witty.' Their voices were menacing. Dandified Julian tightened his mouth severely, his eyes chilled, and said without interest: 'Noël Coward'. The roughs drifted away.

He was always more attentive than he cared to appear. 'Art', a voice declared, further away, 'prompts questions. Only bad art gives answers. You see, Chekhov . . .' Already a gold pencil was travelling over the writing pad beneath the large gin, recently paid for by the speaker. You paid for privileges with Julian.

Here, a lean face, with hot eyes madly staring into different places, belonged unmistakeably to the artist Gerald Wilde, sometimes associated in temperament, certain works and personal habits with Gully Jimson, the painter in Joyce Cary's *The Horse's Mouth*. Admired by Kenneth Clark, Gerald was erratic, unpredictable, carelessly generous, affectionate, fitfully gifted. David Sylvester compared him to Toulouse-Lautrec, and saw affinities with Hogarth and Munch. I was more fascinated by his work – his illustration of an Eliot poem, a more successful cover for the literary magazine *Counterpoint* – than I was by his company. I was once in a sedate Bond Street gallery, otherwise deserted save for the small, perfected, silent figure of Vivien Leigh beneath a slanted, broad-brimmed black hat, stuck with a single violet. The silence due to the pictures was smashed by a whoop, a view halloo, as Gerald Wilde at his wildest bounded forward as if into a circus ring;

he embraced me, he kissed me, he was very drunk. Then he swerved on Vivien Leigh, from whom any resemblance to gutsy, unflinching Scarlett O'Hara vanished as rapidly as she did herself, leaving Gerald bawling, 'Drink, more Drink!'

Count Potocki was no rival either to Wilde or Maclaren-Ross. He always wore a velvet cap, an ornate medallion dangling against a lengthy cloak, befitting one who regarded himself as King of Poland. About this time he challenged Paul Potts to a duel when Paul said that he had had the pleasure of meeting him at David Archer's bookshop. He should have said the *honour* of meeting him. Gallantly, Potts offered to fight him with garden spades, but this was deemed highly dishonourable and the engagement lapsed. Paul Potts? He was the only man I knew said to have been paid £500 not to write a book about George Orwell, with whom he had lived for a while on Jura. Paul was a tall, beaky Canadian, sometimes called the last of the bohemians, sometimes the People's Poet – he had written a poem beginning 'The people of England have asked me . . .'

He stuttered in eagerness to protest, to sympathize, to scrounge; he could be a self-lighting Catherine Wheel, exploding with revelations of failed loves, political enormities, personal insults. Likewise his writing. It was unstoppable. He wrote on hypocrisy, contemporary sainthood – though republican, he revered King Christian of Denmark who, defenceless, yet led successful rescues of Jews from the invaders – he wrote on Israel, on Silone, on Orwell (though not a book).

He attracted stories about himself, few, no doubt, true to the letter. In gratitude for dinner, he turned to his hostess: 'Are you interested in money?' 'Well . . . I suppose so.' 'Good.' He gazed at the rareish Cromwellian table: 'Here's a nice table. Nice . . . but I'll give it more value.' And, pulling out a boy's pocket knife, he carved his name on it. Visiting your home more informally, his departure would leave, like footprints in the snow, gaps in the bookshelves. Our friends Ronald Veltman, education officer and film maker, and his wife, the artist Joan Ingram, always generous to him, graphed inflation by Paul's demands, rising steeply from sixpence in the late Fifties.

I was once in Soho, late at night, sheltering from rain under a tree with John Raymond, literary critic, whose mother, the actress Iris Hoey, had been admired by Arnold Bennett. Out of the drizzle, into the yellow spill of light, loomed Paul Potts. 'Aren't you John Raymond?' John, like Priestley, like most of us, suffered no morbid embarrassment at public recognition. He smiled, he virtually preened himself: 'Yes, indeed.' 'I thought so,' Paul Potts said, slugging him very hard.

More embarrassing was an episode at the Whitestone Pond, Hampstead, where I was escorting a youngish, fairly well-known painter and her 5-year-old daughter, who stepped into the water. Her mother expostulated: 'Darling, that's the third time you've gone into the dirty water and soaked your nice little dress. You must come out at once, and if you do it once more, I will have to tell Daddy ¯...'

She was interrupted by a roar as, out of some bushes, stormed Paul Potts. 'You bloody, bleeding, intolerable Fascist, hasn't anyone ever told you that we fought a war to get rid of people like you?' And, on this text, he punched her backwards into the pond. Then, like the Demon King in a pantomime, he exited with a dispatch which I would not have credited to him. When the lady emerged, sodden and dazed, the only man in view was myself, and a promising relationship was fatally ruptured.

Paul had considerable knowledge of social workings, confiding that *The Times* and *Observer* printers were operating a market for stolen property; that the latter's owners meekly paid weekly wages to the terrorist-style claimants of jobs long vanished; that union leaders sabotaged articles inimical to their interests, personal or collective.

Randall Jarrell wrote that a good poet is one who, in a lifetime of standing out in thunderstorms, manages to be struck by lightning five or six times; a dozen or two dozen times make him great. Paul was seldom struck by lightning, yet achieved a personality that survives. He thought Ezra Pound perhaps the one truly great amongst the many near-great Americans who had followed Whitman in his vocation, and had joined the campaign to save Pound from indictment and probably execution, but, demonstrating his own literary integrity in a life only fitfully honest, wrote 'To Ezra Pound' on the poet's release in 1958:

> I waited to ask you this
> I could not ask you in prison
> I waited until you were free.
> But why, why did you let them use
> Your name and your greatness
> As so many pennies to put
> Into the meters of their gas machines?

6

Characters and Occasions

MY LONDON LIFE at this time was crowded, filled with unexpected turns, small yet enduring events, the anguish and joys of comparative youth, if not quite holding to Pound's lines from *Lustra*:

> And the days are not full enough
> And the nights are not full enough,
> And life slips by like a field-mouse
> Not shaking the grass.

There were those on view who shook the grass.

C. V. Wedgwood's translation of a novel, *Auto-da-Fé* (1946), by the Jewish Bulgarian, Elias Canetti, who was awarded the 1981 Nobel Prize for Literature, roused much argument. The novel was, he would say, intended as part of a '*comédie humaine*' of madness. It created a world as self-sustained as that of Beckett and Kafka, without possibility of a saviour, a revolution, an escape. To some it was a European master-piece, others had reservations. Philip Toynbee, in *Horizon*, allowed it an impressive capacity to imprison the reader within five hundred pages, to block every chink of light. He also found it turgid, repetitive, with nothing but pain, bitterness and horror as norms, an Inferno without a Paradise. Particularly, he attacked its apparent premise 'that madness is in some sense . . . superior to sanity', a childish romanticism unworthy of Canetti's remarkable mind. The nature of obsession, Toynbee concluded, is to be blinkered, and he contrasted the work with the novels of another contemporary, Henry Green, which derived not from narrow obsessions but from hallucinations which saw far and wide over landscapes, as if through strange-coloured glass. Canetti excluded reality, Green might be introducing new revelations of reality. For myself, *Auto-da-Fé* was profoundly impressive, original and slightly boring, in Toynbee's words, a plea for the dignity of madmen. It made me curious about the now-famous author, with his seeming obsessions with power, money, books, chess and physique, his distortions exposing unappetizing truths.

Canetti was no recluse. For lunch, I would go for soup in one small restaurant and would find Canetti. Then I would cross the road for a cutlet and there was Canetti. Finishing with a coffee at a third place a few yards off, I would yet again see Canetti, in all three the hub of a respectful little group. He had the Continental habit of rising to shake hands, a ritual which in these contexts must have been irksome. Cafés fuelled his incessant curiosity about new faces, new shapes of being and feeling: 'All that is demanded of you is to watch and listen . . . their marvellous variety alone rekindles your delight in the human race.'

From a distance he appeared a carefully stacked arrangement of squares of various shapes, surmounted by thick spectacles and a forest of brown hair. The very large squarish head readily suggested a leading character in the book, who kept therein his immense library. Indeed, he seemed to be perpetually reaching into himself to extract and open a volume. His way of regarding you was always very solemn, one's most rapid utterance being weighed, tested, scrutinized again, then answered, usually at length.

Canetti – to call him 'Elias' would have been like addressing Flaubert as 'Gus', or offering to tip Attlee – was a chunk of history, had known pre-war Berlin, Frankfurt, Vienna. At mention of Georg Grosz, Franz Werfel, Robert Musil, von Hofmannsthal, he would often begin, 'when I last saw him . . .' He had known Stalin's victim, Isaak Babel, a veteran of the Russo-Polish War of 1921–2, author of *Red Cavalry* and *The Odessa Tales*. 'I am a master of the genre of silence,' Babel said of the Stalinist censorship. At mention of Brecht, Canetti recalled a supper with him and the satirist Karl Kraus, Brecht at 30 resembling an old pawnbroker in a shabby cap. He told Canetti that he could write only when the telephone was incessantly ringing. Canetti much admired, but disliked him: courageous, but with his retreat already assured; cynical, sarcastic, tricky, a sharp-eyed talented wide-boy. His view was reinforced by Brecht's scrupulously copyrighting his works in the damnable West, and although a Communist East German, clinging to his Austrian passport and his addiction to plagiarism.

As a teenager in Vienna in 1924, Canetti had attended Kraus's three-hundredth lecture, and had compared the vibrant, devoted audience to the Wild Hunt, as if trapped in the hall, disciplined but periodically reverting to type. He thought him idealistic and high-minded, constantly railing against the prostitution of thought, behaviour and language by ignorance, flunkeydom, fashion, turpitude, arrogance and bone-laziness. Kraus's pen spared none: not dictatorship, not Freud, not England. 'The English are not idealists. For all their devotion to commerce, they would not sacrifice their whole lives to it.' I was delighted to learn in 1954, from Erich Heller, of his devotion to Offenbach, of whose music he gave public recitals.

In print, talk, on the radio, Canetti would discuss Kafka, on whom he was an authority, rating him the greatest expert on power, the avoiding of it, submitting to it, seeking every humiliation, yet seeing it in all its dimensions, even through the eyes of its victim. Canetti himself was fascinated by power and its roots. He had experienced its externals, very young, a witness to the post-1918 collapse, conflicts, inflation. Watching Frankfurt demonstrations in 1922, following the murder of Rathenau, he was deeply attracted to the indignant marchers, and, joining them, felt 'an absolutely astonishing process: for one was not something lifeless, either beforehand, when isolated, or afterwards, in the crowd. And the thing that happened to you in the crowd, a total alteration of consciousness, was both drastic and enigmatic. I wanted to know what it was all about. The riddle wouldn't stop haunting me for the better part of my life. And if I did ultimately hit upon a few things, I was still as puzzled as ever.' Later, in 1927, he had seen Viennese crowds burning the Palace of Justice, infuriated by official injustice: ninety were shot in the street by police, Karl Kraus plastering the city with posters demanding the police chief's resignation.

Canetti was then writing his Fifties book, *Crowds and Power*, acclaimed in the USA, jeered at by Geoffrey Gorer in Britain, and his dissertations were more vital than coffee-bar chatter about 'Dylan', or Auden's war effort. He said, probably quoting himself, that the distinction, always fluid, between types and individuals, is the true concern of the genuine writer. At this many of us would become self-consciously despondent, before being gripped once more by his references to Wallenstein, the Gilgamesh epic, a Bantu superstition, the nature of superstition itself. Crowds reinforce superstition: within their clamour we relive the barbarian invasions, medieval witch-hunts, children's crusades, the assault on walls, temples, libraries. We see empires collapse, mediocrities raised briefly on shields, ministers of the interior fleeing to the interior. There is also the crowd in E. M. Forster's *A Passage to India* transforming an English matron into a Hindu goddess, 'Esmiss Esmoor'. Clemenceau had watched it all in Paris in 1871; had

Louis Napoleon withstood the seething crowds bawling for war, he might have prevented the Great War, the Bolshevik and Nazi revolutions, a hundred million corpses. Most of us grew up with dangerous crowds stamping ever closer.

Pondering what forces individuals to become a crowd, the effects of crowds on politics and violence, the duel between crowd instinct and personal instinct, Canetti was convinced that, unlike Freud, he knew crowds from within the crowd, the anthropological realities behind frantic headlines and reasoned articles. Nietzsche had described the unconscious as wild dogs howling in the cellar. Canetti wrote: 'The dissolution of the individual in the crowd was the enigma of enigmas for me. I had never forgotten how gladly one falls prey to the crowd.'

Once Canetti courteously asked what I was working on: a novel about the Anabaptists of Münster in 1533. At once he spoke without a pause about Jan van Leyden, the charismatic Anabaptist leader, his relations with Luther, the possible influence of the sixteenth-century German radical Thomas Münzer on Albert Schweitzer, the deficiencies and merits of the historians von Ranke (an ancestor of Robert Graves), Burkhardt and Huizinga, the treatment of Jan van Leyden in Meyerbeer's opera, *The Prophet*, a connection with a rite known only to a certain rather obscure tribe in West Africa. In Canetti's presence, if I muttered, truthfully, that the day was fine, I would simultaneously think that by some sleight of perception, he knew better, and rain was falling fast.

He shared with his admired Kraus a passionate belief in the unpredictable powers of the written word. He was no conversational dictator, he induced most of us to talk more than usual, and he listened, the great head seeming to toll. He has said: 'I enjoy listening. I have always enjoyed listening. This seemingly quiet, passive tendency is so violent as to constitute my innermost concept of life. I will be dead when I no longer hear what a person is telling me about himself. He may thus live forever, Man's love of this being his second-most urgent joy.'

I myself, alas, impaired Canetti's gregarious curiosity, being one of those he remembered from his early café society, 'who came right into the midst of this noisy turbulence in order to keep quiet – a minority but a highly conspicuous one: mute, pinched face-islands in the seething landscape, turtles who knew how to drink, and whom you had to ask because they never reacted to any questions.'

*   *   *

'I tell you what, young man . . . I don't understand these so-called paintings. I understand Rembrandt down to the last brass button.

There's nothing you can tell me that I don't know about Constable. But this ugly stuff of yours I don't understand and don't wish to.'

'I'm with you there, Jack. I love art. I've been told I'm an expert, by my own wife. But this stuff.'

'You are both absurd buffoons and understand nothing at all, least of all yourselves. As for Rembrandt, you can't even spell his name. So bugger off, back to your damp cheese.'

The third observation came from a tall, coffin-shaped youth, in brown corduroy, pallid under thick, black, polished hair, whose brown contemptuous eyes gazed unblinking at two stuffed City gentlemen with tightly furled umbrellas. This was David Sylvester, arranger of the exhibition. I stood behind, with Hugh Cruttwell, in the tiny gallery of the Arts Theatre Club, watching the comedy.

The paintings were what was still termed avant-garde, pronounced in tones graded from reverence to perplexity to dislike; then to hatred, hysteria, madness. I began to see much of him. Always talking, he was to be seen dropping used handkerchiefs in pillar-boxes, addressing Norman Douglas as 'Doug' and Maclaren-Ross as 'Macclaret', speaking, too loudly, about English cricket during a Wigmore Hall Beethoven recital. Though younger than myself, he appeared very much the elder. He knew of the Olympia Press, Paris, with publications mostly banned from Britain – I had to hint that my own manuscript was being considered there; he spoke familiarly of giant unknowns – Giacometti, Magritte (on both he is today a world authority), Klee, Janko Adler, Oskar Kokoschka (such a name is half the battle), Wittgenstein, Sartre, Jaspers. He seemed almost as abundant as Prokosch, flourishing introductions to Orwell, to Henry Moore, to Michael Hamburger, poet, translator, foremost scholar in German literature; to Jocelyn Baines, who had just started his book on Conrad; to William Coldstream, Victor Pasmore, Benedict Nicolson. I was bemused that one so young should know so many.

Intolerance can promote success but is seldom a wise companion, and David, with his brash, good-natured insolence, knew it. Like Canetti, he had the unusual taste for listening. Whatever you said, whether about the movements of a wasp, the tint of the sky, or Francis Scarfe's shirt, a disgusting anti-Semitic lampoon, the origins of Christianity, the resonant platitudes of Dr Billy Graham, a contrast between the physique and the brain power of the entertainer Sabrina, he would brood over with the same concern as he would over Pasmore's opinion of Magritte, or John Gielgud's reasons for so admiring *The Tempest*, a remark attributed to Aquinas or an idea filched from Aldous Huxley. He would flatter bores by murmuring at intervals, 'very, very interesting', carefully writing down their juiciest absurdities. The art critic Eric Newton called him 'the Boy David'. Francis Bacon was an intimate. Once a hand touched my arm. 'Who is that appalling young man?' 'He knows more about Bacon than do most living men and possibly all women, but one.' The questioner, porcine in build, with bulging forehead and meaty eyes, reddened with suspicion.

I dazed myself by calculating David Sylvester's possibilities: a novelist, perhaps, of the Wyndham Lewis stamp; a literary critic, of course, contradicting, then silencing Leavis. I saw him explaining Ezra Pound's 'Homage to Sextus Propertius' to a startled Nigerian, 'the difference, you see, between Milton's involved syntax . . . the very economy of Pound leading to a syntax hard to follow . . . often charged with obscurity'. He could have been a music critic, relegating the long-standing repute of Bernard Shaw; a Cocteau, with a hint of Oscar Wilde, a flavour of Rimbaud; a profound philosopher, showing Ayer the door; something of a comedian, as I suspected Jesus had been; a theologian. David, after prolonged debate, fell into Roman Catholicism, then fell out of it, swift as a dropped catch, which, essentially, his conversion was. Already he had written for *Penguin New Writing*, soon he was Arts Editor to *Encounter*. He gave a nod to Cyril Connolly in a Dean Street restaurant, and smiled pleasantly at Herbert Read.

His enthusiasm for the arts, cricket, human oddities, curious behaviour, literature, made me breathless. In a café, he generously read aloud Henry Reed's *Chard Whicklow* to the waitress, and it was so impressive that she thought he was reporting a fire, and scurried away to ring 999. Once we were on the last bus from Fulham, late at night. We saw a man seated behind us, we looked at each other, then nodded. David spoke:

'Excuse me, sir, but it's quite an occasion. Has anyone told you that you look exactly like *The Idiot*?' The man's stare was unamiable; and I had to intervene: 'Yes, you know . . . Dostoevsky's *Idiot*.' He did not know, and began such an uproar that the conductor ejected him from the bus.

With genuine disinterest, David indulged a flair for promoting relationships as he might arrange paintings, effecting unexpected juxtapositions. He encouraged Ken Taylor, a Yorkshire youth and Test Match cricketer, and William Coldstream enrolled him at the Slade as a promising artist. Through David, a businessman would find himself on the Third Programme, discussing the latest Fellini film, a zoologist giving his opinions of Matisse at the Institute of Contemporary Art, a totally humourless critic pontificating about Humour at some well-attended gathering. During the Fifties, David had full scope for uniting diverse people, generations, nationalities, for unlikely purposes, in his cricket team, the Eclectics. Painters – Terry Frost, Roger Hilton, Pasmore – would run out such critics as Adrian Stokes (follower of Melanie Klein, tennis partner of Ezra Pound) and Basil Taylor (natural athlete, swooping on the ball and throwing it back in one swift, gliding, perfected motion). An ill-tempered racialist editor would open the innings with a cheerful Jamaican student: Clement Freud, gourmet, keeping wicket, might be offered a half-chewed doughnut by an energetic fast bowler impatient for the fray. The team could include D. S. Carne-Ross and Iain Fletcher, editors of *Nine*; Ian Scott-Kilvert, classicist, poet, translator of Cavafy, friend of Isherwood; Jim Fairfax-Jones, owner of Everyman Cinema; J. P. W. Mallalieu, Labour MP and writer. We also had one actual international cricketer, Arthur Wellard, mighty hitter for Somerset, Test Match all-rounder.

I once captained the Eclectics against a south-west London mental hospital, on an unusually hot day. Winning the toss, but mindful of our opponents' disabilities, I volunteered to field. After some boiling hours, we had taken no wickets, over two hundred was on the board, and chirps, cackles and antics from the onlookers at last demonstrated that we were playing not the patients but the doctors.

Through the decade, David and I talked, talked in lush bombsites and spartan cafés, in unfamiliar flats and Kent hotels, at the Oval and on a tram to Greenwich, on a Putney tennis court and during a baptism, about the need to read Djuna Barnes, the coming importance of Richard Wollheim, Jesus's puzzling remark, or joke, about making friends with the Mammon of Unrighteousness; we talked about Hollywood, and Donskoi's superb Russian film, *The Childhood of Maxim Gorky*; about Gerald Wilde's latest movement, about Desmond MacCarthy's belief that art should somewhere, somehow, suggest the desirability of life; about Fred Astaire's father, Herr Austerlitz, resigning from the Imperial and Royal Army because of having to salute his brother; about Field Marshal von Moltke, who smiled only twice in his life – at his mother-in-law's death, and at being told that Stockholm was impregnable. 'David, you talk in metaphor.' 'Almost always better than simile.'

He became a renowned critic, much applauded in art schools, and mounted exhibitions in many countries. His excitement about this I could align with my own, for compiling anthologies: the calculated deployment of space, the relating of one selection to another to reveal new qualities in each, the sensation of windows opening, unexpected perceptions being born . . . two poems, different in style and language yet obliquely similar, can change the colour of the page, two contrasting yet mysteriously linked pictures transform the texture of the air.

There is a type, once called a Man of Parts, sometimes regarded with cautious respect and sometimes with rank suspicion. One such was Leonard Nicholson, though what his parts were, I never precisely ascertained. In the Fifties, already white-haired, he had a youthful face, sharp, light-blue Nordic eyes, a brisk step. A senior civil servant, he was a statistics adviser to the Cabinet, thus, in some crapulous way, responsible for a considerable amount of unpopular history. His treatise on advanced taxation was unlikely to be set to music: his sister, very dear to him, wrote her own treatise, on Mexican music.

Leonard was a curious creature, one of those which England is so adept at producing. At a dinner, he would sit, saying nothing, implying nothing, boring everyone until, without warning, he would push back his chair, help himself to a last drink, curtly announcing, 'due back at Number Ten', and, at the door, 'I take it that I may come again', leaving behind awed murmurs: 'Brilliant man', 'Fascinating . . .', 'Splendid talker', 'Man of secrets, man of power'.

He himself gave frequent parties, in which intellectuals – Hans Keller, Milein Cosman, John Willet, Bernice Rubens – would mingle with such Cabinet ministers as Judith Hart, financial advisers like Thomas Balogh, titled journalists like Wayland Young. He provided no food, plenty of drink and no introductions, so that once a celebrated face rose up at me, rather severely: 'Is your name Nicholson?' 'Well . . . yes.' 'Ah.' The face relaxed, 'Thank you so much. A most agreeable party. Are you possibly free one night for a dinner . . . Garrick . . .' Thus began a series of pleasant meals, only slightly jolted when, 'you see, my dear Nicholson', made me glance abruptly over my shoulder.

Leonard, like Merlin, would emerge unexpectedly. Once, in the Vale of Dedham, I saw movement amongst some bushes. Leonard pushed up, in a red cap. 'Birdwatching.' And disappeared. In Wales, in what might be loosely termed a reading party, we glanced at the window. Leonard. In Cumberland, there was Leonard pulling himself over a crag. In the shoe shop of a small Cornish town, a familiar voice: 'I need riding boots of best quality.' Leonard again.

He was apt to introduce 'my fiancée', always a different girl, very young, very startled, incredulous, usually attractive, though he never married. At Queen's Club, he won many points with his tennis service, a practical example of winning without aces. First, he bounced the ball and caught it a number of times, as if counting eggs or telling beads, occasionally pausing for an operatic glance at the nostalgic Edwardian setting or the pleasures of a July sky: then he lifted his racquet, slowly, as though in abstruse measurement, and took aim, but instead of serving, resumed bouncing the ball. Ceasing this, Leonard would find a few coughs came in handy, then an adjustment of his headband, another pause, to invite a passing stranger to his next party, then an aggrieved inquiry, 'Are you ready?' until, frowning as if over his famous statistics, and with the demeanour of a churchwarden passing the plate, he delivered a ball so slow, almost hovering, that one assumed a guileful spin that was not there. I suspected someone very lonely, perhaps cruel, and my wife thought him the most attractive man she had yet met.

William Gerhardie had worked in the British Embassy in Russia during the Great War, and his early novels, *Futility* and *The Polyglots*, had been much praised by H. G. Wells and Evelyn Waugh and gained him commissions from Lord Beaverbrook, though his prose style, influenced by the more complex European masters, was rarely suited to the *Daily Express* or the *Evening Standard*; he had written a book on Chekhov, and did not dissent when addressed as the English Chekhov. He was annoyed when his publishers demurred at his wish to adorn the jacket of one of his novels with a recommendation from E. M. Forster. 'I have not read Gerhardie myself, but I am told by Graham Greene that they are very good.' At his house in Hallam Street, he was usually, like Canetti, the hub of obsequious admirers, administering to his wants, which were numerous and varied. Amongst his visitors was Olivia Manning who, while admiring his genius, was never obsequious and indeed often sharp-tongued about the lack of genius in almost all others save Ivy Compton-Burnett. By the Fifties, though he was said to be writing more elaborate novels, from his vantage point of literary sophistication, historical insights and richly endowed language, none appeared. At his funeral in Golders Green in 1977, few of the coterie, save Olivia, were present, and the chapel was sparsely attended.

I would meet him, always at the same party, once a year, from 1950, and he always said the same sentence, accompanying it with a confidential, rather attractive smile: 'I have not read you. Nor, I will go so far to say, will I ever do so. They tell me that you, so to speak, are not going far. You have not yet read me.'

I was probably correct in identifying 'they' as Olivia. He was wrong about my not having read him. I greatly admired him and once, not feeling myself obsequious, I quoted to him, with fair accuracy, a passage from *The Polyglots*, concerning Humour: 'The inestimable advantage of comedy over any other literary method of depicting life is that here you rise superior, unobtrusively, to every notion, attitude, and situation so depicted. We laugh because we cannot be destroyed, because we do not recognise our destiny in any one achievement, because we are immortal, because there is not this or that world, but endless worlds; eternally we pass from one into another. In this lies the hilarity, futility, the insurmountably great.'

I waited expectantly. His pinkish face went glum then, not insurmountably great, it crinkled. 'How did you know that? Whenever people – would-be writers, tag-masters and so on – quote something from my work, it is almost always proof that they have stolen it for their own work. That will explain much, I could say, too much.' He once demanded whether I had attended a university. Rather nervously, I admitted I had, indeed at his own college. This mollified him not at all. 'Ah! Trained folly.' I sensed another quotation, from himself. Greatly as I respected him, I did not luxuriate in his company.

'Look!' A vice-president of the Progressive League handed me a book. 'This is It.'

She was Enid Thompson Browne, who preferred to be known as Brodsky, and who exemplified Max Beerbohm's quip that most women are not as young as they are painted. Years ago, she had approached her stepfather, everywhere called 'Cutlass', having recommended, because of a shortage of rifles in 1940, that the Home Guard should be so armed.

'Papa, I want to get married.' 'My dear girl, marry whoever you like. Not a foreigner. No Jews of course. And certainly not an artist. What's his name?' 'Wolfgang.' Wolfgang was a refugee from Stettin, member of a liberal synagogue, and was currently exhibiting surrealistic paintings at the AIA Gallery.

Enid had sudden exacting enthusiasms, violent colours overlaid on a white screen, and she dived into the early Fifties with an energy matching that of David Sylvester, though with less discrimination. She would divulge a most advanced nudist colony in darkest Hertfordshire, Salvador Dali's telephone number, Faber's latest poet, the state of play between Sartre and de Beauvoir.

'So,' her black eyes strained at their moorings, her tangled hair shook, all teeth were on show, 'you, the ordinary person, man in the

street, will see what is normally seen only by the artist, and only the
exceptional artist at that. Nothing to do with what's socially or bio-
logically useful. The mind, pure, unsullied, at large, drifting through
the universe. All is in all.'

We were dining at Chez Victor; between courses, she handed over
bound proof sheets, many sentences underlined so heavily that they
were barely decipherable. I read aloud, listlessly: 'How can a man at
the extreme limits of ectomorphy and cerebratonia ever put himself in
the place of one at the limits of endomorphy and viscerotonia or, except
within circumscribed areas, share the feelings of one who stands at the
limits of mesomorphy and somatotonia?' I closed the book. 'How
indeed? Jeeves on an off-day?' Brodsky gibbered with irritation.
'You've read the wrong page. You always do. Just listen.'

She read in turn, in vigorous, exhorting tones that reminded me that
she was a contralto in the Bach Choir. Waiters gathered around, their
rather prurient interest suggesting conviction that she had written the
book herself.

It was Aldous Huxley's *The Doors of Perception* (1954) and *Heaven and
Hell* (1956), in which he described his experiment, under medical
supervision, with mescalin, a drug derived from the Mexican cactus,
peyote. Elsewhere, Robert Graves was tracing early Greek concepts of
heaven and hell to visions provoked by 'The Little Foxes', Dionysiac
toxic mushrooms. Meanwhile, Huxley now saw the folds of his trousers as a labyrinth of endlessly significant complexity, deeply, mysteriously sumptuous, like the drapery in a Botticelli, in a heightened
world of Isness and Suchness.

Just possibly, Brodsky would introduce me to explorations of innocent Edens, the sea before the birth of Venus, the sighs of Merlin,
wrinkles on air lustred by gigantic dragonflies and midget alps, the
mind released from obsessions and trends, achieving layers of pure
colour, sensations freed from biological needs. Huxley made his reader
feel a fellow-pioneer of a world undeniably brave, certainly new. So I
gratefully attended Brodsky's mescalin party, in her South Molton
Street home. She had hired, at some expense, a professional master of
ceremonies, tall, swarthy, earrings flashing from black, massy hair. 'I
am', he announced, 'Andreas da Gabba,' as if it were a title, though
a score of smart faces flinched at the cockney accent. Above us, above
the buhl furniture and thickly patterned rugs, themselves a promising
field for visionary distortions, hung a portrait, enlarged from a *Picture
Post* cut-out, of Huxley himself, grave and slightly sorrowful.

Andreas ordered us down from chairs and sofas on to large, many-
coloured cushions. Brodsky, a little in front of us, reclined like the

favourite mistress of some August Personage, whose footfalls seemed already audible. As if from an invisible hat, Andreas produced an oval tray with small, glittering goblets of gin or water. His smile, shrewd, confidential, was almost a leer. His small, ringed hands fluttered, tiny white pellets slid into the glasses. He commanded immediate concentration on a particular object: a rug, a glass paperweight enclosing a toy Bayreuth, a delicately tinted porcelain bowl. We sighed with incipient pleasure, Brodsky's prince was almost upon her. Then we each took a glass, and poised ourselves to breach all known frontiers, and I at once imagined Brodsky as Donald Duck.

We swallowed, we gulped, we lay prone. After some minutes, or hours, I was both disappointed and vaguely proud when, opening my eyes and finding the apartment unchanged, defiantly refusing to transform to a Himalayan ravine, a cracked Bokharan tomb, a Patagonian swamp, Brodsky remained Brodsky, the porcelain not a sniper but a bowl. Around me, however, small moans had begun, well-judged wriggles, as if in preliminaries to copulation, though very soon convincing me that no one was experiencing anything more than I was, that I would have preferred whisky, that the pellets had been less charged than Holy Communion wafers. The only higher awareness I achieved was a blue conviction that Andreas would soon levy a contribution for the victims of some crisis in an unforgettable country which he forgot to name, followed by a sudden wink from Huxley aloft.

More serious scepticism came from Stuart Hampshire, in *Encounter*, in 1954, objecting that Huxley had always been seeking some harmless pill or physical jerks that, without sacrifice of the intellect, would dispense the wisdom of the Buddha. But Huxley disregarded the freedom of the Will, any free act of positive belief, and relied on physical and mental inertia. 'Omit from art the mind's own act of construction, and one may compare or prefer a mescalin vision of one's trousers to a Cézanne or a Seurat . . . But surely the enjoyment of a mescalin vision is a passive enjoyment, and the enjoyment of a Cézanne is not. Works of art are not mere decoration, like agreeable wallpapers, curved table legs, ornamental ceilings, they are challenges to investigate . . .' Mescalin visions were beautiful and interesting, but comparatively unimportant, and Hampshire judged that Huxley was 'a nineteenth-century naturalist who observes with delight the brilliant variety of human molluscs to be found in the rock pools of history. He can, therefore, easily ignore men in discussing art, and God in discussing religion.'

Ernst Jünger, with whom the pacifist Huxley would have had little in common, had also experimented with hallucinogenic drugs and later told Nigel Jones: 'Young people have nothing today. In my time there was the Fatherland or religion. They still need something transcendent today, and I understand that. I don't regret my drug experience – it had a major influence on my life. But to dabble in drugs you need to be intelligent, if you do not master them, they will dominate you, and destroy you . . .'

As the Fifties closed, stories circulated of a drugged student stabbing himself in what he imagined was his third eye, a girl stepping from a high window, a boy circumcising himself with a broken bottle in his advance from catatonia to mysticism. Huxley was rebuked for encouraging wholesale drug-taking, though he wrote to Thomas Merton in 1959: 'I have taken mescalin twice and lycergic acid three or four times. My first experience was mainly aesthetic. Later experiences were of another nature and helped me to understand many of the obscure utterances to be found in the writings of the mystics, Christian and oriental. An unspeakable sense of gratitude for the privilege of being born into this universe. "Gratitude is heaven itself," says Blake – and I now know more exactly what he is talking about. A transcendence of the fear of death. A sense of solidarity with the world and its spiritual principle . . . Finally, an understanding with the entire organism, of the affirmation that God is love. The experiences are transient, of course; but the memories of them, and the inchoate revivals of them which tend to recur spontaneously or during meditation, continue to exercise a profound effect upon one's mind.'

7

Optimism and Nostalgia

FOR T. S. ELIOT, the modern world was an immense paradox of futility and anarchy, a view at least plausible whenever one picked up a newspaper. The crushing of Hitler and Mussolini had helped lose Britain her rank as a Great Power, her Empire, her naval supremacy, her economic and psychological self-assurance. The wartime loss of Singapore and the Yalta Conference were already being rated the worst defeats since late medieval England lost France and a later England lost America.

Yet I sensed little of this, save amongst the elderly, in 1950. Stalin still ruled, grey and inexorable, in Eastern Europe, but had been worsted by the Berlin air-lift. Loss of Empire, not in itself catastrophic, would be balanced by more pronounced Western co-operation, and the foundation of the West European Iron, Coal and Steel Community, if yet without British participation, promised just this. Raised on the anti-imperialism of Leonard Woolf, and another Left Book Club favourite, Leonard Barnes, and George Orwell, few intellectuals had regrets for the Empire. Poets would angrily quote Maud Gonne's words to Yeats: that England and her Empire meant famine in Ireland, opium in China, pauperism in England, disturbance and disorder and robbery everywhere. Anti-imperialism was enhanced by the efforts of Continentals to maintain their colonial empires. Marcello Caetano, Portuguese ruler, issued a memorandum in 1954: 'The African natives must be directed and organised by Europeans, but are indispensable as auxiliaries. They never produced any useful invention, any technological advancements, nor any significant contribution to human evolution. They must therefore be regarded as production units, organised, or to be organised, exclusively by whites.' I remember the irritated incredulity at a literary party when an Indian left-winger, Sarda Pannikar, published *Asia and Western Democracy*, and acknowledged the Indian Civil Service, which the Republic had inherited from the Raj, as an imposing and truly magnificent administration.

Meanwhile the 1948 foundation of Israel would compensate for gigantic wrongs, despite Arnold Toynbee's forebodings that it would reinforce destructive nationalism. Wars in Korea, Malaya and Algeria did not undermine the unlimited hopes for the United Nations fulfilling the international ideas of H. G. Wells and Toynbee. For others, the Yangtze Incident, in which a British frigate successfully ran the gauntlet of Chinese Communists' guns, supplied a draught of stalwart heroism. When England regained the Ashes in 1953, with three pre-war heroes in the team, it seemed a return to an Anglo-Australian balance of fortune, a gleam from the Golden Age. The climbing of Everest, the four-minute mile, the successful staging of the Olympic Games, all within a few years, showed much that was well with national interests. Orchestras, ballet companies and opera were reaching new audiences. Benjamin Britten, Henry Moore, Michael Tippett and Margot Fonteyn were being acclaimed internationally. Britten's *Billy Budd* (1951) and Tippett's *The Midsummer Marriage* (1955), with sets by Barbara Hepworth, made a resounding impact in ways excitingly different. And there was soon to appear the benevolent incorruptibility of Jack Warner's television family policeman, Dixon of Dock Green.

Bertrand Russell won the Nobel Prize for Literature in 1950. The Director of Unesco was the liberal humanist Julian Huxley, Aldous's brother; within the World Health Organization was a world figure, the nutrition expert Dr William Boyd Orr. Nationalism, imperialism, obscurantism and insularity were crumbling; so was disease. British science and engineering had split the atom, had produced radar, penicillin and the turbo-jet, had pioneered plastics and electronics, but without flag-waving.

A symptom of this, if disdained by Eliot, Waugh, Betjeman, Coward and Graham Greene, was the 1951 Festival of Britain, the last flourish of Attlee's dying government, designed to exude 'fun, fantasy and colour' to a nation still burdened with ration books and identity cards. The Festival's *Lion and Unicorn* tableau, like the White Knight, representatives of eccentricity and humour, gave saving grace to a people harassed by 'Work or Want'. Like Prince Albert's *tour de force* a century before, the Festival celebrated arts and sciences, knowledge and potential. Work by Moore, Epstein, Graham Sutherland, Felix Topolski, John Piper and Barbara Hepworth shared space with a scientific Dome of Discovery, with the witty and the whimsical, with fountains and mobiles, a dragon, a crazy railway. The immediate impression, as I tramped through it with David Sylvester, was of lightness and breadth, giving a cheerful riposte to the heavy solidity of St. Paul's, the Abbey, Parliament. Particularly memorable was the slender, vertical Skylon, a steel and aluminium column reaching to an immeasurable possibility, yet also a gently ironic interrogation mark, 300 feet high, querrying the sententious and pompous. Harry Hopkins remembered the Festival in 1964, dubbing it a ceremonial re-erection of the Maypole: 'Churchillian historical rhetoric had resounded well enough from the sounding board of war; in the age of the *Pax Americana*, it rang a little hollow. So the "Festival Style" was clean, bright and new. It looked neither to classical Athens, nor imperial New Delhi, nor to chromium-plated sky-scraping New York, but to the modest, model social democracies of Scandinavia.' This 'contemporary' style affected advertisements, shop lettering, furniture, fabrics, clothes: it meant colourful texture, elegant simplicity in design, deft inventiveness – chairs curved and holed, supple and glistening, if sometimes uncomfortable – space implied within limited contexts.

If the authorized 'spontaneous expression of citizenship' seemed grabbed from a Moscow hand-out, citizens needed no prodding to saunter, dance, gape, grumble, chuckle and wonder. They spoke of 'the new Britain', as they soon would of 'new Elizabethans'. Regulars used the Festival precinct as a club. There, Jocelyn Rickards, girlfriend of A. J. Ayer, small, with a dancer's feet and liveliness, lustrous, witty and intelligent, refilled the glass of a tall, 'hugely sexy' stranger, saying, years afterwards, that she had arrived with Freddie Ayer and left in love with Graham Greene.

The decade also witnessed what a journalist called the Revolution of Rising Expectations. History was now thriving, the future had a future. The Welfare State was continuing innovations begun by Lloyd George and Churchill in the pre-1914 Liberal Government. Attlee had implemented the wartime Beveridge Report, without important dissent. Sir William Beveridge himself was a Liberal, suggesting no socialist revolution: 'The aim is not to destroy inequality. That cannot be done. Inequality will always be with us. It is, to put it bluntly, simply a more efficient method of compelling people to make wise provision for their own emergencies and for their future.' No wild utopianism there! The costs in taxation were high, but Britain could 'take it'. Stoicism was to prevail for a few years more. The onslaught of a Labour Minister, the fiery, Polish-born Emanuel Shinwell, addressing the Electricians' Union, was in terms deplored by most politicians of all parties: 'Organised workers are my government's friends . . . as for the rest, they don't matter a tinker's cuss.' This must have embarrassed Attlee, if not Aneurin Bevan, triumphant from having pushed through the acclaimed National Health Service, against opposition from the doctors.

Churchill had condemned Labour's regimentation and controls, its abandonment of India, its indifference to United Europe, though after his own return to power in 1951 there was no spectacular break and considerable consensus prevailed. It was part of what, in his book of that name, David Rees called 'The Age of Containment', as he surveyed post-war world politics. The consensus was reinforced by an influx of royalism. When George VI died the next year, rather surprisingly, he was ostentatiously mourned in India, South Africa and certain areas of the USA. The Duke of Norfolk, Earl Marshal of England, barked: 'The public will wear black,' surely the last occasion when such a style was tolerated.

Coronation junketings glittered around a young Queen and her cricketing, outspoken consort, smiling, but more of a Mountbatten than he might appear. Elizabeth Longford noticed that the carpet in the Abbey had been laid with the pile facing the wrong way. The Queen's coronation attire was fringed with heavy gold and the pile obstructed her advance at the start, forcing her to ask the Archbishop to help get her moving, 'and with a holy pull she was off'. The Coronation was the incentive television needed to persuade large numbers to buy a set for the first time. Keeping up with the Joneses, some houses sported TV aerials, though lacking the actual set.

On radio, the Third Programme, like the Overseas Service, won much respect abroad, with drama, poetry, new music, discussions, and lectures presented daily. I was thrilled by Benjamin Britten's and Edward Sackville-West's verse drama, *The Rescue*, and by the verse plays of Louis MacNeice. Bertrand Russell gave the first Reith Lectures, Shaw's *Man and Superman* inaugurated the drama policy; there was exhilaration in hearing the words cascading out of the air, back in 1946, to start two famous decades of listening: 'Your friends are the dullest dogs I know. They are not beautiful: they are only decorated. They are not clean: they are only shaved and starched. They are not dignified: they are only fashionably dressed . . .'

Long-playing records blared out cheerful tunes – 'Come on a – My House'; 'Getting to Know You'; 'If I'd Known You Were Coming I'd a Baked a Cake'. Parties were lavish, fanned by Stock Exchange profits. The Bolshoi Ballet performed at Covent Garden. Olivier,

Richardson and Thorndike had set standards by no means élitist in the Forties, giving inexperienced theatre-goers revelatory concepts of 'plays' at their seasons at the New Theatre, and the Fifties did not revoke these. Holiday camps replaced the clogged bathrooms and post-breakfast lock-outs of the earlier dispensation. Adult Education thrived; by 1958, public libraries were lending nearly 400 million books annually. The Arts Council had been established in 1946, its chairman, John Maynard Keynes, announcing that it aimed to create an environment in which to breed a spirit, to cultivate an opinion, to offer a stimulus to such purpose that the artist and the public could each sustain and live on the other in that union which has occasionally existed in the great ages of the past.

Trades unions were starting to endow the arts: the new Council of Industrial Design showed that there was more to life than nylons. New Towns – Harlow, Stevenage, Crawley – the promise of seventeen new universities, the actual building of scores of new schools, suggested a new Britain of light architecture, rain-free shopping arcades, friendly neighbourhoods, all generations at peace within libraries, parks, clean spacious homes and gardens, the gap between Them and Us continually narrowing.

This mood I largely shared, seeing scant evidence for Camus's assertion, in 1951, that the secret of Europe was that of no longer loving life. I met few who worried about fractured egos or lack of identity, having found in the war unsuspected reserves of being. I felt that we now had not only the will but also the apparatus for a more humane attitude towards crime, health, sex, women and children, colour, other countries. Margaret Gowing, historian of the early Harwell, centre of British atomic research, writes: 'Most people remember a strong sense of idealism, which expressed itself not only in a belief in internationalism and international atomic energy control – but also in a desire to do something to demonstrate the peaceful uses of atomic energy as a counter-balance to the bomb. There was a belief that a whole new world would open before them – a medical revolution through the use of radioactive isotopes, and a new clean source of power which would end the pall of sulphurous smoke over the cities.'

These hopes were not wholeheartedly confirmed by older, hardened writers, Edward Upward, Huxley, John Sommerfield, Jack Lindsay, Greene, Malcolm Muggeridge; nor by new names, Doris Lessing, Anthony Burgess, Angus Wilson. I found little fiction or poetry set in a New Town, until Wilson's *Late Call* (1964), showing older people trailing misgivings about the New Britain like a sea anchor. The hygienic blandness of a New Town, meticulously plotted with parks, social centres, neat, tight front doors, might yet lack the old organic liveliness, noisy street markets, backyard encounters, in an atmosphere of remote controls, departmental factions, gadgetry. Wilson's middle-aged Sylvia Clavert is beached in such a town with her headmaster son, a choice Fifties specimen, a New Man, progressive, knowing, *contemporary*, pushing, who bewilders and alarms her with a relentlessly up-to-date kitchen, all glittering knobs, thermostats and technological kinks.

Not herself well-educated, once in 'domestic service', Sylvia is nevertheless rooted in an older, more accessible England with traditions tough, sometimes brutal, yet, to her, reassuring. With more insight than her all-seeing son, who is too busy to observe, acutely, very much, she realizes an innate desolation in a town that is not a community, where affluent gimmicks are not supplements to life but a way of life. In a much later novel, Tony Peake's *A Summer Tide* (1993), a character declares: 'It was a very flat decade, the Fifties. One-dimensional, suburban. Materialistic. The outlook was limited, pinched. People watched their feet, not the horizon.' I remember it differently, but perhaps my own pages will contradict me.

Academics began pondering 'sociology', a new discipline, largely from North America, in which the imagination was enriched by Marshall McLuhan, Vance Packard, David Reisman, with such suggestive notions as the Lonely Crowd, the Global Village, the Organization Man. A Chair had been founded at the London School of Economics, an Oxford lectureship in 1950, followed by Chairs at Leeds, Nottingham and Birmingham. The American historian John Clive, an authority on Lord Macaulay, Gibbon and Carlyle, sensing his own discipline to be under siege and fervently believing that history, all-important, is not a science but an art, had no temptation to research such subjects as 'the connection between siblings and baldness amongst clock workers in South-East Ohio, 1823–59'. Some established writers deplored both sociology and optimism as facile short-sightedness. A. L. Rowse, once a Labour candidate and, until Suez, a Labour supporter, from All Souls, Oxford, was deploring 'the Idiot People'. G. M. Trevelyan remarked that the age had no other culture than that of American films and football pools. 'Democracy has cooked the goose of civilization.' Arnold Toynbee was heard to say that technology would become a Third World War. Evelyn Waugh was not easily imagined luxuriating in a Butlin's Holiday Camp, or presenting prizes at a New School. A proper government, he considered, should be unconcerned with the sick, the old and the destitute. His *Love Among the Ruins* (1953) satirized an English dictatorship dedicated to welfare planning, state guardianship from cradle to grave.

Throughout his career, Angus Wilson sharply noted current trends and ironies which, as always, were ample: miners refusing to work alongside Polish fellow-workers, a Labour government using troops against striking dockers. That essential services were now nationalized, 'belonging to us', had not prevented strikes, the People striking against itself. The union boss Ernest Bevin was viciously attacked for anti-Semitism as a result of his efforts to maintain friendships with oil-possessing Arabs. The electricians' union, indicted in court for criminal vote-rigging, had denounced Attlee for failing to use his huge parliamentary majority to enforce more emphatic egalitarianism. Maynard Keynes was scrupulously impartial, designating Conservatives as the Stupid Party, Labour the Silly Party.

The atmosphere of older traditions re-emerging after the delirium of the 1945 Labour electoral triumph remains in Angus Wilson's story, *Such Darling Dodos* (1950). Here, Harriet and Michael, post-war undergraduates, visit the older Robin and Priscilla, once Thirties progressives but now 'dodos', still engrossed with Fabian tracts, hunger marchers, Wellsian-Freudian-Marxist dismissal of religion, patriotism and profitable business. Robin had published many 'hard, little bright-covered books', crammed with statistics, facts, right-wing enormities and social injustices.

The occasion is unpromising. 'When Robin remarked that Michael must find chapel a bore, the young man stroked his moustache and murmured that he doubted boredom was a possible reaction when something of the kind was so badly needed. Harriet too wondered if freedom was quite the issue when one looked at India, after all responsibility was important.'

The mid-Sixties youth idol Bob Dylan was to ordain 'Nostalgia is Death'. In the early Fifties, this would have been largely unheard of. Nostalgia did indeed offer temptations to sentimentalize pre-war holidays, labour relations, domestic harmony, county cricket and league football, Anglican services, to wallow in B flat minor. I remembered, or thought I did, rainless Augusts, deep bluebell woods, small trains chugging across buttercup fields. J. B. Priestley spoke of long-lost 'tuppenny teas', rich, oozing, curranty, with homemade jams and bread, and thick slabs of butter, and his novel *Bright Day* evoked a pre-1914 popular culture of home music, amateur theatre, travelling opera, new libraries and arts societies, enthusiastic teachers agog with Shaw, Wells and Havelock Ellis, cyclists exploring new, fresh countrysides, good companions everywhere. Even teddy boys imagined they were apeing a departed glamour.

Elsewhere, Edmund Hockridge could extract sighs and tears, singing, in *Dear Miss Phoebe* (1950), his 'I'll leave my Heart in an English Garden', and Donald Peers entranced the nation with his masterpiece: 'In a Shady Nook, By a Babbling Brook ...' Sandy Wilson's *The Boy Friend* lulled us with tinkling tunes and butterfly romances, mild ripples derived from the Twenties. Sporting susceptibilities were stirred by the sight of Wilfred Rhodes, great cricketer even before the Great War, still attending games, though long blind; and of Percy Chapman, mighty hitter and handsome crowd-pleaser of the Thirties, unshaven and sloppy, drinking himself to death in Kentish tap-rooms, ostracized in the Long Room at Lord's and, perhaps wisely, refused drinks at the bar.

Around me certain words and names were gathering elegaic patina: Roadhouse, P & O, Guitry, Blue Moon, Turkish Baths, Jermyn Street, Baden Baden, Hispano-Suiza and Le Touquet, where Bulldog Drummond and his fellow thugs dispatched their wives when the game was afoot. Other words were losing caste without much nostalgia. Proletarian was one. When, in 1951, the Dean, slightly drunk outside the Black Horse, Soho, congratulated a beefy lorry-driver on being a member of the Proletariat, with the Future in his hands, he barely escaped a knock-out. Cyril Connolly's pre-war novel, *The Rock Pool*, glowed with enticing evocations when reissued.

As a small-fry hanger-on, I thought this writer arrogant, conceited and greedy, a connoisseur of guilt and *Angst*, and found ironical his sneer at Huxley's 'competent intellectual vulgarity', but was grateful for his editorship of *Horizon*, often a gleam in a black night, and his idiosyncratic perceptions. I would savour his novel in deserted bars, reliving an adolescent evening on a terrace in Mediterranean twilight; far below, glimmering water spread from dipping, darkening cliffs and, along the curved sea-line, small ancient towns winked like regalia; pallid moths circled the table lamps which flipped unnatural tints over terracotta pots, sham-Pompeian vases, coarse roses, while, far out, gaudy ships edged towards the low moon, a wave moving like a white muscle – 'With the silvery heave of a dolphin out of the water, the force, the beauty of the present moment seemed to flash into something almost visible and then sink back into the natural current of the afternoon.'

Connolly hauled back the years of *Orient Express*, the young Graham Greene, Max Miller glittering at the Brighton Hippodrome, *Harbour*

Lights, the *Flying Scotsman*, early Auden, Prokosch of course hovering in the wings: 'The hulls of large yachts were visible through the arches, his napkin had violet stains, the mosquitoes hummed in the torrid air. Brooding over a bottle of Chianti and scratching his chin, he made up his mind to go into the Bastion. It was the hour when the soft light of southern cities holds the clearest promise of release and adventure, when a light going on or off is a portent and the lowering of a blind seems like a sign from heaven.'

Nostalgia, though with more inescapable melancholy, pervaded John Piper's paintings, a romanticism of ancient mansions in ragged twilit woodlands, abandoned or ruined cottages, bombed churches, lonely waters under stormy skies, great threatened medieval barns. His pre-war abstraction was left behind. Piper's friend John Betjeman was becoming a celebrity, reading his poems, enthusing over Victorian architecture, mourning failing countrysides, recalling childhood delights in Cornwall, yet with sufficient undercurrents of fear, pathos, loneliness, lust, sin, illness and death to add some critical appreciation to the massive public response. Known before the war as a minor poet, journalist and mild eccentric, he had then served as Press Attaché in the Dublin Embassy, probably not a very exacting post; later, from Blenheim Palace, administering the arts and science division of the British Council, and seen by Ralph Glasser 'in baggy beige trousers, hanging sack-like ... Despite what seemed arrogant posturing, and certainly a core of toughness, he had a timid, gentle streak, carefully protected.'

His architectural preferences were often derided by professionals. John Summerson, in agreement with the astringent Nikolaus Pevsner and himself an authority on Georgian London, Inigo Jones, Wren and Soane, rebuked Betjeman's Victorianism as an amateurish, self-indulgent, self-propagating cult. Deploring his popularity, other writers observed snobbishness, facetiousness, the facile, disfiguring a small but undoubted talent. A. Alvarez's 'the upper-middle class, or Tory ideal, presented in its pure crystalline form by John Betjeman' was no recommendation to most ambitious young poets. He was, in a phrase then fashionable, as 'committed' as any, not to abstractions – Freedom, Progress, People, Party – but to the near and the tangible, a curious building, a secluded street, a death from cancer. His Highgate and Perivale meant real places, his characters had faces and oddities. He deplored much of Fifties England, if less stridently than Osborne, less tetchily than Priestley, as he saw religious and communal traditions shredded for the inorganic, the ready-made and the plastic, for novelties and blaring slogans.

> ... The children have a motor-bus instead,
> And in a town eleven miles away
> We train them to be 'Citizens of To-Day',
> And many a cultivated hour they pass
> In a fine school with walls of vita-glass.
> Civics, eurhythmics, economics, Marx,
> How-to-respect-wild-life in National Parks;
> Plastics, gymnastics – thus they learn to scorn,
> The old thatch'd cottages where they were born.
>   (from 'The Dear Old Village')

Philip Larkin, in *Listen* (1959), considered Betjeman 'one of those rare figures on whom the aesthetic appetites of an age pivot and swing round to face an entirely new direction'.

Larkin himself, during the Fifties, was acquiring a reputation amongst critics superior to that of Betjeman, while sharing his dislike of an England seen as a place of growing union power, pupil power, anarchic literary and artistic modernism, faked reputations, mass immigration. In 'At Grass' (1955), a symbolism is provided by once-famous race horses, relegated to the peace of old age, the classic Junes and stop-press columns long dead. 'Church Going' (1955) was perhaps the most popular poem of the decade. Both he and Betjeman, bypassing Eliot, without debts to Auden, carried reminders of the moods and vision of Thomas Hardy, who remembered the church services of his own childhood.

> So mindless were those outpourings,
> Yet I am unaware
> That I have gained from subtle thought on things
> Since we stood psalming there.

Eliot, Pound, Arnold Toynbee and Jung all applied antique civilizations and remote cultures to their critiques of the present. Betjeman and Larkin, less ambitious, looked back only a few years, without sensational novelties of thought and technique, but with effect scarcely negligible.

Bernard Kops made Sam Levy, pickled-herring seller, ruminate in his play, *The Hamlet of Stepney Green*:'Whatever became of Whitechapel? Teeming with people, so gay, so alive ... where are they? Where are the old men with the long white beards, where are the women selling beigels? ... everything is dead and being put into tins, smaller and smaller, good-bye cabbages, good-bye oranges, good-bye silver fishes ...'

In another play, *The Winslow Boy*, Terence Rattigan optimistic-
ally appraised traditional English justice, without reference to Lord
Goddard. In the Cinema, Herbert Wilcox and Anna Neagle, his wife,
a pre-war favourite, presented such romantic pieces as *Spring in Park
Lane, Maytime in Mayfair* and *The Courtenys of Curzon Street*, displaying
reassuring vistas of graceful bay windows, footmen polishing silver
heirlooms, venerable butlers dedicated to the Family as loyally as any
official to the Party, pert, uniformed maids galore: the affluent gentility of what was, with deepening irony, being called Gracious Living.
Here, as in *The Boy Friend*, was the imitation of a past, quieter, more
elegant and probably more bogus than Fifties realities.

Post-war British Cinema shirked much of the present and all of
the future, serenading instead traditional decencies, little-man forti-
tude, public-school leadership and self-deprecation, the absurdity of
foreigners and contemporary art. With Labour in power, some producers accepted scripts recounting individual raids on stuffy local government, bureaucratic controls, union despotism, police officiousness,
restrictive licensing laws, clock-watching employers and courageous if
unheroic non-conformists.

The decline of Empire and loss of colonial adventures was partially
balanced by the Ealing Comedies, stressing regional quirks, individualistic disrespect, an inventive aptitude for bloodless, anti-social behaviour, and with some of the Festival whimsy and fantasy. Satire was
gentle, the crookedness amiable, 'political awareness' negligible: not
quite a never-never world, the acting from seasoned favourites usually
called 'polished'.

The Second World War itself was generally confined to stiff-lipped
British heroes who flew, sailed or marched their way to victory, or
escaped from prison camp. Here Jack Hawkins's resolute chin proved
as useful as Clive Brook's before him. The Nazis were mostly stage-
property; their distinctive contribution, the Holocaust, was never
seriously examined, nor the murderous, gigantic land battles in Russia.
An almost Victorian set of wartime virtues – bravery, self-sacrifice, class
solidarity, patriotism, decency – were themselves nostalgic, reinforced
by the charm of such performers as Kenneth More, Richard Todd,
Michael Redgrave, Olivier, Richardson, Guinness and Coward. Con-
spicuously missing was the irrational, the sexual, the inconsequential
and over-simple, the crazed logic of Kenneth Erskine, the Stockwell
Strangler, on arrest: 'I wanted to be famous.'

Nostalgia was repeated in such popular war books as *The Cruel Sea*,
The Wooden Horse, Boldness be my Friend, themselves often filmed, and
stories of individual adventure and colourful experience – *The Kon-Tiki*

Expedition, Elephant Bill, The Jungle is Neutral. Alain Bombard sailed the Atlantic alone in a small boat, existing mainly on plankton, then writing a best-selling account.

Masculine nostalgia for crumbling paternalism and domestic slavery was expanding in the face of the undramatic but persistent broadening of women's rights, in all but the Church, West End clubs, the Marylebone Cricket Club, and the sharing of the bill in expensive restaurants. Increasingly, women were entering professions, abandoning drudgery, departing early to work, asserting independence, power, status. Billy Rice, father of Archie, Osborne's ruined 'Entertainer' (1957), lamented the passing of women of his generation:'They were graceful, they had mystery and dignity. Why, when a woman got out of a cab, she descended. Descended. And you put your hand out to it smartly to help her down. Look at them today. Have you ever seen a woman get out of a car? Well, have you? I have, and I don't want to see it again, thank you very much. Why, I never saw a woman's legs until I was nineteen. Nineteen.'

Since 1953, many, though not the Rices, were discussing Simone de Beauvoir's *The Second Sex*, a feminist tract on the need for women to redefine their roles, hitherto subservient, for men to shed their discontents, maladjustments and unimaginative selfishness which made them exploit women not only as beasts of burden, but also as pegs on which to hang their weaknesses.

Lionel Trilling, tall, elegant, handsome, very courteous – he tended to 'remind' you of books unknown to you, to begin, 'You remember . . .' probably certain that you did not, though in no way condescending or malicious – reminded me and, I remember, Muriel Spark, of Henry James's *The Bostonians*, which he had apparently quoted in his *The Opposing Self* (1955). Writing in 1886, James gave one character a didactic voice, very different from that in which, a little later, H. G. Wells and Arnold Bennett were to envisage the New Woman, independent, courageous, intelligent, long before de Beauvoir and Greer: 'The whole generation is womanised, the masculine tone is passing out of the world, it's a feminine, a nervous, chattering, canting age, an age of hollow phrases and false delicacy and exaggerated solicitudes and coddled sensibilities, which, if we don't soon look out, will usher in the reign of mediocrity, of the feeblest and flattest and the most pretentious that has ever been known. The masculine character, the ability to dare and endure, to know and yet not to fear reality, to look the world in the face and take it for what it is – a very queer and partly very base mixture – this is what I want to preserve, or rather, as I may say, recover.'

To have recommended this to Fifties students would have been to risk one's neck, or worse. As for Trilling, I have never met anyone to whom I was more immediately attracted. He must have been a splendid teacher, though his later students became more restless with his friendly, liberal humanism, tending to equate his regard for Jane Austen with support for the Vietnam war. I only twice saw his quiet, slightly ironic smile slightly strained: when Muriel said she found Dickens unreadable, and when Philip Toynbee wrote that Trilling's one novel, *The Middle of the Journey*, was 'the best novel by a non-genius since E. M. Forster'.

8

Stalin and After

THE RUSSIAN JEWISH poet Itzik Feffer wrote a poem about Stalin. I do not know its title, but this is easy to imagine:

> When I utter *Stalin* I mean good.
> When I utter *Stalin* I mean courage.
> I mean eyes shining,
> I mean ceaseless activity.

> When I utter *Stalin* I mean yes,
> Wherever you call me I am there;
> You are my present, my yesterday,
> You are my tomorrow.

Stalin did eventually call him, to a firing squad. What could have been his last words? Stalin had continued the long-rooted Russian anti-Semitism which Marx had thought a capitalist-nationalist aberration: Jewish theatres, presses and synagogues had been vandalized and suppressed. Moscow Jews were assaulted by police as 'street hooligans'. Czech Jewish Communist officials were hanged after the infamous Slansky trial in Prague in November 1952. Stalin's death in 1953 saved the thirteen Jews of the 'Doctors' Plot', forced to confess to conspiracy to murder Soviet leaders. In the previous year, twenty-six leading Jewish writers had not been so lucky and had been shot on farcical charges.

Hailed as the creator of a modern, industrialized Russia, Stalin had transformed politics into unprincipled theology: reasoned opposition was the heresy of 'Enemies of Society'. His career also suggested the truth in Malraux's assertion that Marxism was no doctrine but a form of will power. He had been a swollen moral enormity, with his disregard of law, capricious personal rule, Party purges, mass executions and torture. His secret police, like the SS, had such extra-mural interests as managing factories, developing building sites, organizing black markets and currency frauds and illicit arms sales, selling drugs, blackmailing. Breaking his promise of free elections, his minority puppets reigned throughout Eastern Europe, only Tito's Yugoslavia successfully resisting, perhaps assisted by the Korean War, which made Stalin hesitate to use Hungarians against Belgrade. His brutal collectivization policies retarded Russian agriculture for a quarter of a century and, by murder and famine, killed many millions.

Russia had remained obsequious, *Pravda* daily committing what Eliot called the sins of language. An editorial, of 1951, was a hymn: 'Never was there a man so varied, so rich, so fruitful, so omnipotent, a genius . . . he astounds by his wisdom, by the irreproachable conclusions of his advice to masters of every trade. There is no other man in the world who can see so clearly into the future as Stalin.' Back in 1936, André Gide, passing through Stalin's birthplace, felt it appropriate to send the Secretary-General a telegram thanking him for Russian hospitality. The postmaster jibbed at *you*, insisting on 'You Leader of the Workers' or 'You Lord of the People'.

Bertrand Russell wrote that Tsarist Russia allowed a thousand times more freedom than Stalin. His reign recalls the words of the French terrorist Hébert, in 1793: 'To be safe we must kill everyone.' Stalin himself remarked to Khrushchev: 'I trust no one, not even myself.' Stalin's Commissar for Justice, N. V. Krylenko, subsequently shot, had pronounced his master's legal ethic: 'Every judge must keep himself up-to-date with State Policy and remember that his judgement in any particular case is intended to promote the contemporary outlook of the ruling class, and nothing else.'

The Russian poet Ilya Selvinski had told Isaiah Berlin in Moscow, in 1945, to speak loudly for the benefit of concealed microphones, as did he himself: 'I know that we are called conformists in the West. We are. We conform because we find that whenever we deviate from the Party's objectives it always turns out that the Party was right and that we were wrong. It has always been so. It is not only that they say they know better than we do: they see further: their eyes are sharper, their horizons are wider than ours.'

Stalin, like Shaw, considered writers 'engineers of the spirit' and he read widely. Milovan Djilas, himself a writer of some distinction, had been protesting about Russian liberators looting and raping in Yugoslavia. In his *Conversations with Stalin* (1961), dedicated to Aneurin

Bevan, he reported Stalin as saying: 'You have thought the Red Army ideal. It isn't, never can be, even if it didn't contain a certain number of criminals – we opened the prisons and shoved everyone into the Army. I'll tell you an interesting story. An Air Force officer needed a particular girl and a gallant engineer rallied round to protect her. The officer pulled out his gun. "Ekh, you stay-at-home mole!" And killed that gallant engineer. He got sentenced to death. But somehow I got to hear of it, asked a few questions – my privilege, as wartime commander-in-chief, and I freed the major, sent him to the Front, and he's now a national hero.' Stalin continued that in East Prussia, the victorious Red Army had massacred fleeing Germans, soldiers and civilians alike, men, women and children. 'We give our troops too many lectures; allow them some initiative.'

Like Churchill, Eden, Beaverbrook and, very briefly, H. G. Wells, Djilas admitted a humane, sentimental fondness for Stalin, a fellow-Communist, yet judged him 'the greatest criminal in history, uniting the criminal lunacy of Caligula, the refinement of a Borgia, the brutality of an Ivan the Terrible'. Robert Conquest, in *The Great Terror* (1968), calculated that Stalin killed more peasants in 1932–8 than the total casualties of the Great War.

Nadezhda Mandelstam, widow of Osip, the great poet, has written: 'We were all the same; either sheep who went willingly to the slaughter, or respectful assistants to the executioners ... Crushed by the system each of us had in some way helped to construct, we were incapable of resistance. Our subservience only egged on the regime's activists.' This was complemented in America by John Steinbeck during the McCarthyites' persecution of Arthur Miller. 'If we had fought back from the beginning instead of running away, these things would not be happening now.'

Much of the Stalinist terror had been known to such British writers and public servants as Shaw, MacDiarmid, Jack Lindsay, Kim Philby, Anthony Blunt, Donald Maclean and Guy Burgess, but many treated it with unconcern or, like Sartre and Brecht, deflected it with references to racialist imperialist America which Stalin was resisting. Pierre Trudeau, later Prime Minister of Canada, praised Stalin's efforts to create 'the new man'.

An adept politician, Stalin fooled Roosevelt and, briefly, Churchill, who in 1942, more unexpectedly, had found Stalin 'a truly great man', with humour and deep cool wisdom, and praised his lack of illusions. Joseph Losey, the gifted film director, had met Stalin before the war and found it 'impossible to think of him as other than warm, lovely'. Bernard Shaw told Stephen Winsten in 1945: 'Hitler has no sense of humour. I was pleasantly surprised to find when I met Stalin that he has a wonderful smile, somewhat like mine. We understood one another, though we could not converse directly together. You see, being myself the most foreign of all foreigners, an Irishman, I understand him.'

Brecht praised Stalin as 'the justified murderer of the people', and said of the executed Old Bolsheviks, 'the more innocent they were the more they deserved to die'. Sartre's 'saint', Jean Genet, denied the existence of the Gulags, Sartre himself extolling Russia for preserving freedom, though John Strachey must, by 1950, have repented his calling Stalin's empire 'the Kingdom of Freedom on earth'. Strachey and Victor Gollancz – who famously rejected Orwell's *Animal Farm* – had founded the influential, pre-war Left Book Club which must have assisted Labour's 1945 electoral victory. The Webbs appeared disinclined to abandon their belief that Stalin possessed less power than the American President and was circumscribed by effective courts of appeal. Hitler had reflected: 'What luck for rulers that people do not think!'

The passing of such a figure, towering, menacing as a thundercloud, while cleansing the air also induced a brief silence in which to recollect, ponder, hope, a sensation captured in Doris Lessing's story, 'The Day that Stalin Died'. Some felt a sudden gap: the cloud had been oppressive, yet also protective. Stalin himself had wondered how the little people would cope after his departure. Some did not even survive his funeral, killed in the tidal shifts and pressures of the crowds.

However, any initial optimism excited by Stalin's death was unjustified. Victorious Chinese Communists were already agitating against 'obscurantist feudal Tibet'. James Cameron was assailing the West's client, South Korea, as a 'Belsen, a screaming torture chamber with the United Nations flag flying over it'. In America, rumours were hardening into facts: that the government was employing European war criminals, Nazi scientists, runaway collaborators, in the Cold War. We heard that in certain American states, as in pre-war Germany and Switzerland, the 'feeble-minded' – the improvident and feckless, sick and tiresome – were being forcibly sterilized, as indeed Aldous Huxley had proposed for the mentally defective, in an essay on Population in 1934.

In Russia, capital punishment of Party rivals seemed discarded, but the slave camps, including Kolyma, Vorkuta and Cherenko, remained undisturbed. Khrushchev, when reaching full power, might have abandoned slavery as a vital economic ingredient, but he retained it as a punishment. Edward Buca, sent to Vorkuta in 1945, was still there in 1966, surviving to publish his experiences of officially promoted prostitution, cannibalism, and a general vileness in which captives were thrown into 'trough-like holds and lay there in piles, or crawled around like ants in a basket. Virtually nothing was given them to eat. Then they tossed them into the tundra to work – and there they were allowed nothing at all. They were just left to die, alone with nature.'

Professor Hyman Levy, a British scientist and an admirer of Stalin, visited Russia in 1957 and discovered, 'coupled with a cast-iron bureaucracy, a form of gangsterism that battened on an unassailable socialist basis'. He was expelled from the British Communist Party for his subsequent book, *Jews and the National Question*, assailing the full extent of Russian anti-Semitism between 1948 and 1952.

In East Germany, within weeks of Stalin's death, Hilde Benjamin became Minister of Justice, a post she kept until 1968. She at once announced her premises, often unnoticed by those who belaboured Lord Goddard: 'There must not remain a single judge who is not a partisan of the revolutionary struggle. If a judge tries to be objective, he is himself guilty of the crime of neutrality, and deserves punishment.' From 1953 onwards, however, periodic strikes and demonstrations occurred within the Soviet Empire. The 1953 outbreak in East Germany prompted Brecht's famous verse in *Die Lösung*, in which, being told that the People had lost the government's confidence, he suggested that it might be simpler if the government dissolved the People and elected another.

President Tito of Yugoslavia was much admired by Winston and Randolph Churchill, and Brigadier Fitzroy Maclean. He had some repute in Britain as a decentralizing, near-democrat, 'a Communist with a human face', courageous defier of Stalin in 1948. Not yet widely known in Britain was his feat of killing 30,000 anti-Communist compatriots who, having assisted the German armies, like anti-Stalinist Ukrainians and Russians, had sought refuge in Austria, relying on Anglo-American sympathy but fatally receiving the reverse.

George Mikes, a Hungarian expatriate, small, merry-eyed, beguiling, affectionate teaser of Britain and America in such books as *How to be an Alien*, and *How to Scrape Skies*, benign at bars and parties, doughtily combative on the tennis court, often confessed to cherishing facile and superficial generalizations because as a rule he usually found them true. He travelled to Yugoslavia in 1955 and, in *Encounter*, reported what he found: 'Two hours after crossing the Yugoslavia frontier, I was sunk in a gloom worthy of Koestler or Dostoevsky. I wanted to die, I wanted to abolish the human race; and I wanted to turn back and never again set foot in Yugoslavia. Between the Italian frontier and the outskirts of Rijeka (Fiume) I had seen two hundred and fifty-six portraits of President Tito. Not one single motor car or lorry ... In the main street of Rijeka loudspeakers were howling. Someone was delivering what sounded like a political harangue. After each sentence, an unseen audience of twenty thousand burst out shouting and applauding, though the people in the street did not seem to be particularly stirred, or, indeed, to pay any attention whatever to the hullabaloo. Having made some inquiries, I was directed to a restaurant, where I was served a poisonous meal by a murderous-looking waiter.'

British progressive opinion, still grateful for the stupendous Russian war effort, was tolerant of much of this and, for an impressive variety of mixed motives, not least as a declaration of British independence, was more disposed to display anti-Americanism. This, though, was unaccompanied by any inclination to boycott American films, music, cults, drugs or slang. Addressing a post-war Labour gathering, Denis Healey, a rising young Labour politician, exceptionally intelligent and widely read, probably expressed a majority opinion: 'If the Labour Movement in Europe finds it necessary to introduce a greater degree of police supervision and more immediate and drastic punishment than we in this country would be prepared to tolerate, we must be prepared to understand their point of view.'

Objections could usually be routed by a reference to our ally America, whose atomic policy, segregation of Blacks, and McCarthyism were now supplying a parallel and more publicized human nastiness. Senator Joe McCarthy, intellectually negligible, was a loud-mouthed and dishonest political hack with a limp which he claimed was the result of a war wound, though actually it was acquired falling downstairs. Nevertheless, for some years his tirades and accusations outclassed presidential speeches, together with party leaders, generals, movie and sports stars, in the grab for public attention. By the 1950s, encouraged by Stalin's crimes and by pro-Russian agents and supporters in America – the Hiss, Rosenberg, Fuchs and Gold trials, and the Korean war gave his ranting some plausibility – he was agitating about 'a great conspiracy, on a scale so immense and an infamy so black as to dwarf any previous such venture in the history of men'. He named General George Marshall, revered spokesman for the Marshall Plan, as always and invariably serving the policy of the Kremlin, which itself had rejected the Plan as a capitalist trap.

McCarthy's henchmen assiduously followed up such accusations, blacklisting, blackmailing, denouncing, dismissing teachers, scientists, editors, civil servants, writers, librarians, actors, movie directors. They censored newspapers, enforced internal exile, withdrew passports, using the police-state apparatus they claimed to be fighting. Books by Edmund Wilson and Auden were withdrawn from libraries. Arthur Miller, his play *The Crucible* deemed subversive, was given a prison sentence, quashed on appeal. Lillian Hellman, not herself always very honest in her own polemics, courageously resisted, calling it 'the Scoundrel Time', and was blacklisted. Many were unable to resist: Joseph Heller, Elia Kazan, Clifford Odets, Edward G. Robinson, Jerome Robbins. Others tried to, and their careers folded. Still others, like Losey, had to work under false names.

Another who withstood the new Inquisition was a Texan media personality, John Henry Faulk, who won a fortune in a libel action and whose subsequent book, *Fear on Trial*, echoes some passages of Nadezhda Mandelstam: 'The terrible thing is that many of those victimised, and the American people as a whole accepted this sentence of Guilty. They accepted the right of the vigilantes to bring charges, to make the decision and to pronounce the sentence. And we all kept quiet. We felt that silence would make us safe.'

All history, Croce wrote, is contemporary history. In 1955, writing a book on the French Revolution, I repeatedly found modern parallels with events long past, attitudes which should long have been eliminated: particularly the Jacobin Law of Suspects, which allowed random denunciation or official mistrust to exterminate a life; or the Law of Prairial, under which juries could be offered not factual evidence but 'moral proof' of the accused's crime. Georges Couthon, in 1793, spoke a language typically twentieth-century: 'For a citizen to become suspect, the accusation of rumour is sufficient.'

McCarthy became wilder, his victims now including homosexuals, Blacks and a variety of non-conformists. He accused the State Department of employing several hundred Russian spies and obeying policies dictated by them, thus inferring treachery or supineness on the part of John Foster Dulles and President Eisenhower himself. Here he overreached himself and, like Robespierre in crisis, he refused to name the conspirators. By 1955 he was finished, dying an alcoholic in 1957, though persecution lingered a few years more. What his British opponents on the Left overlooked was what existed in the USA but not in Communist countries: the force of moderate public opinion, even though liable to erratic swings, predictable cycles, accident and fashion.

In 1953, British intellectuals joined ranks in anti-American fury over the Rosenbergs' execution as Russian agents, though their actual guilt was little discussed. I saw Bernice Rubens, witty, mercurial, irreverent, poised to slap the right-wing *Encounter* editor, Irving Kristol, for murmuring that they were, after all, guilty. To be repelled by McCarthy was not to refute the existence of spies in America and Britain – Pontecorvo, Nunn May, Burgess and Maclean, Klaus Fuchs – whose activities ensured betrayals, sabotage, political changes, deaths.

Fuchs had fled Nazi Germany and, before departing to America with impressive British credentials, had worked for the Foreign Office, with Graham Greene as his junior. A gifted physicist, his secret passing of atomic secrets to Russia was held, like the Rosenbergs' espionage, to have encouraged Russia to prompt her ally, North Korea, to invade the South. Later, he confessed himself rigidly divided by Marxism into two mutually exclusive areas – the personal and the political, each with its own freedom. Back in England, having confessed, he refused to give full details to the security officer, protesting that the latter had not been completely cleared for security. Tried before Goddard in 1951, he stated: 'My Lord, I have committed certain crimes for which I am charged and I expect sentence. I have also committed some other crimes which are not crimes in the eyes of the law – crimes against my friends.'

He aroused frenetic debate at the Gargoyle, the Partisan, the Black Horse, the Prompt Corner.

'He's sabotaged Anglo-American atomic co-operation. They'll never trust us again.' 'But that's marvellous!' 'But ... treason!' 'An outmoded concept, dearie. He merely gave away some beastly secrets. And a very good thing too. A lesser man would have sold them.'

Some hailed him as a Stoic, or Futurist, loyal not to some stale and greedy country but to humanity in its furthest reaches. Patriotism, gratitude to hosts, was obstructive, thus evil. He should be rewarded as forerunner of a new consciousness, a new Honours list. 'He hated cruelty. Loathed bull fights.' 'But so did Himmler.' 'How unkind can you get, Charles?'

None of us then knew that his Marxist sincerity had not made him protest when a Black academic colleague was dismissed because of his colour. On his release from Brixton Prison – in Russia traitors were summarily shot – he ended as a dutiful Stalinist in East Germany. Rebecca West assessed him as a brilliant scientist stranded in immaturity, even adolescence.

More reassuring than sensational trials, exposures, hatred, was the

Japanese Maidens Project, when in 1955 a group of Japanese girls, ravaged internally and externally by blast and radiation at Hiroshima, scorned by their neighbours, some rejected by their families, were welcomed in America where medical, psychological and cosmetic expertise restored and rehabilitated most of them.

9

Developments

TRANSFORMATION FROM THE vividly coloured Empire to the some-what nebulous Commonwealth was methodically hastening. Rejection of British rule in the Empire did not entail rejection of the English language, which was indeed being invigorated by Commonwealth novelists, poets and journalists with fresh viewpoints, perceptions, allusions, imagery, humour, landscapes, cities and examples of justified grievance.

Since Tagore, Indian writers had become familiar to British readers, and in the Fifties several had some reputation: Mulk Raj Anand, Dom Moraes, Khushwant Singh (a Sikh as resolute, tireless and wily on the squash court as he was professional in novel writing), R. K. Narayan. The last, admired by Graham Greene, was also being compared to Chekhov, with his stories about Malgudi, a town fictional but surely not imaginary; stories quiet but shrewd, about extended families, peasants, busybody officials, young brides, calculating in-laws, wide-eyed children, fathers complacent but credulous, moneylenders, doctors, lawyers, vague, chattering hangers-on, story-tellers, and with strangers and new values endangering tradition. Tender but not soft, acutely observant, Narayan's apparent simplicity could hold the intricacies of a Chinese carving.

Climbing rapidly in esteem and popularity, V. S. Naipaul from Trinidad eventually went on to win many literary prizes and receive a knighthood. A fellow West Indian, Derek Walcott, was from tiny St Lucia, and Robert Graves thought he wrote better English than most of the English. He was still over-influenced by Eliot, Auden and de la Mare, but was to reach a poetic individuality that established him in a Boston Chair and won him a Nobel Prize. He had a refreshing refusal to grouse about British colonialism. George Lamming, from Barbados, not in the early Fifties a devotee of Naipaul, could be met in London, where he read from his *In the Castle of the Skin* (1953: a novel compared in the *New Statesman* to *Huckleberry Finn*) at the Institute of Contemporary Art. It enlarges the independent country of childhood, with its distorted truths, incomplete judgements, fruitful misunderstandings, lack of necessity for evidence, and constant survival tactics. 'One boy had it on good authority that the king was never seen. Maybe as a baby and later as a boy. But when he became a king no one ever saw him. No one could see him. That's why people often asked you, if you thought you were a king.' This reminded me of my own early belief, long-held, that the reason why George V possessed so many medals was that he personally attended every hanging, after which, very understandably, he awarded himself another medal, pinned on to him by the hangman.

The message I received from the Empire had different import than that of Narayan, Naipaul and Lamming: 'Sir, Respected Madam. I am a happy admirer of all your books and greatly, very much hope that in time I shall find time to read one. Would you then in return despatch me by return and in promptitude the works of Mr Miller, Mr Henry Miller, and any books, columns or essays about the Princess Margaret and her Groupy. Also, if you can venture more, photographs (coloured) of *Salad Days*.'

Other voices spoke from Empire and Commonwealth. Doris Lessing was raised in Southern Rhodesia and later barred from South Africa, a grounding which gave her fiction ample scope to comment on Africa, and a richer perspective when applied to London. Anthony Burgess's *Malayan Trilogy* (1956–9), in the wake of Conrad and Maugham, respected the intricacies of imperial rule. A colonial administrator, of vigorous charm, never easy to fool, he disdained crude confrontations between exploiters and exploited, exorbitant praise and wholesale denunciation, but portrayed individuals through their personal intrigues, rebuffs, hopes and livelihoods, rather than through racial stereotypes and political dogma.

The short stories of Frank Sargesson opened New Zealand to many. From Australia came Patrick White and James Aldridge. Aldridge had fought in Greece and became a correspondent in Moscow. Though a Marxist, he too was no tractarian: knowledgeable about international issues, he was sympathetic to human dilemmas; his writing joined a soldier's experience of swift and perilous action with a humanist concern for moral ultimates. He achieved recognition with *The Diplomat*

(1949), centred within the British Embassy in Teheran but with absorbing excursions into strange and remote countrysides. Sardonic, never bland, but with sufficient literary tact to remember artistry, Aldridge remained a considerable novelist. In Moscow, Isaiah Berlin was informed by the poet Ilya Selvinski that Britain's foremost writers were Walter Greenwood (author of *Love on the Dole*) and James Aldridge, though he had heard of neither.

The Institute of Contemporary Arts in Dover Street was founded in 1949 by Herbert Read and the surrealist painter and friend of Picasso, Roland Penrose. It early mounted, as a declaration of intent, an exhibition called 'Forty Thousand Years of Modern Art', challenging the insular, the conformist, the blinkered. Here, at last, was an informal club where young and old, the famous and the unknown, the native and the alien, could meet, quarrel, borrow money and learn. One saw Dylan Thomas tweaking Edith Sitwell's Gothic hat, youngsters covertly scribbling down I. A. Richard's retort: 'It's never what a poem says that matters, but what it is.' Overhearing this might be the poet Iris Orton, cloaked, brooding, holding herself, someone said, to be the reincarnation of Dr Johnson, and indeed possessing some physical resemblance, indirectly reinforced by the title of one of her poems, *Unwashed Hands*, though the resemblance ceased at the poem itself:

> I am afraid to wash my hands too often
> In case you think I have renounced you
> And their white skin mocks your weariness.
> I am afraid to empty my glass
> In case you think I am not coming back ...

Lee Penrose, Roland's wife, might be on view. She was a photographer with a repertoire of surrealist effects who had worked with Max Ernst, and with her first husband, Man Ray. She had filmed the liberation of Paris, and of Dachau, and in the adjoining canal had seen a floating mass of SS. Reputations – William Empson, Louis MacNeice, J. Z. Young, Wyndham Lewis, Jacquetta Hawkes – mingled with those new but growing: William Turnbull, David Sylvester, Michael Ayrton, Bernard Meadows, Reg Butler, acclaimed for his *Unknown Political Prisoner*, Bridget Riley with her abstracts – fierce vortices, harsh diagonals, strong stripes and dizzy, cunning spots, effecting far more than at first appeared. There was Eduardo Paolozzi, genial, serious, whose resemblance to the actor Oliver Hardy almost infringed copyright. To him a hunk of scrap metal, discarded stone, a screw, any industrial bric-à-brac offered clues, possibilities of something further, analogies of extra lives. From Eduardo, F. W. McWilliam, Butler, Armitage and Chadwick came intimations of live pain and cruelty, a rejection of soft decoration and timid self-expression, then a paring of form and idea into metaphors of dark experiences, into myth: into dream rather than fantasy.

The Director of the ICA virtually throughout the Fifties was the generous, hard-working, no-nonsense Dorothy Morland, widow of a tuberculosis specialist, the Quaker-reared, tolerant Andrew Morland, who had attended the dying D. H. Lawrence. Lawrence dedicated some poems to her, never published and years afterwards stolen, probably by a discerning student window-cleaner. She, assisted by David Sylvester, Lawrence Alloway and Richard Hamilton, provided a continuous forum of lectures, readings, debates, recitals and exhibitions at which appeared Geoffrey Gorer, I. A. Richards, Angus Wilson, F. R. Leavis, John Wain, Philip O'Connor, Philip Toynbee, Peter Green, Stephen Spender. Flashpoints might occur. Graham Greene and John Davenport once arrived drunk and tossed out anti-Semitic remarks during a lecture by Professor Jack Isaacs. Courageously ejected by Dorothy Morland – Davenport had boxed in public rings – in urchin riposte they piled up chairs to block the only staircase.

Alloway coined 'Pop Art', defined later by Andy Warhol as 'liking things', drawing sustenance from the clichés, images and generalities of mass-consumption advertisements. It had remnants of Dada, and of such American Young Turks of the Twenties as Edward Hopper and Stuart Davis. It was the indiscrimination, art without effort, disliked by Stuart Hampshire. In this spirit, Alloway loved the science fiction films at the London Pavilion, particularly the *Quatermass* series, starring Brian Donlevy, a relict of Thirties gangster films. He was subsequently lured to a prestigious American gallery: 'Alloway went Thataway' a headline gibed, at his dismissal.

Another ICA figure, Toni del Renzio – detractors supplied a humbler baptismal name, more demonstrably in keeping with those he sympathetically called 'exploited people' – had earlier founded a surrealistic journal, *Arson*. An admirer of the Greek surrealistic writer Nicolas Calas, he was remembered by Derek Stanford for asserting that poetry begins with the transformation of the Parthenon into a Turkish arsenal, and ends with Marat's blood. This recipe had, by 1955, produced no masterpiece from del Renzio who, despite his democratic professions, also enjoyed claiming kinship with the Romanovs.

Proceedings were not invariably decorous. Leavis lectured, harshly acerbic, in his usual open-necked shirt, and afterwards invited questions,

The Festival of Britain survived Noël Coward's satirical song, 'Don't make fun of
the Festival', and presented a mass of new shapes and possibilities, new architecture,
sculpture, painting, scientific achievements and trends, together with self-mocking
but affectionate humorous images of the British tradition. Thousands came to
scoff, but left amused, enlightened and, at the start of a new decade, exhilarated.

In the Fifties, J. B. Priestley's energies were unabated. Almost
daily, from one place or another, his running commentary
continued and, though indomitably pessimistic,
he produced a row of contemporary
novels: satirical, nostalgic or combative.

By the Fifties, Somerset Maugham had ceased to write plays and novels while, mostly from the South of France, observing developments at home with an eye that had lost little of its caustic lack of sentimentality.

Poet Laureate since 1930, John Masefield stuck doggedly to the metres and interests that had made him a best-seller before the Great War. Not an opponent of Modernism, he cheerfully ignored it. In 1958, he observed that of 300,000,000 English readers, three read him and four criticized him.

Alec Guinness, at ease in the Classics and Ealing comedies, in satire, Shakespeare and T. S. Eliot, had enduring popularity. On screen and stage, he was a thoughtfu presence, of sly or mischievous humour, graceful movement, intellectual depths. His range took him from the Man in the White Suit, an unknown inventor, to such roles as Adolf Hitler, Richard II, Macbeth and Hamlet. As a verse-speaker, h was one of the few actors who could understand not only what a poet was saying but also what poetry itself actually was.

though his baleful stare devalued the invitation. However, Marghanita Laski was present, herself no wallflower. 'Wasn't it you', she demanded, of a shrinking *New Statesman* contributor, 'who wrote that fascinating and very silly piece about the semi-colon?' Actually it was not, but, oppressed by her peremptory delivery, he confessed his guilt. A fervid admirer of Kipling and Jane Austen, Marghanita had written a novel, *Little Boy Lost*, transformed by Hollywood into a film for, rather incongruously, Bing Crosby. She did not see herself as enslaved by Leavis: 'In speaking of modern novelists, and of the Great Tradition, Dr Leavis, you overlooked, I believe, Joyce Cary.' Leavis's response sounded like elastic snapping. 'I would remind the speaker that we are here to discuss literature and nothing else.'

A large crowd assembled to hear a Soviet Professor of Art. Pudgy, he spoke at length, and badly, on the necessity for Social Realism. Afterwards, Stephen Spender asked him to comment on 'the painting hanging behind you', defiantly Cubist, by Picasso, who was lauded by Communists as one of themselves. The Professor played his master-stroke: 'Since it is behind me, I cannot see it.'

A more startling flashpoint involved a close friend of mine, Emanuel Litvinoff. The ICA held a regular poetry platform, poets reading from their own work. At one, with Herbert Read in the chair, Emanuel had been invited to read, to a considerable audience. He had always admired, even idolized, T. S. Eliot, without ever having met him. However, following his own war service and the revelations of the Holocaust, he re-read Eliot and was perturbed that certain anti-Semitic lines remained, which seemed less a historical curiosity than an offensive verdict and, from what he knew of Eliot's character, perplexing.

> The rats are underneath the piles.
> The jew is underneath the lot.
> (from 'Burbank with a Baedeker:
>   Bleistein with a cigar')

Before the reading began, Herbert Read whispered, with some satisfaction, that Eliot himself had just arrived. Nervous, but resolute, Emanuel read his poem, 'To T. S. Eliot', to an astounded audience and outraged chairman.

> Eminence becomes you. Now when the rock is struck
> your young sardonic voice which broke on beauty
> floats amid incense and speaks oracles
> as though a god
> utters from Russell Square and condescends,

high in the solemn cathedral of the air,
his holy octaves to a million radios.

I am not accepted in your parish,
Bleistein is my relative and I share
the protozoic slime of Shylock, a page
in *Sturmer*, and underneath the cities,
a billet somewhat lower than the rats.
Blood in the sewers. Pieces of our flesh
float with the ordure on the Vistula.
You had a sermon but it was not this.

It would seem, then, yours is a voice
remote, singing another river
and the gilded wreck of princes only
for Time's ruin. It is hard to kneel
when knees are stiff . . .

Yet walking with Cohen when the sun exploded
and darkness choked our nostrils,
and the smoke drifting over Treblinka
reeked of the smouldering ashes of children,
I thought what an angry poem
you would have made of it, given the pity . . .

There was immediate uproar. Read was furious, likewise Stephen
Spender who, for this occasion, considered himself as much Jewish as
Litvinoff. Dannie Abse attempted some defence of Emanuel, who
remained standing above us, harassed but dignified. Strangely, Read,
despite his anarchist belief in freedom, tyrannically permitted no such
defence. Eliot himself sat throughout, head forward and meditative,
and was heard to murmur that the poem was good, very good.

For a few days the episode was on front pages. Then it subsided,
though the poem's underlying question was never, for me, satis-
factorily answered.

Wearing his publisher's hat, at Routledge, Read once noticed, in
Poetry from the Forces, a poem from a young soldier and wrote asking
for more, which he published to some critical acclaim. Encouraged, the
poet sent him a second batch and was rewarded by an invitation to
lunch at the Athenaeum: egg mayonnaise for Read, Welsh rarebit for
his hopeful guest. This feast over, Read produced the manuscript. 'We
have made a very great mistake. Your book is very bad. I can find
nothing in its favour. We cannot possibly publish it. You have no
talent, no talent at all.' The book was swiftly accepted elsewhere, and

fortified a growing reputation. I should perhaps add that I always found Read helpful and courteous and was surprised to hear of his outburst to Somerset Maugham, at a party of E. M. Forster's, 'contemptible people who write for money, like you'. Many writers were sent gifts of money by Maugham, sometimes anonymously.

More genial encounters floated around a constant presence in the early days of the ICA: Vera Cunningham, one-time model and girlfriend of Matthew Smith. Now old, resembling Wodehouse's 'stately procession of one', she was always amusing, chuckling, insouciant, friendly to all, and seldom with much in pocket. I fancied she conducted her public life on a One-year Plan. She gave four huge seasonal parties, surviving in the intervals on the hospitality to which these entitled her. In her Hampstead residence – 'home' never seemed wholly appropriate – the famous and the unknown grappled for lavish drink and spirited talk, the last reinforced by a parrot, whose monotonous utterance I interpreted as 'Sod off, Clark', presumably a reference to Sir Kenneth Clark, though the command was never promptly obeyed. At Vera's cremation, a fairly well-known actor began his address with: 'You may all want to know why I decided to go on to the stage . . .'

I was delighted when Vera's paintings were exhibited in London, in 1992, and at once remembered her smile, her generosity, and also one of her parties in particular where a tousled, blue-eyed, burly girl strode in, booted and corduroyed. She was greeted as Clay and was escorting the slender young novelist Olivia Manning, who looked intense and, not for the last time, somewhat discontented. I had read her 1949 novel, *Artist Among the Missing*, and wanted, if not to talk to her, at least to hear her talk. This was mostly denied me. She would open her mouth, but Clay, aggressively lucid, would supply the words: 'Miss Manning, I believe you've met my friend, Ivy Compton-Burnett.' Clay intoned: 'Olivia is a very valued friend of Ivy Compton-Burnett.' 'Miss Manning, is it true that we can soon expect the new novel by William Gerhardie?' Clay glared. 'Olivia does not betray the confidences of Mr Gerhardie.' 'Isn't it dreadful, that wretched little shop in Flask Walk sells Mosley's Fascist rag, *Action!*' 'No, Vera, it's really all right, because it also sells the *Daily Worker*, and as Fascism and Communism are the same thing, they cancel each other out, so to speak.'

At this Olivia Manning was understandably roused. Her mouth, a small one, opened yet again, and her dissent began well enough. 'Actually . . . you see, Fascism . . .' But no. Clay's implacable voice barged her aside. 'What Olivia means to say . . .' At this, only seeming unheard, I muttered: 'God, woman . . . I wish you were dead.'

The next day she was. Squatting on a high ladder, painting a ceiling, she toppled over and broke her neck. The story, however, did not quite end there. On Clay's birthday her mother would, until her own death in 1981, give a party, to which guests were expected to bring a present. I always felt that my own invitation was issued from misleading premises and, though the party was always agreeable, the obligation riled me. I compromised by entering with a flamboyant box of chocolates, which on departure I unostentatiously retrieved.

Poetic confrontations were not limited to Dover Street. All generations crowded to the monthly readings at the Ethical Church, Bayswater, to hear Dylan Thomas trumpet out blasts of Auden, Edith Sitwell or himself, or hear the tweeded, beefy libertarian chairman, Alec Craig, open the meeting with some such announcement as, 'I had hoped to welcome amongst us Mr T. S. Eliot and Sir Herbert Read, that very gentle parfit knight. Actually, neither of 'em has turned up. Nevertheless, I'm more than pleased to greet a relative newcomer to our feast . . .'

Stephen Spender, while reading here, was, to his mild perplexity, jostled by the drunken, warlike Roy Campbell, whose squires soon hustled him back into the night, rumour soon enlarging the affair into a hooting dazzle of fisticuffs.

For many, Dylan Thomas's *Collected Poems* (1952) and *Under Milk Wood* (first broadcast in 1954) lit up the bedsitting room and rented flat, unzipped the earth and sky.

> A springful of larks in a rolling
> Cloud and the roadside bushes brimming with whistling
> Bluebirds and the sun of October
> Summery
> On the hill's shoulder.
> Here were fond climates and sweet singers suddenly
> Come in the morning where I wandered and listened
> To the rain wringing
> Wind blow cold
> In the wood far away under me.
>
> (from 'Poem in October')

Modernists complained of verbosity and obscurity, academics traced some juxtapositions and stylistic manoeuvres back to Hopkins and medieval Welsh verse. The youthful and unprofessional, however, relished a breeze of lyrical tenderness, ribald bawdiness, wayward jokes, mythic springboards and bardic phrases. His personality, unlike that of Eliot, fitted what people considered to be that of a poet: swaggering, dishonest, dirty, amoral, funny, always forgiven by loving friends. At Ostia, he had seen himself as a witch throwing into a cauldron Edith and Osbert Sitwell's genitalia, Auden's foreskin, Spender's left ear, Empson's unambiguous gizzards, Connolly's nose – if he still had one – and Leavis's tail. After his murky death in 1953, I found myself the only man in London who had not known him to distraction. My one interesting sight of him, off-stage, was outside the Lord's Tavern where, with Louis MacNeice, he was watching Denis Compton, and I was surprised by his humble excitement and knowledgeable comments.

It is fair, after so many Thomas stories, hackneyed and squalid, to quote the poet Patric Dickinson, then a BBC producer, who had used him in early poetry broadcasts, now lost, when he read with 'a simplicity and command of breath, absent from the later recorded examples. His performance in Vernon Watkin's "Ballad of the Mari Llwd" was splendid. We stood together in the bar of a pub in Charing Cross Road, and he spoke to me about my poems. He liked them but I "ought to let myself go more" in the way of imagery ... Among other poems he read Thomas Campbell's "Battle of the Baltic" quite beautifully. He asked me if Thomas Campbell was a relation of Roy's – entirely seriously. He had not read the poem before.' Nor, perhaps, have many contemporary readers. Thomas Campbell (1777–1844) began his poem in an idiom unfamiliar now, as in the Fifties:

> Of Nelson and the North
> Sing the glorious day's renown
> When to battle fierce came forth
> All the might of Denmark's crown,
> And her arms along the deep proudly shone;
> By each gun the lighted brand
> In a bold, determined hand,
> And the Prince of all the land
> Led them on.

I resisted a demand from a now long-dead literary editor that I should hire a taxi for her, and perhaps me, to attend Thomas's burial in Wales. She had previously invited me to 'a slap-up dinner'. On my arrival at Highgate, she pushed me, not into the dining-room but into her study. Pointing sternly to a substantial, barely legible, handwritten pile, she ordered me to read it and write my opinion of it, promising me the dinner when I had done so. She then departed to a very audible succession of drinks, having first locked the door.

Kingsley Amis, often a discordant interventionist, later recollected Dylan Thomas as 'outstandingly unpleasant', a poet who wrote but one good poem, 'The Hunchback in the Park', and some isolated good lines; Sir Kingsley judges that Thomas harmed Wales and Welsh literature by such a work as *Under Milk Wood*: 'false, sentimentalising, melo-dramatising, ingratiating'. For myself, literary criticism is a footnote. The most convincing criticism is demonstration, not assertion: Dylan Thomas and Kingsley Amis wrote poems. Let them be compared.

Literary life, necessarily private, could, and sometimes did, continue parallel or wholly detached from public life. In this latter, optimism was renewed in 1955, in many quarters by the resignation of Winston Churchill. His departure might let in fresh air. Ponderous, sententious, he seemed representative of aristocratic and imperialist paternalism, the era of Great Men and their incessant wars, of grandiloquence disguising injustice, magnificence covering moribund causes. We needed, not heroes, not the Flag, but peaceful international co-operation, together with guilty concern followed by unalloyed admiration for the Empire's successor-states.

Adults in my childhood would disapprovingly call Churchill 'Mr Chatterbox'. Not so his successor: Anthony Eden was unmistakably a gentleman, nicely poised between a useful past and a secure future. Debonair, looking like a minor movie star or cigarette advertisement model, he flashed smiles like banknotes, as he had years before when, as Foreign Secretary, he had opposed appeasement and actually resigned. A founder of the United Nations, in 1951 he reiterated that no alter-native existed to the role of law, so that the UN was the only path to follow. In 1954, he had successfully urged John Foster Dulles not to use the atom bomb in Indo-China. A civilized, reasonable man, quietly impressive at international conferences and low-key settlements, more interested in these than in domestic concerns, he had lately achieved a peaceful agreement in Indo-China which, despite the Communists' capture of Hanoi, experts informed me was likely to hold. He had, when very young, concern for Cézanne and modern art, studied Per-sian and Arabic, had brave experiences in the Great War. His reign was unlikely to prove sensational. Few shared Churchill's misgivings: 'I wonder if Anthony can do it.' My experts had not told me that the new Premier was shy, nervy, irritable, impatient from having been kept so long from supreme power.

Meanwhile, jobs were plentiful, inflation was controlled, prices acceptable, labour relations equable: we wandered through Jackson

Pollock's colours, heard smart unimpressive jabber about Françoise Sagan, disputed about *Waiting for Godot* and queued for another Bergman film – those unfamiliar landscapes in calm static summers, menacing autumns, hangman's winters; the remote villages and manors, uneasy towns, taut relationships mingling despair and eroticism, the subtle eyes and trim nakedness, smouldering pasts kindling manic obsessions.

10

The Wednesday Club

BENEDICT NICOLSON AND his closest friend Philip Toynbee founded the Wednesday Club in 1953, meeting regularly for lunch at Bertorelli's Restaurant in Charlotte Street. Both their fathers had attended the Versailles peacemaking in 1919. Harold Nicolson was friendly, sensitive, at parties ready to desert distinguished company to chat with the unknown and doubtless tedious. In the *Spectator*, the *Observer*, on radio, he never lost his style of amused tolerance. Twice he saved Philip Toynbee from deserved military disgrace, perhaps court martial, for behaviour which attracted unfavourable notice from Rebecca West. He would utter opinions unexceptional, even obvious, yet in a way that I did not forget: 'Only one person in a thousand is a bore, and he is interesting because he is one person in a thousand.' 'I do not think it quite fair to say that the British businessman has trampled on the faces of the poor, but that he has sometimes not been very careful where he puts his feet.'

His apparent blandness did not prohibit effective repartee. In a well-known story, lecturing in America, he was heckled. 'What about India? How can you justify the British behaviour to the Indians?' 'Which Indians? Ours or yours? We educated ours. You massacred yours.' Harold usually added, 'They had the decency to laugh.'

Ben Nicolson was the elder of Harold Nicolson's and Vita Sackville-West's sons. Tall, gaunt as if whittled down, his bony, slightly florid face under black hair was emphatically inherited from his mother, with her trace of the Spanish gypsy. He was almost always in the same nondescript suit, as though he never realized that clothes were actually on the market. When he told Harold in 1953 that Summerfields

School, Oxford, had left him with a horror of making himself conspicuous, his father wrote in a diary: 'Considering that his hair is like
that of a golliwog and his clothes noticeable at the other end of
Trafalgar Square, this was an odd assertion.'

I was introduced to Ben, of course, by David Sylvester, thenceforward seeing him regularly for the next thirty-five years. The first
twenty were the most difficult, for shy, awkward, he could be unpredictable; sometimes confiding, even warm, always stingy, sometimes with prolonged and forbidding silences, sometimes downright
ungracious.

'Ben ... Your brother Nigel has given my novel a marvellous
review.' 'Nigel was never a good judge of fiction.' Or: 'Ben,' I
pushed forward a friend, 'you know Ian, don't you?' 'Oh yes! Horrid
man!'

As a child, he had met the current hero, Charles Lindbergh. Harold
said: 'Benjy, Colonel Lindbergh has very kindly offered to take you up
in his aeroplane, "The Spirit of St. Louis". You'd like that, wouldn't
you?' 'No.' At Harold's later expostulations, Ben replied that he had
always been told at home to speak the absolute truth: he did not like
the thought of flying nor, very much, the sight of Charles Lindbergh,
though he did afterwards consent to a short flight.

I remember a National Theatre production of O'Neill's *Long Day's
Journey into the Night*. I was a fellow-guest with Ben, who disliked the
theatre almost as much as he did music – I thought of him when
reading Aaron Copland's view, that if a literary man puts together two
words about music, one of them will be wrong – in a party of about
twenty, he on the extreme right seat, myself on the extreme left. He
sat miserably, during an exceptionally hot evening, encrusted by the
thick fur coat that he refused to remove, in fear of theft, though twice
intervening at a tense moment of the drama in those deep, slightly
magisterial tones, clearly heard throughout the theatre. Once, when
Olivier paused before delivering a particularly momentous speech, Ben
spoke first: 'Peter ... I've decided not to invite Sonia to my party.'
Then, a little later, while the audience were tensed for some response
to a tragic revelation on stage – 'Peter ... Ronald Pickup! Rather an
unfortunate name, don't you think?'

We once had a particularly agreeable lunch; that evening, at a party,
he gave no flicker of recognition, allowed our hostess to introduce us
formally, and continually addressed me as 'Mr Berger'.

Much of this was endearing, and his friends were numerous and
devoted: Isaiah Berlin, Stuart Hampshire, Vitale Bloch, Robin and
Ginny Darwin, Bernard Berenson. Another intimate, Francis Haskell,

quoted Berenson's comparison of Ben to a deep well of crystal-clear water, the effort needed to draw it up being very worthwhile.

Deputy Surveyor of the Royal Paintings, first under Kenneth Clark, then under Anthony Blunt, Ben was also a long-serving editor of the *Burlington Magazine*. An art historian of international stature, he was absorbed in Italian art, and indeed in all things Italian, including, sometimes regrettably, food not of the best quality. He also wrote on Vermeer, Terbrugghen, Wright of Derby, Courbet, de la Tour and Cézanne in addition to the followers of Caravaggio and the artists of Ferrara. 'Ben', Haskell considered, 'was drawn instinctively to the outcasts, the off-beats, the provincial.' As an editor, he demanded lucidity, factual reliability, full seriousness. 'The enemies of scholarship', he insisted, 'are tact and urbanity.' I owe to the art historian John Bury an example from 1958 of Ben's empathy with his chosen masters: 'The determination to hold up mundane themes for our contemplation as visions of dignity and beauty is also the quality which Vermeer, a kindred mysterious being, inherited from his Utrecht predecessor . . . In Terbrugghen's hands, as in those of Gentileschi and the young Velasquez, the appropriation by art of everyday life came as an occasion for showing that what had been regarded up to that time as the accidents of colour and light, as departments of life fit only to accompany, and dance attendance on, dignified moral themes, could become the subject of a picture, with undiminished moral dignity and grandeur. It was this tradition that Vermeer coaxed to a silent and sublime conclusion.' 'Sublime', used by such well-meaning improvers as Robespierre and Ramsay MacDonald, is often surrounded by the pretentious or the ludicrous, but Ben could restore its earlier weight.

In the early Fifties, he was sharing a Pimlico apartment with David Sylvester and Jocelyn Baines, the latter still perhaps remembered at Winchester less for his important book on Joseph Conrad than for setting alight a pleasantly sited, thatched cricket pavilion. Ben was to write of the look of affront that appeared on Jocelyn's face whenever anyone agreed with what he had said.

I first met Philip Toynbee when staying with David Sylvester, currently most pleased with a new, gleaming tennis racquet. Philip arrived to play, without shoes, without a racquet. David lent him an old one which, in singles with me, either my service or his habit of walloping the net-post after a mishit, caused to split, very swiftly. David then, reluctantly, handed over the new racquet. The court was hard and roughish. Philip's method of picking up a ball was to scrape the racquet along this surface, to raise the ball to his hand without having to stoop. David's face, as he watched the inexorable destruction of his cherished implement, had a Picasso-like double-view: the restraint of a host's courtesy at a sharp angle to a bruised accumulation of fury.

Toynbee, swashbuckling, ramshackle, hands seldom far from a bottle, with 'an ugly beauty', a rich, indeed compelling voice, and, through unsatisfactory teeth, a chuckle resembling the last gasp of a soda-water bottle, was grandson of Gilbert Murray, the celebrated classicist, whose translations of Euripides made tough East End audiences hold fast to their seats, a model for 'Adolphus Cusins' in Shaw's *Major Barbara*. Murray's wife, dogmatically egalitarian, refused presentation at Court, because of the numerous common folk likely to be met there. Philip had something of this: militantly Communist until the Ribbentrop-Molotov Pact, he would stay with miners on Party business, but secreting tails and white tie for weekends at Castle Howard.

Ralph Glasser, genuine working-class Glaswegian, had met Toynbee in pre-war Oxford and found him, as first Communist President of the Oxford Union, very bogus in his proletarian self-identification, intolerant in his hunger for certainty: 'Philip gloried in personifying the Party's ethos of paternalism and menace. If, when the time came, it was in the Party's interest to send someone to the firing squad, he said, he will do so without hesitation . . . To be fair, Philip had more sensitivity than many of them. That attribute, allied to a questioning tendency that Party discipline only temporarily held in check, would in the years to come lead him away from its narrow absolutism. Then, in sadness and some confusion, he would seek in vain a substitute for the old certainty – in founding a commune, for example – with which to regain the lost glory of a spiritual leader.'

In his quest, Philip could display considerable spirit. Ben told a story about Philip in the Thirties, being invited to Cliveden by David Astor, future editor of the *Observer*, though, by mischance, on a date coinciding with a visit from the King and Queen. Lord and Lady Astor reluctantly assented to Philip's presence, on condition that, as a piratical Red, he avoided contact with the royal couple. Nancy Astor, disturbed by emphatic sounds rolling in over lawn and hedge and lake, saw from her window Philip haranguing their Majesties on the moral superiority and financial needs of Republican Spain.

He was an impulsive hero-worshipper, of Danton, Cobbett, Nansen, certain Great War airmen, Thomas Mann and, increasingly, some saints and martyrs: he would quote Bonhöffer, 'If you wish to find God, be faithful to the world.' He enjoyed the world, not overlooking some of its grosser attributes. He respected St Teresa of

Avila's belief that more tears are shed over answered prayers than over the unanswered.

Like Ben, Philip had devoted friends, but they had far more to endure than Ben's. Generously compassionate, he could also be an insensitive wrecker. He was a remorseful hedonist in mysterious search of defeat, a melancholic edged with self-mockery and clowning, his intellectual austerity punctured by drink; gamey, idea-loving, often reckless – in one family he was called 'the plunger' for his headlong dives into parties, beds, causes. Tim Tosswell, a master at Rugby, which had expelled Philip, had literally to lock up not only his daughter but also his maid when Philip plunged in for a visit. Jessica Mitford tells that, after death, he wanted to be stuffed like a bear, holding a pint, grinning at people. Julia Strachey called him a real duck, with a good dash of goose thrown in.

By 1950, Philip was chief reviewer for the *Observer*, under the Proustian, Terence Kilmartin. He was also a novelist, beginning in the standard mould favoured by Priestley, Walpole and Maugham; then, swallowing Joyce, Eliot and Pound like elixir, to the dismay of most friends and all readers he rejected narrative fiction. Linear narrative, Philip insisted, must be replaced by conveyance of the multiple and simultaneous associations of each moment – 'simultaneity'. His *Tea with Mrs Goodman* (1947) used a verbal Cubism, in which the breaking of a cup at a tea party sets off multiple ripples, emotional exposures, abstruse inter-connections and cross-references. The broken cup, observed via different sensibilities, relates to Jungian archetypes, Arthurian legends, sexual and mythical symbols and to cosmic metaphor, the technique influenced not only by Joyce, but also by Braque and Picasso, Bergson and Dunne, with their obsession with time.

Like many of his group, Philip had served in the war – though his friends suffered more blows from him than the enemy – and, like them, did not bottle himself up entirely in the arts. Only strenuous protests had deterred him from challenging Neville Chamberlain at the hustings. Unlike Edmund Wilson, who spent a lifetime dodging it, Philip constantly praised income tax, not as a masochistic luxury but as a democratic obligation, even a privilege. Without pontificating about 'commitment' like Sartre and his followers, he joined or led protests, wrote or edited books on behalf of nuclear disarmament, social underdogs, contemporary theology.

He never really escaped the public-school cycle of high jinks, secret societies, compulsory chapel, games, private codes and jokes; revolutionary fireworks, conducted above a safety net of an assured job and family status. He could seldom resist overdoing a joke, an obsession, a 'craze'. Once, in an unappealing story, dressed up as a clergyman in Belgium, in schoolboy fun, he accosted a group of battle-worn soldiers, and demanded if they were 'saved'.

Philip Toynbee had a lifelong addiction to John Buchan novels, and a paragraph in *The Three Hostages* excited an ambition. Here Buchan's Sir Richard Hannay describes the Thursday Club: 'There were a dozen present including myself, and of these, besides my host, I knew only Burminster and Sandy. Collatt was there, and Pugh, and a wizened little man who had just returned from bird-hunting at the mouth of the Mackenzie. There was Pallister-Yeates, the banker, who didn't look thirty, and Fulleylove, the Arabian traveller, who was really thirty and looked fifty. I was especially interested in Nightingale, a slim peering fellow with double glasses, who had gone back to Greek manuscripts and his Cambridge fellowship after captaining a Bedouin tribe. Leithen was there, too, the Attorney-General, who had been a private in the Guards at the start of the War, and had finished up a G.S.O.I., a toughly built man, with a pale face and very keen, quizzical eyes. I should think there must have been more varied and solid brains in that dozen than you would have found in an average Parliament.'

This was too much for Philip, and was the origin of the Wednesday Club. Members included Noel Annan, who had shared a study with Leonard Nicholson at Stowe – a curious pairing – Frank Longford, Francis Haskell, Stuart Hampshire, Rex Warner, Richard Wollheim, Peter Quennell, Robert Kee, Hugh Thomas, Cecil Day-Lewis, J. M. Richards, Kenneth Minogue, A. Alvarez, Ian Scott-Kilvert, Lawrence Gowing, Roderigo Moynihan, Simon Raven, James MacGibbon, Bernard Wall, John Sutro, Ronald Hayman, Roger Lubbock, Gerard Noel, Robin Darwin, Derwent May, Jeremy Potter, Paul Ableman, John Berger, William Letwin, Richard Harris, Ted Honderich, John Minton, Edward Crankshaw, David Caute, George Melly, Bryan Magee, Colin Haycraft, Eric Hobsbawm, Douglas Johnson, Anthony Curtis, Dannie Abse, Terence Kilmartin, Emanuel Litvinoff, John Jolliffe, Nicholas Bagnall, John Bury, Kyril Fitzlyon, Thomas Hinde, George Weidenfeld, Christopher Isherwood and Raleigh Trevelyan; also the Fleet Street journalist Maurice Richardson, whose resemblance to Randolph Churchill almost killed him, from the buffets and free drinks he received in public. He was said to have increased by two stone on the day of Winston's death. He himself once punched Ben for failing to invite him to a party, which had not, in fact, occurred, and for years Ben glowered at him, not because of this but because Maurice had once owed him sixpence, and doubtless still did.

Then there were Raymond Mortimer, James Baldwin, Dwight Macdonald, Theodore Roethke and Zero Mostel, who had been appearing in Joyce's *Nighttown* at the Arts Theatre, and had stalwartly resisted McCarthy's UnAmerican Activities Committee. Harold Nicolson came, also Arnold Toynbee, peering with uneasy curiosity as John Minton was carried away on a table, drunk, and diffidently inquiring whether this was obligatory. I once thought of introducing the Dean, but did not think twice. Lindsay Anderson was invited to join, but did not reply. His proposer resented what he considered Ben's disrespect in not repeating the invitation in more fulsome terms, and resigned, though constantly re-appearing as a guest at someone else's expense. Members bore Anderson's absence unflinchingly, Philip and Ben probably with relief, fearing an outburst from him on democratic rights. The Club was, and remains, a mild dictatorship. Newspapers, furthermore, were alleging that Anderson was withdrawing free passes to critics unlikely to give his production a favourable review. I always thought that, many years later, photographers missed a spectacular expression on Bette Davis's face when a youthful journalist told her she 'must have felt very honoured by working with Mr Anderson' in his 1988 film, *The Whale of August*. Kenneth Tynan was another guest, and lectured us on the wide range of children's rights prevalent at the Moscow Children's Theatre, affecting not to hear a question from Patrick O'Donovan about the range of adult rights on the streets outside the theatre. He also enthused about bull-fighting to Bernard Wall, sensitive to all cruelty, especially towards animals.

At the inaugural lunch, the sight of a small, dapper, alert figure, A. J. Ayer, caused me misgivings, even alarm. In 1953 he was Grote Professor of the Philosophy of Mind and Logic, at London, for me an achievement akin to planting a flag in remote regions of thick-ribbed ice. Ayer had raised his Department from a minor accessory with few staff, books or students, to one large and vigorous. Lecturing, he was mobile, excitable, lucid, witty, dramatic, his speech almost as rapid-fire as Isaiah Berlin's, and I was not surprised when he confessed an early hankering to be a Jack Buchanan, Fred Astaire, song-and-dance man. He could recall the most insipid lyric, and jig a few steps at any opportunity or none. My most welcome gift to him and his later, much loved wife Vanessa, must have been a box of records, *The Golden Age of the British Dance Bands, 1925–1953*.

He had recently been featured in *Picture Post* as one of the 'new Elizabethans', which he might not have relished, though he would have relished being omitted even less. Of his first and most famous book, *Language, Truth and Logic* (1936), he remarked on publication that philosophy had now come to an end. The young loved its disregard of metaphysics and ethical judgements, its bracing analytical exposure of nonsense and what Robin Lane Fox has called his inspiring lack of any religious conviction. 'Freddie,' Vanessa asked, 'what do you think you have established as enduring and philosophically true?' He smiled briskly. 'Nothing. Nothing at all. It was wrong.'

Meanwhile, without interest in, or knowledge of, philosophy, I sat as far from him as possible, though as attracted by his quick smile as I was alarmed by his incisive manner and incomprehensible assertions: 'Heidegger? Certainly not. He raises an occasional matter of philosophical interest, no more, but to seek for any depth is only to realise this emptiness, pretentiousness, monkey-chatter. He praised Hitler, ratted on Jewish colleagues, betrayed Edmund Husserl . . .'

He was reputed to have enjoyed one hundred and fifty women and did not deny it. 'All you have to do is to pay a woman the smallest attention. In this country, no one else does.' Accused of dismantling morality, he retorted that he merely scrutinized others' opinions of noble concepts. An enthusiastic and adroit games player, he also demanded the most careful use of language, the utmost intellectual rigour, which in themselves were moral activities. A cogent sentence, if not axiomatically proving moral worth, at least assisted logic, the search for truth which, had rulers followed his example, might have prevented the war.

Freddie did seem to enjoy confessing his vanity. Many years afterwards, at an evening party: 'Freddie, did you know that Philip Toynbee died this afternoon?' 'I always thought he greatly admired me.' I once found him at Hatchards, examining the indices of a pile of books. 'You're not buying all those?' 'Of course not. I'm looking up the bits about me.'

He had a daughter, Wendy Fairey, by Sheilah Graham, Hollywood journalist and Scott Fitzgerald's lover, but did not know it until she was 46, and he had only a year to live. He greeted her, for the first time since her infancy, with a question about Jane Austen. 'I wanted so much for Freddie to see who I was, and instead I found him fixed on himself. I didn't need him to prove to me that *he* was well read: I hoped he would find that *I* was.' In his will, Freddie left her one book, though this she could choose herself.

My awkwardness with him endured until 1958. Then, at a lunch, engaged in some dispute further down the table, probably, I thought, on the contemporary influence of Gottlob Frege, through Wittgenstein, or about some modification of the Verification Principle, he unexpectedly leaned over towards me: 'Peter, who went in last for England in the Oval Test Match, 1926?' 'George Geary.' It was untrue, but, satisfied, he returned to his discussion. 'Martin – you were in error! George Geary!'

This released me, and I increasingly looked forward to our meetings, particularly after his relations began with generous, intelligent Vanessa, of antique, slightly Egyptian beauty and mischievous smile – she once exchanged shirts with Peregrine Worsthorne at a stuffy dinner table. Our discussions were not intellectual. Historical relativism he brusquely dismissed, not caustic, not contemptuous but like a cricket umpire silently surveying three broken stumps.

'You don't have a mind,' he once assured me, 'but . . .' I waited, tremulous, hopeful, expectant, before he said, 'are you going to Miranda's?' At best, I felt, he might think of me as H. L. Mencken had remarked of President Calvin Coolidge, 'He had no ideas, and he was not a nuisance.'

We enjoyed discussing favourite movie actors – Conrad Veidt, Melvyn Douglas, Astaire, Von Stroheim, not entitled to the 'Von', and who wore most of his face on the back of his neck; Emil Jannings and Paula Wessely, both pro-Nazi; Claude Rains. We swapped the names of 'featured players' during dullish periods at Lord's: 'Eric Blore' – 'Arthur Treacher'; 'Franklin Pangborn' – 'Eugene Pallette'; 'Nat Pendleton' – 'Mischa Auer'; 'Edward Arnold' – 'Jerome Cowan'.

Like Marghanita Laski, he enjoyed a daily ration of thrillers or detective stories. He admired Yeats and Baudelaire, and much enjoyed, though with less admiration, Verlaine and Swinburne. He read much of Dickens and Kafka, 'The Circumlocution Office . . . pure Kafka.' He appreciated Wordsworth, Jane Austen, Angus Wilson, and indeed Noël Coward, often humming the songs and rating *Private Lives* 'admirable'. Thomas Mann he thought verbose, philosophically pretentious and unoriginal. He was seldom silent. If he had nothing to say, he still said it. Like his admired Russell, he often seemed apathetic to colour, landscape and most paintings save those of Vermeer and of himself; he admitted his deficiency in visual imagery, and to finding tedious such poetical conceits as those of Donne. Being driven through a lustrous Irish countryside in 1953 by Robert Kee, he speculated on the consciousness of sheep instead of delighting in water and sky, mountain and field. I only once heard him utter 'beauty', about Denis Compton's batting – and then he looked uneasy, as if caught in some error of logic, and amended it to 'inventive'. 'Beauty' was as unlikely in his professional writing as 'arse' in a Henry James novel. Admittedly, in his autobiographies, *Part of My Life* and *More of My Life*, girls are awarded 'very pretty', 'very beautiful'; he did mention the beauty of autumnal forests in New Hampshire and found Peking 'the most attractive city I have ever visited'. C. P. Snow he found 'unreadable', particularly his Cambridge novel, *The Masters*. 'Tell me, Freddie, do you dislike it because you think it an uninteresting story, or badly written, or merely inaccurate in college detail?' 'All three!'

Of British philosophers, he most appreciated Hume and his belief that concepts and knowledge derive from propositions about sense-experience. That parapsychology was currently being encouraged by his friend Arthur Koestler, made him wince. A famous atheist, he would display ill-natured letters from the religious, one telling him that he deserved that someone close to him should suffer a terminal illness, which indeed occurred with Vanessa's distressing death. Only once was he momentarily abashed. At the Wednesday Club he was discussing miracles with Martin D'Arcy, a Jesuit who reputedly contributed to Evelyn Waugh's 'Father Rothschild'. 'Miracles!' Freddie was contemptuous. 'A careless misalliance of words and thought ... historical nonsense, wishful thinking and make-up. They never happened, they will never happen, can't ever happen ... combination of fortuitous circumstance, misinterpretation, iconographic complexity, sheer luck, misapplied interpretation of rigged evidence ... the corruption of mysticism ...' He was interrupted by an intervention, presumably from sheer luck and fortuitous circumstance and not from D'Arcy – a large whirling fan which unexpectedly broke loose and, travelling above us the length of the table at less than average speed, finally fell between them, smashing Freddie's wine glass and leaving D'Arcy's intact. D'Arcy suddenly looked understandably smug.

Though unsympathetic to Marxism in theory and practice, Freddie was officially invited to China in 1954 as part of the celebrations of the fifth anniversary of the Communist conquest, along with Rex Warner, Hugh Casson and Stanley Spencer. He liked Rex Warner, respected Casson, but found Spencer 'a vile little man, boring on an unwholesomely lavish scale, intolerable ... interested only in himself and women'. The last two objections sounded curious from Freddie, but the rest was unquestionable. Spencer would belabour at length what he called, too often, the vulgarity of law and morality, and found pleasure in inflicting and receiving pain, with women. For the artist, and his joyous creativity, all must be forgiven, all permitted. A third, and unremitting topic, was Cookham, Spencer's Berkshire village. He talked of Cookham by day and by night, in bed and at table, its beauties, oddities, natural features, its usefulness to himself. He contrived an interview with Chairman Mao, presumably depicting Cookham, more Cookham, nothing but Cookham, and after Freddie's return, I imagined new maps of Great Britain being issued to Chinese schools, marking Edinburgh, London, Heathrow and Cookham. Like Kenneth Minogue after him, Freddie was a tireless attender of international conferences, as if qualifying for a David Lodge novel.

Freddie, though a socialist, was an Old Etonian, and sent a son to Eton without any moral flap. Despite sneers at his morality, he was a responsible citizen, like Shaw, Wells, Russell, finding voluntary civic activity compatible with professional work. In the war, he served in the Welsh Guards. He chaired the Society for Homosexual Law Reform which, by 1967, had helped legalize the rights of consenting adults. He campaigned against racial discrimination in sport. For a while he was chairman of his local Labour branch, organizing, canvassing, writing a pamphlet for the Westminster Housing Association, from a step-ladder haranguing busy shoppers in Berwick Market. He recalled 'a Sunday afternoon in which we marched, or rather straggled, in a long procession all the way from the Embankment to Hyde Park, calling out slogans of which the most popular was "Caviare for the Upper Class, Peanuts for the Working Class". This was made to sound as though it were something that we were demanding rather than a protest.' He was an unsuccessful candidate for the Great Marlborough Street Ward. More lengthily, he sat on the Plowden Education Committee, also campaigning for the abolition of grammar schools in favour of egalitarian comprehensives, though not availing himself of such beliefs for his own children. My affection for Freddie, after its inauspicious start in the Fifties, increased without setbacks, and I remain haunted by a wretched day, when for Vanessa's funeral, a Christian one at that, we descended his stairs together, Freddie suddenly old and hunched, muttering 'What a farce it all is!'

Amongst other regular members of the Wednesday Club was Stephen Spender. In 1953 he had changed little from the description in a poem by George Barker, who saw him as a poet with his soul upon his shoulder:

> Let me see now not the irregular fountain
> Whence poems rose like crystals, glittering truth,
> But the tall chap with a leg like a flying buttress,
> A hand for a saw, a face worth a fortune,

> But for the distorted torture of the mouth
> Which to his words of truth bore such a witness.
>   (from 'To Stephen Spender')

Despite deep personal preoccupations, he did not lock himself away in words. He had been in the Fire Service during the London Blitz, had worked in the Political Intelligence section of the Foreign Office in 1946, studying the effect of Hitlerism on German intellectuals. In *Forward from Liberalism* (1937), he had argued against Fascism, arbitrary imprisonment and unemployment, and that the liberal freedoms should be targeted on social justice, active resistance to dictators – he seemed to exclude Stalin – without sacrificing free speech, free movement. The Liberalism of Gladstone and Asquith had been too much geared to the interests of employers. Freedom was more than the open market, unrestricted competition, licensed overcharging and underpayment.

Injustice and cruelty always hurt him. Briefly, in 1936, he had joined the Communists and been rebuked by the Party Secretary, Harry Pollitt, for lack of class hatred, for objection to the Moscow show trials and the Old Bolsheviks' executions. This Pollitt, in 1939, had acclaimed the war against Hitler, but then, on Kremlin orders, swiftly instructed 'the workers' to sabotage war production. Spender had to recognize the mysticism within Marxism, attractive to intellectuals with a love of theory and a distaste for facts. The British Communists, he wrote, believed in making the poor militant, but not in loving their neighbours. 'Truth for them was a slave which waited on the convenience of a small inner circle of leaders.' His 1951 autobiography, *World Within World*, had chilling descriptions of cynical changeabouts like Pollitt and William Rust, selecting volunteers for probable death in Spain while risking nothing themselves. And, 'It seemed to me – as it still seems – that the unique condition of each person within life outweighs the considerations which justify class and privilege.'

His poems did not explain the universe or demand Party allegiance, but revealed the world, particularly, I thought, for the inarticulate and the lonely, giving me a world not of marches and slogans, but of windows, solitary evenings, sudden intensities, friends and 'the grave evening demand for love'. Revolution remained desirable, but from 'change of heart', not firing squads. At Bertorelli's I remember a brash young guest accosting him. 'I've always thought you ten feet tall, I've looked up to you so long.' Of a Spender poem, William Coldstream reflected: 'Very Stephenish, full of slightly embarrassing and very strong feelings, very personal, very big and over life-size in emotion, but very original and striking.'

Peregrine Worsthorne, much younger, was at odds with the leftish flavour of the Club, debonair, lucid, unpredictable in his responses, in debate always striving to add a fifth side to a square, disappointed if politeness restricted contention, easily bored. After working in America for *The Times*, he did not share the general disgust for Senator McCarthy. McCarthy himself he thought a foul-mouthed boor, yet necessary, as their 'brutal battering-ram' to break 'Ivy League Washington's protection of well-connected Communists in high places', and preferable to liberalism's constant excuses for Russian terror, one-party dictatorship, show trials, the occupation of Prague, and the barely credible tolerance by the British establishment of known traitors. That Russia was, assisted by Western agents, an atomic power only increased the urgency for Western resolution. McCarthy thus symbolized American democratic vitality. This was scarcely deferred to by Philip, Ben and others, hating Fascism far more than they did Communism. Perry was always pro-American and felt it hypocritical not to be, dependent as we were on American financial and military support. He admired President Eisenhower, was sympathetic to Nixon, sceptical of the United Nations, disliked the Welfare State, union power, mass immigration. A patrician Tory, markedly independent of the Conservative Party of property speculators, entrepreneurs, go-getting salesmen and inarticulate old-timers, he could exhibit Churchillian romanticism: Churchill had suggested reviving Attainder to dispose of Nazi war leaders, Perry wanted to restore the concept of Outlaw against terrorists. He had had his share of actualities.

During the war he had been, with David Niven, in Phantom, a task-force dealing with dispatching the swiftest possible information from scenes of action. There was often an older man too, quiet, friendly but reticent, to whom he spoke, perhaps lectured, incessantly. The other listened as if gratefully, certainly without complaint or rejoinder, though in post-war Cambridge, Worsthorne was disconcerted to discover that his erstwhile fellow-warrior was Professor Michael Oakeshott, already renowned as a philosopher and writer. In 1945, Perry was the first to report that the Allies had reached the North Sea.

I was not really aware of Perry until reading his 1956 article in, I think, *Encounter*, which convinced me, wrongly, that I would dislike him for supercilious smartness: 'The most hopeful thing about a country like India today is that, in fact, India is governed by a liberal aristocrat who openly behaves like one. Mr Nehru, educated at Harrow, has no nonsense with democracy ... infinite harm has been done to English and American universities by trying to teach democracy as a coherent political theory. It has prevented the generation of

Asians who are now in charge of their countries' governments from learning the great lesson that we had to teach them; that their function was not to emulate Western democratic politicians of today but Western liberal teachers of the last century.'

This was very much Perry, confident but not swaggering, coolly reasonable, giving little comfort to any political party and none to fashion, difficult flatly to contradict, mildly irritating, particularly to David Sylvester, who regarded a right-wing intellectual as a self-contradiction. Charming, he could also be teasing, indeed mischievous, with well-plotted frivolity. Once, we argued at length about Africa, he professing disbelief in any African contribution to civilization, I the reverse, with amply researched historical and cultural references. At tea, in a crowded hotel lounge, he said, not loudly, but very clearly: 'Yes, you always maintain that the African is inherently barbarous, incapable of moral, physical or intellectual effort. I, on the other hand ...' People rose in unison, like Canada geese, flapping, outraged, glaring at me as they passed in contempt and hatred, awarding Perry sympathy, indeed compassion.

Perry could also be tactless: visiting Auschwitz, he apparently remarked that it reminded him of Stowe, his public school, which would scarcely have qualified him for the higher reaches of diplomacy. His carefully enunciated four-letter word on television, at a time before it became almost obligatory, delayed his professional advance. 'Do think,' he urged some opponent, 'it can be done, it really can. Just use your brain. Make a real effort. It has been done. Perhaps not very often.' He could easily become restless, politely incredulous that people should make a display of sheer silliness. He was also affectionate, generous, at ease with all classes. His articles were a blend of neat equation, supported by minor paradoxes in the tradition of Wilde and Chesterton, and logical but often unexpected conclusions to reverse conventional wisdom. In 1960: 'To a large extent all moves towards democracy, political just as much as industrial, have the effect of limiting the scope for individual freedom, precisely because by broadening the base of authority, they increase its reach.' He was then married to Claudie, a vigorous, sharp-witted Gaullist-French girl, Flaubert-loving, self-mocking, with idiosyncratic English. 'Perry', she once said, 'wept cats and dogs.' She fascinated me.

I never saw Peregrine Worsthorne and Angus Wilson together. Save in physical appearance and address, they would have made an interesting contrast in debate. Though moderately left-wing, Wilson likewise rejected utopianism, the deception played by 'thinkers' on themselves and their dupes, and on language, producing such unsatisfactory communities as Vardon Hall, refuge for young writers in his early novel, *Hemlock and After* (1952). Like Perry, he was not noticeably modest, or inarticulate, or reticent with opinions, and he too had unusual charm.

His stories and novels, and his play *The Mulberry Bush* (1956), gave a lasting flavour of one middle-class section of the Fifties: methodical social climbing, bitchy parties, hotel junketing, corrupt members of the professional classes, idealists and 'progressives' tainted with snobbery and emotional callousness, and chilling cover-ups of failure, sterility, pretentiousness, possible damnation. At one lunch, very fluent and able, he complained that, assisted by Jane Austen, the English Novel had shied from essentials, reducing Good and Evil to mere Right and Wrong, though Dickens's hunted murderers, George Eliot's *Daniel Deronda* and Henry James's *Portrait of a Lady* attempted to restore the profounder dimension, as did William Golding in *Lord of the Flies*. He also wrote, in 1963: 'I think that confusing novel writing with sociology is the weakest aspect of English fiction at the moment.'

At the University of East Anglia, he must have been an exciting and generous presence, admirable with the young. He befriended and helped the unknown Colin Wilson: I myself received several disinterested kindnesses from him, despite an incident following publication of his *The Middle Age of Mrs Eliot* (1958). During the interval of a play, I noticed Angus, awaiting a friend's return from the bar. Like many of us, he enjoyed a spice of praise, and I started some, routine, but in full sincerity: 'I did so enjoy the book . . . could absolutely identify . . . I do think it remarkable how you can so get under the skin of a middle-aged woman . . .' To my horror, I was interrupted by a voice from the crowd: 'That's all very well, Peter, gushing away like this . . . you must remember that Angus is a bit of an old woman himself!'

Two members who, like their friend Lawrence Durrell and, further away, Vladimir Nabokov and John Updike, showed no signs of adopting the 'kitchen sink' sensibility were Robin Fedden and Patrick Leigh Fermor. Fedden reminded me of the outwardly casual Englishman-at-large, often played in movies by Leslie Howard, himself actually Hungarian: the amateur Buchanesque adventurer who worsts the villain by charm, integrity, concealed resolution and shrewdness. He had fought in Egypt, worked for the National Trust from 1951 and, while Secretary of the Historic Buildings Committee, had published

Crusader Castles (1951), and later, *Ski-ing in the Alps*. His book on suicide explained, though with no damaging effects, how best to crucify oneself. Ascending some lonely peak in the Pyrenees, his party was surprised to discover a tiny post-office, and quickly sent a telegram to the aged Hilaire Belloc: 'Yours is still the best book on the Pyrenees.' He later wrote his own: *The Enchanted Mountains*. He had stores of surprising information, suddenly announcing that 30,000 different roses had been identified by 1950.

His small masterpiece, *Chantemesle*, concerns a French house and region where he had spent some period of his childhood. The book celebrated privacy, with reticences more powerful than the explosions from temperaments less subtle. Old woods and pools, herons and egrets, books and paintings, could have been reduced to mush by clumsier hands. The region, geographically, was small, but with imaginative depths never wholly chartable, and the sunlit summers cast dark shadows ahead – to the Occupation, treachery, revenge. Meanwhile, it provided hallucinations from light and landscape, substantial beauties of hills and the water between islands, crowded with feather and fin, the flash and swoop and glide. Reading, I felt the lure of a distant horn, the apparition of an unsuspected manor house, the infinite resources of silence, a bizarre drowning. The *Grand Meaulnes* suggestiveness reinforced rather than jarred, for Fedden's perceptions were distinctly his own: 'The few children in our part of the valley met, each combed, frilled, starched, at various houses for fêtes and goûters. The seasonal ritual, set in motion by our parents, drew us like a flock of twittering birds, armed like birds in beak and claw, to terraces and lawns, dispersed us under heavy August trees, or set us to dance, self-conscious and suddenly older, round gilt drawing-rooms where formal Louis XVI chairs were ranged against the walls.'

Patrick Leigh Fermor, before the war, had made a lengthy walk glittering with small bizarre incidents, and exotic survivals from old, monarchical estates and memorable landscapes, through the former Habsburg Empire, and Greece; through farms, hovels, mansions, castles, forests, mountains, with history flowing like wind or as settled as summer dust. During the war, in Crete, he personally captured the German General Kreipe, an adventure later transformed into the movie, *Ill Met By Moonlight*, Dirk Bogarde impersonating Leigh Fermor. Relations between captive and captor, in a situation which lasted for three weeks, naturally began with some stiffness, which softened when the General, thirteenth son of a Hanoverian pastor, exclaimed at a magnificent mountain view and began a Latin quotation from Horace, which the younger man then completed.

Paddy's books, particularly his *The Violins of Saint-Jacques* (1953), a West Indian novel and subsequently an opera by Malcolm Williamson starring Owen Brannigan, fiercely reacted against kitchen-sink austerities, the dehydrated greyness of social-realist polemicists. I would open this book at random and be at once transported to territories simultaneously new and familiar: 'The clear sad sound of French hunting horns sailed into the stillness of the night. Somewhere in that far off lighted circle, the three *piqueux* of the Count's pack from Beauséjoux were standing under the leaves in their scarlet coats, their black cheeks expanded over the mouth-pieces of their slender and curling instruments, sending over the waters of the Antilles notes that set ghostly finger-tips creeping up the nape of Berthe's neck under the thick and disordered pile of plaits. The fanfare played the children's song about the good King Dagobert, then the sequence of the grave and formal little tunes, so unlike the brisk twanging of English hunting horns, which marked the incidents of the chase in France as solemnly as the movements in the pavane. They rang in the distance like the secret voice of all French forests; the spirit of the tapestried and the unicorn-haunted penumbra of their alley ways and of the great druidical trees when the bare winter branches are clouded with mistletoe.'

Like Alec Guinness, V. S. Pritchett had an erratic childhood of back-door escapes from duns; also of alarming oddities, outsize paternal speculations, small, vivid adventures. His memories reached back before the Great War, to homes, schools, livelihoods remote from the public school, Oxbridge backgrounds of most members. In his teens he was working humbly, in leather, then sold shellac in Paris, daily passing great writers in their cafés but ignorant of all of them. Excited by such as Belloc and Unamuno, he walked across Spain, *Marching Spain* appearing in 1928, a young man's book, over-written, breathless, yet with sudden convictions, swift conclusions, flashing with images yet not flashy, anticipating the VSP seated amongst us.

Looking at his stocky, unassertive, always friendly presence, I felt that he could have made no enemies. Unassuming, yet aware of his worth – his stories had few rivals in English – he would enter our room, smiling diffidently, still, after so many years, apt to cram his hat into his pocket, his talk always interesting without being chatty, stocked with anecdote and memories. Staying in a country house, he had a fellow-guest who unexpectedly went mad and wrote eleven plays in one night. His mother had a favourite music-hall song:

At Trinity Church I met me doom,
Now we live in a top back room,
Up to me eyes in debt for rent,
That's what 'e done for me.

Dying, her last words were, 'Ah! Illuminations.'

At table, always part of the talk, he seemed never far from the leather-works, the Spanish bar, Irish cabin, Corsican doss-house, New York bar, all rich with human material that could have burst one of lesser stamina. Genius, he said, is spiritual greed. To imagine that twinkling face bored or despairing or jeering was impossible. Only his friend Graham Greene could have matched his world of exceptions, small independent rebels and victims, absurd plausibilities. Something about him invited confidences from shepherds, weekend cyclists, debt-collectors, floor-walkers, salesmen, servicemen who had come down in the world, Home Guards, colonels' daughters, suburban misfits on a spree, dockside boozers, aunts' lovers, sailors, malevolent or puzzled loners who see only bits of our world and who talk and ramble in whatever is left to them of their own, like the man who disparaged birds, as 'individualists gone mad'.

'Expenses, the most beautiful word in modern English,' V. S. had reflected in 1946, while rejecting an extravagantly lucrative offer from Global Enterprises to write a propaganda pamphlet extolling and doubtless embellishing an American company's war service, to be 'a valuable historical record'. He was offered thousands. Cheerfully, though unsuccessfully, he suggested millions. 'If we sell our souls we ought to sell them dear.'

I learnt much from him. During the war, his weekly *New Statesman* essay made him a one-man university, and during the Fifties and thereafter, his lessons, delivered with certainty but without hectoring or conceit, braced me to confront my craft with, as it were, serious humour.'One of the reasons why bad novels are bad is not that the characters do not live, but that they do not live with one another. They read one another's minds through the author.' 'The Russian novelists of the nineteenth century owe everything to their response to the man or woman sitting alone in his room, to the isolation, inertia, the off-beat in the human character.'

Reading a paragraph in his Fifties' critique of Gosse's *Father and Son*, I reflected on how different my attitude to the seventeenth century would have been had I read more V. S., and less Dumas. 'Outwardly the extreme puritan appears narrow, crabbed, fanatical, gloomy and dull; but from the inside – what a series of dramatic climaxes his life is, what fascinating casuistry beguiles him, how he is bemused by the comedies of duplicity, sharpened by the ingenious puzzles of the conscience, and carried away by the eloquence of hypocrisy.'

Like Orwell, V. S. Pritchett could offhandedly reveal what had always been obvious, though usually unobserved until he indicated it. On London, for instance, he wrote in 1962: 'One's first impression is of a heavy city, a place of aching heads. The very name London has tonnage in it. The two syllables are two thumps of the steam hammer, the slow clump-clump of a policeman's feet, the cannoning of shunting engines, or the sounds of coal thundering down the holes of Victorian terraces.'

Another regular was slim, neat-dressed, neat-faced William Cold-stream, Slade Professor of Fine Art, with a perky humour very much his own. Confronted by a Coldstream painting of a domestic interior, David Sylvester demanded the significance, pictorial, symbolic, even moral, of a dullish block of furniture obstructing the foreground. Bill replied mildly that its significance was in its having been too heavy to move. Earlier he had worked in films, collaborating with Auden, Britten, Cavalcanti, John Grierson in the GPO Film Unit. He could now be found, randomly, yet never wholly surprisingly, at the school, in his studio, the Lord's pavilion, the Gargoyle Club, on a dance floor with poets and musicians, or listening to an ancient record of 'Bye Bye Blackbird', on a street, chatting to a wartime army companion, at a meeting of the Artists' Benevolent Fund. He loved committees, the politics and factions, subtle changes of fortune, small dramas, after-wards examining all the doodles, invariably deciding that his own were the worst.

I had just heard of him during the war, reading Auden and MacNeice's *Letters from Iceland*. In one letter, 'Last Will and Testa-ment', they leave bits of English life to prominent people. To H. G. Wells, Shell-Mex House; to Isaiah Berlin, a saucer of milk; to Lord Berners, the architectural follies of fifty countries, providing he wrote the history of the King and Queen. Prophetically, '. . . and the Slade School I choose/For William Coldstream to leave his mark upon.'

Within Bill's quiet irreverence could be discerned an obdurate dignity of mind and person. A. J. Ayer distinguished between his intrinsic seriousness and lack of solemnity, appreciated his wit, and shared his loathing of humbug.

*   *   *

Graham Greene occasionally appeared, casual, courteous, eyes often wandering and indeterminate until abruptly stilled into sharpness, or gleaming with curious complicity at any mention of sympathy between Catholicism and Communism. He was knowledgeable about Paris brothels and Saigon sexual theatricals, and gave Jocelyn Baines information, not about Joseph Conrad but abstruse details of tribal mating habits and contraception. He left unsaid much that, for me, added mystery to his charm; he was more hesitant than aloof, interested and indeed helpful in others' work. He had worked for the defector Kim Philby in M.I.6, always defended him and, bafflingly, maintained that more religious freedom existed in Russia than anywhere else. He held Castro a personal friend, had been on some covert mission to Ho Chi Minh, had been threatened by 'Papa Doc' Duvalier in Haiti, was contemptuously anti-American and 'Coco-colonization' and was said to be risking his chance of the Nobel by an affair with a Swedish actress. He was still travelling, when he wished to, for M.I.6, though we did not know this and suspected, indeed, that he worked at times for Russia. Like Coldstream, he mingled bouts of melancholy with a teasing quality – after his death, his wife referred to his addiction to practical jokes, particularly during periods of manic depression. This may have helped his view of the writer as independent and outspoken, a bit of grit in the State machine, which gave us an exciting, even adventurous view of our vocations: 'The virtue of disloyalty'.

His vocabulary of grace, salvation, damnation, was as incomprehensible to me as Schönberg, his support of liberation theology very sympathetic. I found his sentences exhilarating: an African girl with a baby in her arms, 'who smiled and smiled like an open piano'. Corpses in Vietnam water, 'like an Irish stew containing too much meat'. The celebrated 'seediness' of his fiction held for me a perverse exoticism, enriched by the hunted underdog, the cripple, the petty crook, the eerie. Like his admired Buchan, he saw the jungle encroaching on the brilliant roadhouse, the deceptive peace of a silent cul-de-sac. Mauriac and Buchan, he would say, were his foremost mentors, though in print he would add Marjorie Bowen, Rider Haggard, A. E. W. Mason. His Catholic orthodoxy was often suspect, and he smiled gently, without replying, when Philip Toynbee asked him to confirm the story that the Pope, receiving him in the Vatican, reminded him, on parting: 'Mr Greene, remember, that I too am a member of the Church.'

Greene was then allowing five pounds weekly to the impecunious, almost unknown Muriel Spark, on condition that she did not pray for him. I believe they never met, but he admired her talent. During the war she had broadcast official misinformation to the Nazis, and in the

Club's early days was winning scars as secretary of the Poetry Society, battling with such aged, sub-Tennysonian poets as Marie Stopes, whose poems for the *Poetry Review* could have been written by Wodehouse's anti-heroine, Madeline Bassett: 'I feel as though we held each other's hands/Like babies in a field of daisy chains.'

Muriel too was Catholic, particularly respecting the Holy Ghost, too often taken for granted. For me, Greene remained remote, unknowable, beyond reach. Through the years, an occasional smile of recognition, a hand raised from across a crowded room, once a rueful shrug.

The Club's invisible, unofficial president was, not wholly unanimously, E. M. Forster, whose by now sanctified remark that he hoped he would have the guts to betray his country rather than betray his friend was still, in the Fifties, much approved by older members, though betrayal of their country by Quisling, Laval and Pétain had not obstructed betrayal of friends. Some club members agreed with Auden's comparison of Burgess and Maclean's flight to Russia in 1951, with his own departure to America in 1939. He said that such actions were necessary as the only way finally and effectively to insult England.

Prokosch, naturally, had known Burgess at Cambridge, where he, Burgess, seduced undergraduates and disapproved of Auden's *Spain*: 'the purest balls, totally bogus, utter poppycock ... what I loathe is all these poets who preach their communism with an Oxford accent'. Prokosch's view of Burgess lacked warmth. 'He had long-lidded eyes and an insolent sensual mouth and he stank of sweat, gin, beer, urine and cabbage. He was the only man I'd ever met whom I disliked instantaneously.' Prokosch conceded, however, that beneath this lay not only shrewdness but also a chaotic idealism, even a dark, subversive charm.

I never met this paragon, and was sometimes in a minority, though not a rowdy one, at the Club's opposition on grounds of freedom, liberty, legality and anti-authoritarianism, to the Nuremberg Trials, the Rosenbergs' execution, American imperialism and de Gaulle's return to power in the 1958 Algerian crisis.

The Wednesday Club was, and remains, all-male, though once Bill Webb, wise and genial literary editor of the *Guardian*, teasingly or absentmindedly slipped in the gifted novelist Angela Carter, undeterred by Ayer's sharp 'What's *that*?' as though probing the Verification Principle. I met her only on this occasion; our relations did not prosper. I said: 'I think I'm correct in saying you've a new book coming out soon.' She scowled. 'What exactly are you trying to infer from that?' This numbed me, but V. S. Pritchett, recognizing my plight, intervened, and started some talk that engrossed her throughout the lunch.

Recollections flicker past. Lord Longford once argued that no action, however useful and virtuous, could acquire full moral stature unless accompanied by Christian belief. Another Catholic, Bernard Wall, quoted some poem about the Lamb of God, prompting Patrick O'Donovan to mention Chesterton saying that where there is animal worship there is human sacrifice. At a 1958 lunch, during a sudden silence, a Russian prince, of bubbling charm and vivacious memories, announced, 'I want to tell a few slightly discreditable stories about F. W. We were on holiday together and . . .' The stories were numerous. F. W. had avoided tipping a waiter, F. W. had been sick in the Louvre, F. W. had tried to seduce a servant, F. W. had bilked a taxi driver . . . Finally, as the prince paused for refreshment, his neighbour said mildly, 'Excuse me, but I *am* F. W.'

'Yes, yes, of course.' The prince was imperturbable, and told a few more stories, leaving me admiring him for his coolness in crisis, and F. W. for his Forsterish tolerance.

Canetti, soon to receive the Nobel Prize for Literature, as a guest announced: 'I have a flair, some have called it genius, for telling at a glance what profession a person's father enjoyed. For one example, this charming young lady . . .', he indicated the waitress, 'her father was and perhaps is, a butcher.' 'But, Herr . . . my father is a rabbi.' 'No! You are wrong.'

In 1955, Haldor Laxness received the Nobel Prize. This name stimulated me into inspecting the list of previous Nobel literature winners and, at the next lunch, I challenged anyone to name more than six. The names included Sienkiewiez, Gjellerup, Sillanpää, Karlfeldt, Kawabata, Björnson, Lagerkvist, Echegaray, Pontoppidan, Sholokhov, Sully-Prudhomme. None, after a thick lunch, roll very readily off the tongue, and I won my bet.

Anthony Burgess suspected the Club was an insider's ring to fix reputations and debase his own, though he declined my invitation to test this in person. Meanwhile, deprived of his company, I learnt as much trivia at Bertorelli's as from Oswell Blakeston. Julian Jebb told of Sir George Sitwell stencilling his cattle with Chinese willow-pattern, to improve the landscape: Philip Hope-Wallace alleged that Henry Irving, driving home in a hansom after some theatrical triumph, was asked by his wife: 'Tell me, Henry, do you intend to spend the rest of our married life making a fool of yourself in public?' Irving stopped the cab, stepped out, raised his hat, and, very properly, never spoke to her again. I myself repeated Patricia Hutchins's story of Ezra Pound learning that his name in Japanese meant, 'This picture of a phallus costs ten yen.'

In general, the table talk was seldom lofty. Robin Fedden grumbled about the inactivity of the middle-aged cock. Someone remembered his grandfather seeing a sheep-rustler slung over a Welsh cliff, minister and choir attending. Julian Jebb, without leaving the table, was violently sick when Bernard Wall volunteered that he considered Edith Sitwell a poet. Michael Oakeshott recalled the swindler, Horatio Bottomley, on a public platform, bawling, 'There ain't no flies on the Lamb of God,' adding afterwards that for an extra five quid he'd '. . . 'ave give 'em the Lord in all 'is glory'. A bore, who insisted on detailing his bad health, nervously retired when told that his symptoms exactly reproduced those of a man in a Kipling story, preliminary to his changing into a wolf.

The last time I saw Harold Nicolson was while sharing his taxi after a lunch. He seemed very reluctant to leave for his empty flat in Albany, and we drove repeatedly round Hyde Park while he talked, slowly, sadly, the talk of an old and failing man, yet with a moving intimacy . . . about Lady Colefax, Lord Curzon (about whom he had written a book), Wilhelm II, Paris 1919, the influence of a classical education on good manners, his pre-war novel, *Public Faces*, in which he had fluked a prophecy of the atomic bomb, and much else.

John Raymond usually left early: 'I'd better go home now, and write up my journal.' For many years we lived in some dread of this journal, fearing that some gaffe, triteness, misquotation or innuendo would be embalmed in it, and I suspect that, hearing of his death, most of us first felt relief at the possible demise of the journal, before sincerely regretting his departure. It never surfaced: probably it had never existed, possibly an executor prudently, or angrily, destroyed it.

Once, when both Ben and Philip were absent, the two senior drinkers, John Raymond and Maurice Richardson, acted as hosts. Several prospective members were present, awaiting high-minded discussions over an austere repast, and staring about them like Vatican tourists wondering whether to tip the Pope. The meal began with champagne, then continued with brandy, without any food, Maurice continually dodging out to a nearby bookmaker, and at the end, John stumbling off to his journal, the entire bill for seventeen being left to the visitors. They were never again seen at the Club.

I recollect all this forty years later with affection and a sense of lost opportunities with figures, considerable if not titanic, so many of them dead, but for me still living, resurrected by their smiles, minor affectations, unexpected disclosures, and stories. Harold Nicolson delighted us with a recollection of his housekeeper's comment at the execution of Mussolini: 'Serves him right! To think of a gentleman like that driving about in a car with a lady who was not his wife!'

11

Youth

IN THE EARLY Fifties the poet Edmund Blunden, author of *Undertones of War*, a Great War classic, while we waited to bat and sometimes during wicket-keeping, recalled songs of his boyhood, some of which I had heard in my own youth, almost all by now unthinkable in schools.

> Be British was the cry
> As the ship went down.

and

> What so'er you find your duty,
> Do it, Boys, with all your might:
> Never be a little truthy
> Or be little in the right.
> Trifles even lead to heaven,
> Trifles make the life of man.
> So in all things, great and small things,
> Be as thorough as you can.

In 1955, I several times teasingly read aloud from Captain Scott's last letters: 'We are showing that Englishmen can still die with a bold spirit, fighting it out to the end ... I think this makes an example to Englishmen of the future.' This had been piously received when a teacher read it to us in 1935, but now, in Hampstead literary salons and at the ICA, audiences assumed I was being sardonic and gave appreciative titters. Later, I slightly amended it, as if it had come from the Warsaw Ghetto, in 1944, or from Mao, or from Che Guevara, and it was respectfully applauded. Had I announced that it was by Brecht – himself much influenced by Kipling – they might have been awed into silence.

Outwardly, in the early Fifties, situations appeared much as before. Conscription was sending youths to fight in Korea, Malaya, Kenya and Cyprus, and to safeguard West Germany and the Suez Canal. Though heroes were becoming 'role-models', the radio hero Dick Barton, Special Agent, was nearer to Dick Hannay or Bulldog Drummond than to James Bond. But much was changing. In this decade of James Dean, Bill Haley and Brigitte Bardot, teenagers – a word now, like student, more often used – were taller, better nourished, better paid, already feeling themselves adult, thus often at odds with adults. In one of her stories, Gillian Tindall wrote of the early Fifties as 'a beastly time to grow up in', with pre-war adult values clashing with new, more casual attitudes, the opening of 'the Generation Gap'. Girls were reaching puberty two years earlier than in 1938 and courting could begin at 12, though elders tended not to see this and relied on memories of their own childhood.

The new standards were milder, more sensible, less arbitrary but, as at the Reformation, the loss of solid, paternalistic rulings left considerable uncertainties. Psychological sophistication and tolerance might cause confusion, or lack of respect for parents behaving like elder siblings. 'Lindy doesn't care,' a child complained, testing his mother with bad behaviour, striving to goad her into a flash of genuine feeling, even passion, but eliciting only bland forbearance, amused forgiveness. Still oppressed by the war, apologetic for 'the Locust Years', many adults harboured, or boasted of, much 'guilt'; useless, boring, self-indulgent and sometimes damaging. For some of these, their children, guiltless of Holocaust, Stalin, the Indian Partition massacres, pre-war unemployment and hunger marches, Munich ... the Match Girls' Strike, the Slave Trade ... the Norman Conquest ... were Always Right, but this could divide as often as it united. Youthful alienation, though age-old, was probably more explicit. J. D. Salinger's young Holden Caulfield spoke for many: 'If somebody at least listens, it's not too bad.'

Adults had their own problems. Alfred Charles Kinsey's reports (1948–5) on sexual behaviour yielded disconcerting information liable to disrupt the marriage vow, with revelations about husbands' recourse to prostitutes and masturbation, women's pre-marital and post-marital sexual adventures, the devaluation of virginity, the claim that 30 per cent of American males had adult homosexual experience. They opened horizons of wishful thinking, exposed vast areas of sexual incom-

patibility, ignorance and misunderstanding, and a slow but resolute
reassessment of women's roles, needs and rights. Kinsey, who died in
1956, was an authority on wasps, of which he had catalogued some
three million; for his human studies, he had interviewed five thousand
men and women. His statistics and citations convinced rather more
that their own sexual antics had been timid and perfunctory, while the
teachings of Dr Benjamin Spock forced them to reappraise attitudes to
their children, who should now be allowed all freedoms compatible
with brute survival.

Reeling with joyous sexual abandon and surrounded by uncontrolled
offspring, wealthy parents indulged in fashionable quackeries, unmiti-
gated by common sense. Children, they enthused, had rights, deserved
privileges, were owed rewards for existing. Stories sped across the
Atlantic, glum or hilarious, of parents dispatched elsewhere, or to early
bed, making way for teenage parties. A London mama liked her
daughter to address her in public as 'Old Cow', to ditch the inhibitions,
a service delivered regularly and without zest. Her brother was known
as 'The End', having been incautiously named Endymion. Philip Larkin
noted the forcible reintroduction of a servantless middle class to its
offspring, in which many misunderstandings and worse were liable
to erupt.

The virtual extinction of nannies left children in the care of parents
who, in richer suburbs, rejected sterner concepts of right and wrong,
and excused damage to guests, animals and furniture as 'self-expression',
a concept not confined to children. The ICA's exhibition of Chim-
panzee Art incited serious critical discussion. For children themselves,
the *Sunday Pictorial*'s annual exhibition of paintings attracted over
20,000 entries, the last hundred being judged by Maurice Field and
Herbert Read.

'Self-expression' could of course include voluntary work in Africa,
Asia, Israel, scientific expeditions to wildest Patagonia, animal photo-
graphy in Canadian forests or Persian mountains, crossing Central Asia
on roller-skates and with packets of nylons, ballooning to celebrate the
centenary of Jules Verne's *Five Weeks in a Balloon*. In a world of second-
rate professionals, older people were refreshed by the exploits of first-
rate amateurs. To work in a kibbutz, to relieve famine, assist irriga-
tion, join the Peace Corps, seemed an authentic fresh start, a relief from
history, though the Press preferred to report the more sensational
aberrations of the young.

I understood from Wilhelm Reich and his devotees that domestic
sexual freedoms would resolve problems of violence, race, perversion,
poverty, even death, thanks to that useful word 'integration'. 'We're

going to see the matron strip,' schoolchildren enthused in a Herbert Farjeon revue. Young sensitivities were relieved by 'Three Blind Mice' being republished as 'Three Kind Mice', the carving knife cutting off not tails but slices of cheese. Another tiresome word was 'sincerity', Simone de Beauvoir pronouncing in 1953 that the headlong sincerity of de Sade entitled him to be hailed as a great moralist. She could have said the same of Himmler.

Much was auspicious: new universities and schools, the school-leaving age raised to 15. London's first comprehensive school, Kidbrooke, was hailed as the answer to the divisiveness of the Eleven Plus and snobbery. National culture was to be powerfully assisted by Labour's leading savant, Anthony Crosland, who vowed to eliminate 'every fucking grammar school in the country'. Also by the Dean, in 1955 working with an educational publisher selling text-books produced so cheaply that they collapsed within three months, and then had to be re-ordered. The Dean offered his biography of Wellington, based on the psychological effects of the Duke's possessing a vestigial tail, necessitating a special saddle and desk-chair. This, for some reason, was refused, and he and his employer soon hated each other like motorists and, like motorists, collided.

The far-sighted had forebodings. Television would replace print: dance, drama and travel offered options that encouraged a preference for subsidized 'self-expression' rather than a routine job, and on the applicant's own terms. Family and Party loyalty, domestic bliss, were being shirked, particularly by those with affluent parents, who furthermore professed a vague but noisy anti-materialism. Elsewhere, publicists noted that 9½d. per head was weekly lavished on the Royal Family, only 4d. on youth services. Heywood, in Lancashire, had fifty-three pubs but no youth clubs.

J. B. Priestley, in *World Review* (1949), had wondered whether words were losing magic: 'The younger members of my family, though brought up in a house crammed with books, are intellectually and enthusiastically devoted to music, art, ballet, film, but seem to care little for literature, and are quite different from what their mother and I were at their age. And their friends seem to be much the same. Young people appear to me to be living far more through the eye and the ear than we did at their time of life; but of course the opportunities to do this are much greater now. I rarely find young people arguing about poets, novelists, essayists, as we used to do. The bookshop has many new competitors.'

The word 'square' was uttered frequently, sometimes hurled, denoting conformists and most people over 30. 'Bobby-soxer' was invented. 'With it' became a synonym for being in fashion, particularly youthful fashion. George Melly and his jazz were 'with it', likewise Ayer, in his role of corrupter of the young. Fame, Rilke had said, is the sum of misunderstandings that gathers about a single name.

To be 'with it' embraced Sartre's Existentialism, and intellectual parents debated Free Will and Determinism. A friend, Maurice Cranston, asserted: 'One had rejected, under the influences of such men as Freud, the old-fashioned notion that children have complete free will and were wholly responsible for their deeds. Freud, and others like him, have made us more compassionate, more understanding, less ready to blame and punish the young, precisely because they have shown us, in terms of their own determinist psychology, that children with Genet's sort of history, often *cannot help* doing the kind of thing that Genet did. [Lying, thieving, talking treason, seducing boys.] But Sartre's psycho-analysis is directly opposed to Freud on this question. His absolute libertarianism makes children morally responsible agents no less surely and severely than does the free-will dogma of Victorian Christianity ... Sartre has spoken of the moral teaching of existentialism as "austere": where it restores the notion of juvenile culpability, it can only be described as harshly reactionary'.

In the aftermath of war, throughout much of the liberal West, youthful spokesmen were denying that any cause was worth a life, in a world of ludicrous conferences, nuclear bombs, old men. Reason was suspect, emotion was not. Chalked on city walls, like a password, was Blake's 'Rather murder an infant in its cradle than nurse unsatisfied desire.' The sober efficiency of Montgomery, the managerial qualities of Mountbatten, the determination of 'Bomber' Harris, were meaningless or worse in the milk bars, cafés, dance halls and unofficial youth clubs, where a duffle-coated youth achieved brief fame for allegedly being sacked from Sandhurst for wearing mittens.

T. R. Fyvel, in *The Insecure Offender*, showed Britain, West and East Germany, Sweden, Italy and the USSR, despite their different regimes, sharing many youth problems – emotional frustration, hooliganism, intelligent illiteracy, vague fears. Attending an international conference in 1950, he heard a leading French socialist bemoan the political apathy of French youth, made cynical by the black market and un-neighbourly values of the Occupation, the savage vendettas around the Resistance and Liberation, the factionalism which had forced de Gaulle from office. Fyvel replied that in Britain he at least found no such cynicism. What then, he was asked, was British youth's belief. 'I gave the first answer that came into my head. "I imagine they believe in what Mr Attlee is always calling 'our way of life'." ' This could bear several interpretations: dislike of intellectuals, of rhetoric, dogma, populism; mistrust of foreigners; a Fabian belief in the State as a useful service for redistributing immoderate wealth and supervising or initiating public services, and attending to Fair Play. If not attracting much youthful cynicism, by 1951 this outlook was scarcely bracing the young for fervid work or providing passionate ideals. Political scepticism was to be assisted by a 1959 *Observer* article by Attlee himself, confessing that he, Churchill, Truman and Acheson had been ignorant of the genetic effects of the atomic bomb; also by war criminals like Krupp and ambiguous geniuses like von Braun, back in business, in the Cold War.

There remained those completely outside the pull of sport, study, travel, art and a belief in the future. Groups of young males stood on urban streets ignoring the songs blaring from cafés, eyeing not passers-by but each other. They had hairstyles like silk curtains, like spokes, like upturned blades; hair tinted, laminated, bejewelled, crimped, bunched, recalling the rich Hanoverian macaronis. They were what Attlee deplored as unproductive spivs and drones, in white shirts, black stove-pipe trousers, longish coats, black string ties; shirts could be frilled or pleated, waistcoats elaborately flowered. Teddy Boy became their popular nickname, in dandy association with Edward VII, though this might have been disputed by some who remembered King Tum Tum at Marienbad, in green cap, pink tie, white gloves, grey slippers and brown, very brightly checked, overcoat. I see them now, standing, as if exiled from home, impassive, staring, a few surreptitiously preening: suddenly, without a sign, they quiver like birds before flight, and are gone.

Increasingly, youth was adopting the motorcycle, a declaration of independence, linking the provinces to the major cities in inarticulate conspiracy, the heavy machine itself proclaiming both individual mastery and group solidarity, relieving personal tensions, electrifying the moment with speed, risks, noise. Talk was starting about juvenile crime and parental irresponsibility, accompanied by more nostalgia, for wartime discipline and the comradeship and social cohesion of the Blitz, though some recollected an abortive parliamentary attempt to extend the death penalty to looters.

Fifties writers found useful themes from the young: provincial universities – the hurrying go-getters, academic humbugs, literary frauds, conformist toadies, the pretentious, the unimaginative, the falsely tolerant, or the plain stupid – disrespect for elders, fractious homes, the need for new roles, the need too for honesty, sympathy, decency. Sexual dilemmas, generation conflicts, war traumas, the anarchic impulses of 'the crazy mixed-up kid' enacted on the screen by James Dean, were treated seriously, in an added awareness that Fifties youth possessed unprecedented strength, by spending nine hundred million pounds annually on motorcycles, cosmetics, clothes, cigarettes, the new long-playing records, drugs. Advertisers found it worthwhile to flatter this spendthrift population. Prominent 'youth novels' were William Cooper's *Young People*, John Wain's *Strike the Father Dead*, Bernard Malamud's *A New Life*.

Fifties youth culture – jazz, sex, classlessness, racial harmonies, drugs, vitality – was championed by Colin MacInnes, in whose novels, *City of Spades, Absolute Beginners* and *Mr Love and Justice*, was revealed for many a London of racial tensions, unusual joys, relations complex beneath ostensible callowness, generation feuds, underground fraternities, covert drug shops, illicit meanderings, with the young mocking their elders as 'you taxpayers' and with Blacks abused as 'spades'. MacInnes, related to Kipling and great-grandson of Burne-Jones, was an authority on Black culture, music halls, cricket, prostitution, pornography, the police, Allied soldiers' behaviour in defeated Germany. He witnessed the 1958 Notting Hill race riots which he claimed had been planned, savagely aimed at particular areas, groups, individuals, homes, clubs, with yelling mobs showing faces descended from those in Gillray, Rowlandson, Hogarth. He had pronounced sympathy for youth, particularly West Indian. 'I'm really a teenager,' he told the Wednesday Club, though his white hair and rheumy eyes made one hesitate to agree.

Black self-respect must have been fortified during the Fifties by the prowess of the Turpin brothers, Dick and Randolph, in the boxing ring, by Althea Gibson winning the Ladies' Singles at Wimbledon in 1957, and by the growth of the West Indies into an international cricketing power.

J. D. Salinger, in *The Catcher in the Rye*, was accepted by middle-class youth as speaking for it with magical charm, though 'charm' would have disgusted the teenage anti-hero, Holden Caulfield, to whom the word 'phoney' came more readily and which was eagerly adopted by Western youngsters, to cover politicians, teachers, parents, lawyers, bishops and the general establishment. An adult literary critic compared him to Huck Finn, his peregrinations a nearly perfect lament for all lost youth.

The young stampeded to buy another American, the pagan, priapic rhapsodist Henry Miller whose *Tropic* books were still banned in his

native America, and not yet easily available here. His boastful aggres-
siveness towards women was often forgiven, for his frenetic sexual
explicitness, windy rebelliousness, tall stories, even for his turgid
philosophizing. However, Brigid Brophy denounced him as a male
bully and philistine. He had been praised by Havelock Ellis, Marcel
Duchamp, T. S. Eliot, Blaise Cendrars. Pound told him that he had
out-Ulyssesed Joyce. Lawrence Durrell remained an intimate. John
Wain thought him 'a great big something'.

He was now in California, publishing *Big Sur and the Oranges of
Hieronymous Bosch* in 1958, a thick chunk of impetuous life, introduced
by an announcement that the Law had imposed some deletions. The
Fifties had not changed him. He still discharged frantic convictions,
untrustworthy reminiscences and vast digressions, ranting against
technology and officials, his prose poems enlarged by hit-or-miss
similes: nuns paddling resemble old demented haddocks trained to
stand upright. The book was a sprawl, now bawdy, now merely
sniggering, the emptying out of a mind vapid when striving for
greatness, but fun when recollecting or observing, without bothering
about the prophetic or the didactic.

Amongst 'comics', and children's periodicals, the public-school
orientated *Magnet* and *Gem* were dead by the Forties, though
having contributed Billy Bunter to popular mythology. Middle-class
fictional schoolboys were replaced by the supra-human: Captain
Marvel, Wonder Woman, Superwoman, extending the tradition
of Tarzan, even Biggles. Leslie A. Fiedler in 'The Middle Against
Both Ends', a 1955 essay, argued that Superman was not the adulation
of a Hitler or Stalin, rather of the archetypal Cincinnatus that has
possessed the American imagination since Washington: the leader
who appears in crisis, rescues the land, then retires to obscurity.
He said that comics 'reduce to manageable form the threat of science,
the horror of unlimited war, the general spread of corruption in a
world where the social bases of old loyalties and heroisms have long
been destroyed ... Their gross drawing, their poverty of language
cannot disguise their heritage of aboriginal violence, their exploitation
of the ancient conflict of black magic and white ... They are our not
quite machine-subdued Grimm, though the Black Forest has become,
as it must, the City; the Wizard, the Scientist; and Simple Hans,
Captain Marvel.'

By contrast in England the opposition to urban squats and fraudulent
advertisements, addressing a huge, largely young middle-class audience,
largely took the form of J. R. R. Tolkien's mid-Fifties *Lord of the
Rings*, pseudo-saga, of Icelandic and Anglo-Saxon parentage, appealing

to archetypal and mythical patterns of quest and initiation, innocence confronting guile, of supernatural dragons, talking creatures only half-human, short cuts of magic, long cuts of mysticism, in starkly remote landscapes. Auden told the sceptical Philip Toynbee – himself devoted to the original sagas – 'Tolkien . . . as good as Tolstoy . . . no, better!' Toynbee rated them sentimental fustian. 'Don't read them,' he told me, 'they're not drugs but they're adhesive, like stamps . . . stamps of an exiled government.' Schoolchildren enjoyed the sense of evil – actually very tame – and human weakness striving with a world polluted by betrayals, lies, universal conspiracy, to be redeemed by purposeful adventure. Adolescents enjoyed the mixture of idealism and pessimism, unpretentious dedication, the strange and the common-place, which held a sense of esoteric belonging, the allure of a secret garden, a secret society.

Youth had no glamour for William Golding, and his awareness of evil was keener, more naked than Tolkien's. His *Lord of the Flies* (1954) entered the school syllabus as a development of an innocuous Victorian children's classic, *The Coral Island*. It attacked Fifties optimism and most of its premises. The Enlightenment had assumed that humans were rational, perverted only by bad government and stale but power-ful beliefs inherited or imposed; that human equilibrium could be restored by wise legislation, scientific knowledge, benevolent parents and teachers. Golding's novel disputed this. *The Coral Island* boys grappled with misfortune, those in *Lord of the Flies* – the title of Baal, Old Testament pagan god of evil – with far worse. Evil is less forced upon them by shipwreck and hardship than rises from within them, from some psychic or genetic inheritance, as if in an old homily on Original Sin, the joker in a pack which includes a saint, a sacrificial martyr and an innocent.

The novel was rejected by fifteen publishers until accepted by Charles Montieth at Faber's, despite a report that it was dull and pointless. Nothing in it blamed the children's cruelty, superstition and terror on abnormal training, lop-sided societies, irresponsible adults, poverty, rotten environments; few of the Nazi leaders, either, could seek such excuses. Golding dug far beneath the Fifties, beneath the century itself into the primal urges. He ripped away the apparatus of school uniforms, good manners, formal discipline, liberal teachers, harmless toys, to probe tissues of myth, primitive symbols, black fears and twilit temptations, suppressed or sublimated but always ready to pounce, even overwhelm. It was a dimension away from the sanitized certainties of Wells and Shaw.

*   *   *

Continuing from the Twenties, 'progressive education' disdained any notion of original sin, its premises seemingly confirmed by war and atrocities. Adults were corruptible, children were sinned against – by external discipline, punishment, rewards, competition, false teaching, social mores, lack of love. Self-expression was favoured, and Ayer for a while sent a son to a progressive school. Later, Freddie was apt to murmur that, to express one's self, one must first possess a coherent self.

Education, Bertrand Russell taught, as did Wells, was the key to the new world, not violence, religion or conventional morality. It could in one generation produce the millennium – health, freedom, honesty, happiness, kindness, intelligence. Love was the essence: love of children and of humanity, at the expense of nationalism, dogma, inflexible justice, ancient, nonsensical feuds. Curiosity must be fed, spontaneity and independence encouraged.

A schoolteacher myself in 1950, I was excited by this. If intelligent people behave in a certain way, then certain results must follow. Hitherto, admittedly, I had had the misfortune to feel sceptical, as I did about the Socratic premise that knowledge induces virtue. Most of my favourite writers were scoundrels, and I had seen virtuous loving homes produce criminals. Nevertheless, my experience, compared to Tolstoy, Wells and Russell, was negligible: I must look further, read more widely. Intellectuals had damaged the world as heartily as anyone else, but the world was being repaired: UNO, Unesco, WHO ... magic letters. I resolved to attach myself to a progressive school and drank Russell in gusty pints: 'A generation educated in fearless freedom will have wider and bolder hopes than are possible to us, who still have to struggle with the superstitious fears that lie in wait for us below the level of consciousness.'

The most celebrated progressive teacher of the time was A. S. Neill, with his Suffolk school, do-as-you-like Summerhill: *That Dreadful School*, as he titled one of his books. 'Leave well alone and encourage everything,' Robin Bond, A. S. Neill's art teacher, said of art for young children. Summerhill had no inhibitions against swearing, nakedness, cheeking adults, avoiding lessons. Neill held that older systems had trained the intellect and 'character' to the detriment of the emotions: preference for the IQ, against the EQ – the emotional – too often warped children into conformity, colourlessness, timidity. 'Summerhill deals primarily with the emotions.' With all this I tended to agree, doubtless influenced by the fact that my own IQ had been officially rated unusually low. As a teacher, I was given some IQ cards to distribute. The first question entailed completing, 'Good as ...' 'Black as . . .', invitations to cliché, and I read no further. Subsequently, Professor Burt, a prominent IQ enthusiast, was accused of falsifying crucial results, and my feelings collapsed in laughter.

Whatever its final effects, Summerhill recognized the central problems: of authority, sex, anti-social behaviour, hypocrisy mincing about as good manners, violence. The rules, often transitory, emerged from below, were not handed down from above. On a question of whether smoking should be allowed, Neill was outvoted by the majority of children, and had to submit, and allow it.

Much less famous than A. S. Neill in the Fifties, but as impressive was George Lyward. Presiding at Finchden Manor, Kent, seated in a large overcoat, very unobtrusive, scarcely speaking, like a Taoist, he appeared to do nothing and achieve much, to name everything without seeing it. Michael Burn, the novelist, wrote of Finchden Manor in 1956 that it was not quite a school, or an experimental commune, or a convalescent home, certainly no institution, but giving respite from conventional morality, examinations, conventional standards, over-exacting adult demands, which had weakened the young will to survive, move on, laugh, be spontaneous and playful, lose resentment. Reviewing Burn's *Mr Lyward's Answer*, Harold Nicolson wrote: 'The very casualness or fluidity of treatment obliged a boy to lose his resentment against what he was expected to be, or feel, or do, and to replace it by an act of personal choice.' Lyward disproved Maugham's remark that there is no kick in the milk of human kindness.

Throughout the Fifties I served, or was at least present, at Burgess Hill co-educational school, Hampstead, beginning in the questing spirit of a dedicated pilgrim. The school had been founded in the Thirties by a consortium, largely anarchist, which included Herbert Read, and was well-tuned to the messages of Russell and Neill. Read himself was a composite perhaps particularly English. Tall, slim, handsome as Trilling, with fastidious bow-tie and discreetly tinted socks, he was a pacifist, decorated for gallantry in the Great War, an anarchist who accepted a knighthood, devotee of Wordsworth, tireless promoter of the new in art and poetry, and art critic, poet, social critic. He had in *Poetry and Anarchism* (1935) confessed: 'To me it seemed just as important to destroy the established bourgeois ideals in literature, painting and architecture as it was to destroy the established bourgeois ideals in economics.' For him all politics was local politics: 'a sense of the fraternal between man and man is an essential part of the anarchist sensibility'.

Burgess Hill, therefore, was to be a forum for learning without compulsion, living without authority – authority itself too often identified with cruelty. Education was simple, and must be founded more on biology than economics, Kropotkin, not Marx. Nazi vileness could be traced to the Allied blockade of 1918–19 and childhood deprivation. To induce respect for another's flowers, give a child a garden. To reproach a liar merely induces the fear which induces lying. Lessons are not competitions for marks but co-operation for truth. Minorities, dissidents, eccentrics deserve rather more than their fair share. A third-rate person with a first-rate idea is a public nuisance.

When Bertrand and Dora Russell set up their school after 1918, they were convinced of the emotional injuries caused by repression, and had announced: 'We allow children to be rude, and use any language they like.' At Burgess Hill this was followed wholeheartedly, particularly by the staff. Hideously conventional and thus morally contaminated, at home with traditional courtesy, classical music and literature, enjoying Hollywood, but desiring redemption, I myself was the pupil, the children my teachers, at least in the byways of sex, popular culture and magistrates' courts. I certainly departed having learnt more than I taught, though retaining an ingrained scepticism for majority opinion. I partially accepted the validity of EQ while feeling that few claims could be made for Mussolini, Göring, Goebbels or Beria being sexually repressed.

Burgess Hill, with shaky finances and equipment daily shattered and infrequently replaced, was no clean, well-lit place; rather, a reminder that a state of nature can be a state of chaos. In this it resembled Summerhill, as it did in its assumption, opposing Golding's, that juvenile crime was due to abominable adults, faulty social arrangements, the tyrannical weight of history. The pupils were from rich, nervy families, from embassies, from despairing if sceptical local authorities, from transient voyagers, from neighbours, from the careless, and from world-improvers like Brodsky. The community, with a bank overdraft guaranteed for some reason by the first Mrs J. B. Priestley, numbered about seventy, the children ranging in age from around 8 to the indeterminate, though all, I thought, were under 40, one boy very heavily moustached and with specialized information about Portuguese brothels. From cook to principal, all were paid the same. The latter was Geoffrey Thorpe, who had been at Charterhouse with Robert Graves, had taught Spender and had known H. G. Wells. He had also carved on his father's tombstone 'Thorpe's Corpse'. His rule was benign, occasionally galvanized by some three minutes of barely creditable ferocity.

Much idealism remained from the Thirties, with its devotion to Gandhi and constant collections for the League of Nations. No punishment was permitted: a child of 10, with an expression of importance, lectured me that of the last 1,845 adults condemned to be flogged before 1948, those spared subsequently had the better record. Lessons, of course, were voluntary. No child was to be encouraged to learn to read or count until psychologically ready for this, and if this took several decades – as for one girl it did – no great matter. (She became literate only in order to read aloud to her own child, until the latter impatiently snatched the book and read it to her.) Compulsion, I should know, stunted organic growth, contaminated free, roving thoughts with facts and information, caused, as all doctors recognized, cancer. I had qualms, for this seemed to ignore an element prominent in myself, but surely unexceptional, that of bone-laziness. I was sternly rebuked. Voluntary lessons, by presenting choice, developed individual responsibility, the absence of which nourished Fascism. I should also remember the importance given to play, dance, fantasy, by Dickens, Ellis, Freud and Huizinga.

Clearly, I was no man of the Fifties. Reading Thomas Hardy to a few tolerant 'pupils', I realized that scarcely a word was comprehensible: 'Flossy catkins of the later kinds, fern-sprouts like bishops' croziers, the square-headed moschatel, the odd cuckoo-pint – like an apoplectic saint in a niche of malachite – snow-white ladies'-smocks, the toothwort, approximating to human flesh, the enchanter's night-shade, and the black-petalled doleful-bells.'

'In need of a doctor,' a boy commented about me, later comparing me, unfavourably, to my predecessor, Bernice Rubens, prestigious for her Dance of the Seven Veils in a production of Wilde's *Salome*. Essentially I was agreeing with Peregrine Worsthorne, who had already told Kurt Hahn, founder of Gordonstoun, that to attempt to make a boy morally and physically brave was insufficient. 'That might even be the easy part. The difficult part is to teach him not to oversimplify, not to believe that he has the answers, above all not to believe that he can always tell the truth because so often there is no truth to tell.' If only, Perry considered, life was a choice between good and evil as in Nazi Germany – from which Hahn was a refugee – it would be child's play. In England, however, a child should be prepared for 'the moral murkiness, ambiguities and ironies of life'.

I soon found myself no idealist bringer of light but merely that old tribal asset, a teller of tales. Fifties sophistication had not exorcized a relish for stories, particularly black comedy and the inconsequential. King Christoph of Haiti, I reported, quelled a mutiny by inviting suspects to step forward and shoot themselves. At the Battle of Laffeldt, Lord George Townshend saw a Prussian officer's head blown

off, and remarked, 'I had not realized that Shieger had so many brains.'
Tolstoy, on the road, met a lizard and, bending down, was overhead
by Gorky: 'I say, old fellow, are you happy? I'll tell you something,
I'm not!' Lord Dufferin and Ava dreamed of an ugly man carrying a
coffin. Years afterwards, he refused to enter a lift in a Paris hotel
because the liftman was the man in his dream; the cable broke, the lift
crashed, killing all its load. Hermann Göring, Grand Huntsman of the
Reich, hung a text in his study, 'Whoever tortures animals harms the
Germans' feelings.' A. J. P. Taylor, in print and in talk, was a useful
reservoir, knowing of Mr Theodore Yates, agitated by his conviction
that the Second World War had been partly caused by his sin in not
becoming a Roman Catholic; and of G. N. Clark, who secured the first
Oxford Chair of Economic History by arguing that he was ignorant
of economics and wanted to learn.

Nevertheless, I too was young, anxious to share, convince, excite.
I remembered H. G. Wells's definition of education as the building
up of the imagination, and grabbed at a sentence by Sean O'Faolain,
currently reviewing fiction in *The Listener*: 'Imagination is a soaring
gull, and opinions no more than a gaggle of ungainly starlings chattering angrily in a cornfield. Opinions breed anger, nourish hate, ossify
the heart, narrow the mind.' Obstinately, risking an empty classroom,
I thrust forward my discoveries: Viktor Khlebnikov's poem:

> Peoples, years, and every creature
> In an endless river go,
> As the passing waters flow.
> In the supple glass of Nature
> Stars are nets and fishes we,
> Gods the midnight's fantasy.

The empty classroom, if unflattering to my vanity, did not immoderately distress me. Though I had learnt much from the personalities
of my own teachers, classroom curricula had affected me less, and I
could remember playing truant, sitting in a tree and reading *The Time
Machine*, *At the Villa Rose*, *Jeremy at Crale*, *Bulldog Drummond at Bay*.
More could be implied than bluntly taught. I appreciated style which,
like love, can only be demonstrated. That Stalin's Russia was spending
double Churchill's education budget was, in itself, meaningless, or,
if meaning there were, it was unpleasant for the Russians. Harold
Macmillan, at Pratt's, at the Beefsteak, enjoyed quoting Professor J. A.
Smith's comment that one Oxford curriculum, save for aspiring dons
and schoolteachers, would be absolutely useless except that, after hard
and intelligent work, the student should be able to detect when a man

is talking rot. Macmillan said that, for him, this was the main, if not the whole purpose of education. This improved on Lord Melbourne, who maintained that education had ruined upper-class health uselessly, and rendered the working class unfit to be good servants and labourers. He also avoided church, for fear of hearing something extraordinary.

A tiresome girl, who pointedly avoided my classes, enjoyed repeating to me, 'Those who are taught most, know least. Those who can, write: those who can't, teach.' Ending her litany with, 'George Bernard Shaw'. This actually rather pleased me, which disappointed her. The children liked what I could tell them about GBS, and applauded his style: they felt that, with his mockery of exams, punishments and compulsory textbooks, he was on their side, and his death produced a disposition to hoist a large portrait of him in the hall, labelled for the benefit of parents and inspectors as 'Our Founder'. In a brief craze, children would excuse almost everything with 'as Shaw says ...' Despite his beard, his spindly appearance convinced one wiseacre that Shaw was female which, put to the tyrannical School Meeting, was carried by majority vote, and the craze lapsed. The School Meeting itself usually approximated to Canetti's description of those crowds seen in his youth.

Those who boycotted my classes would often condescend to go for walks or play tennis with me, frequently confiding with some spirit.

'Do you believe in God, Peter?'

'Well, you see ...'

'Do most people?'

'Probably.'

'What's He made of?'

'I don't think it's like that. Like electricity or love ...'

'Nonsense. God's made of iron.'

Children usually write well, from their fresher perceptions. Ezra Pound heard a girl wanting not to turn on the light, but open the light. 'She was using the age-old language of art. It was a sort of metaphor but she was not using it as ornamentation.' A Burgess Hill girl with a ring through her nose, set an essay on Public Parks in some external exam, began, 'There was once a man named Parks. He named his son Public, so ...'

Once another avoider of classes and deft thief handed me a dirty scribble. His own? Stolen? I never knew, though he looked fiercely possessive.

Up within the Welsh hills and mountains
Where the lonesome bedraggled sheep graze

Where the rocks cling to their mysteries,
And the whispering stream talks to its mystery
As it dips between rustic bracken
The peaceful cottages silently moan
When the rain rives and spears them,
And the lightning cracks against their stern bodies
   They cry when it's over

As the melancholy drops of rain fall sadly
Down down bouncing from windows
Sky becomes pale and drooping
As sudden dashes of wind blow at the wild wet mint
That sways mournfully
And the dejected bloom sags as she rocks herself to sleep
Now the pools darken guiltily
Sky darkens in its pale sickness
Then my heart trembles and I retire to bed like a thief.

In the Sixties he became a financial consultant whom I once, unwisely, consulted. Afterwards, I showed him his poem. He smiled indifferently. 'Not at all literary, is it! No big deal. Old hat. This must mean you taught us very badly . . . admittedly I was sensible enough to leave lessons well alone.' We never spoke again but in 1975 I passed him in the City walking with a pretty girl unknown to me. He did not recognize me, or pretended not to, but I heard the girl murmur, 'Wasn't that Peter?'

Neill used to speak of Problem Parents, and these could be more difficult than their children. One boy regularly pillaged Hampstead shops. Quiet remonstrance was blocked by his mother, a refugee from Communist Prague who rejoiced in his activities for exalting the freedoms long denied to herself, also obeying Herbert Read's injunction to undermine bourgeois institutions. Once she took my hand: 'My feelings . . . they are like pets. Very gentle, very sad,' her eyes moistening on cue, until she unexpectedly guffawed, 'Do you realize that, in its simplest form, a tumbler is merely a cylinder with one end closed?' Another mother grazed on her son's income as a child actor, demanding that he be taught nothing, for extra knowledge might distract him from his work. I taught him strenuously but indeed he learnt nothing. Erich Fried had a son with us, and was apt to boast that he was totally fearless through possessing 'cast-iron balls'. He invited me to test this by kicking them. This I declined, but not so Naomi, a pupil who then affected a limp. Erich was visibly distressed, but not on behalf of Naomi.

Anarchist convictions made some teachers reluctant to give leadership or issue 'value judgements'. Both would devalue the young and impale them on adult prejudices. Thus *Hamlet* could be neither better nor worse than *Getting Gertie's Garter*. Grammar, spelling and decimal points were starting points for democratic discussion, not despotic facts. I would get sensations of watching people morally superior to myself reluctant to put one foot forward for fear of hurting the feelings of the other. This attitude induced periodic listlessness, a dangerous, 'What shall we do next' paralysis. The children wanted to be consulted and to advise, but could be bored by too much free time. They would wonder 'Who am I?' with many small scraps of evidence but no very clear notion of what to do with them. A touchy, rather aggressive youngster muttered wistfully, 'Juliet should punish us . . . she lets us off too much.' Freedom rather easily became a dogma as emphatic as that which it aimed to supplant. Few could relax this, each of us was intolerably correct, and so children could become oppressed by unending noise and self-expression.

Not all adults were self-effacing. I remember a middle-aged American idealist, styling himself Walt, after Whitman, and Doctor, for a thesis, abandoned after a shaky start, on the text of *Casablanca*. He was disappointed with America – 'I introduced the barbecue . . . no one noticed' – and gave lectures to slightly bored children on the merits of *Lolita*, and on the world's future. 'Fortunately, Western women are increasingly resembling men, becoming sturdier, heavier, gruffer. Their traditional allures are passing to the Afro-Caribbean, thus restoring Black dignity.' Our girls failed to applaud. Distinguished outsiders would address pupils, staff, and parents – Herbert Read of course, Donald Winnicott the psychologist, Alexander, of the Alexander Technique. Hearing of this, the Dean volunteered his rather carnal knowledge of the court of Edward II which, intellectually unexacting, was long remembered.

Burgess Hill, known locally as 'Licensed Premises', possessed one notable advantage, the absence of a Staff Common Room. Teachers collect malice, envy, disappointments and frustrations like poisoned knick-knacks but, lacking a central meeting place there, they dispersed them less openly. Left much to myself I could have some simple pleasures. 'Do you like jam?' two smiling putti addressed a stolidly suited HM Inspector.

'Very much.'

'We're so glad. You're sitting in a great lump of it.' Simple lives, simple humour.

But I had seen more than simple jokes: an absence of snobbery, racial, cultural, social; an easy friendliness between generations; spontaneity and generosity. Children could acquire the self-assurance so often credited to Eton. I took one boy, Arthur, to a Chelsea party. Drinking well, if without refinement, he plucked my sleeve. 'Peter, who's that man? With the corrugated face?' 'That is Auden. W. H. Auden. Poet.' 'We'd better go over and have a word with him.' 'Well, I don't . . .' I, unwilling for the famous writer to be disturbed, looked with some disquiet as Arthur crossed the room.

'Ah, Auden! What are you up to these days?'

'I am writing an opera.'

'That's interesting. So am I. I'll tell you about it.'

He did so, at some length.

I learned finally that what should happen very seldom does happen. Stalin, Himmler and Goebbels were raised on Christian principles. Baron Stockmar proudly averred that the education of the future Edward VII was designed to make him the Perfect Man. Isaiah Berlin should have resented his Surbiton prep school and London public school, but was very happy at both. Surveys among the Hungarian Young Communist League revealed 17 per cent unaware of Lenin, 31 per cent ignorant of Stalin. In the French Revolutionary prison, the Conciergerie, the Duc de Châtelet, with centuries of high breeding and culture behind him, cried and complained after condemnation. He was rebuked by Catherine Eglée, a young whore from the rue Fromentau: 'Monsieur, in this place those without a name manage to get one; those who have a name should know how to live up to it.'

Individuals, despite a few thousand years of civilization, can harbour unconscious or conditioned prejudices. I had been arrested by a story told about himself by the benevolent, public-spirited, richly educated Gilbert Murray. During the war, he had entered a blacked-out railway carriage and, fatigued, querulous, found no seat. Inwardly he cursed 'the Jews' for having grabbed them all though, when his eyes finally became used to the faint light, he realized that none of the others were Jews.

I was to become further disillusioned with Burgess Hill, but can sometimes see those Fifties children, touched with radiance in butterfly summers, brimful of the future; then they became artists, editors, teachers, bird-fanciers, actresses, media-types, nuns, drug addicts, suicides, misfits, conformists, convicts, cosy parents and nothing in particular. They taught me much.

East London was different, but not totally different: I was giving talks in Stepney youth clubs, and roaming small street markets under flaring jets, strange foreign alleys, ribald pubs, listening. 'Treatin' me like coupla pot-'oles! Oo does 'e think 'e is? Big Farouk?'

The club adolescents, many of them Jewish, were outwardly aggressive, jeering, often ambitious but in ways I seldom discovered; poor, shabby, yet boastful, untrustworthy: 'School now. Once a new bloke came. So we crowded all our desks into one corner. So, coming in, he stood geezed up, just seeing an empty floor and us packed in the corner like statues. Dumb, not moving, see. Next day, we smiled an' smiled but only whispered. He'd see our lips, but 'ear nothing. He was old, smashed in the war. We smiled more, as if we loved 'im. 'is face kept twitching, began to fall to bits, and we didn't see 'im no more. Lovely!'

I was hired in 1955 to talk about Current Affairs, in which they had no interest. They could joke obscenely about 'that de-bugger, Mr Cigar' with his two raised fingers, but their MP was unknown to them, the Labour Council, like schoolteachers and social workers, merely ruffians out to plunder. They were quick-witted, sceptical, full of repartee and perky humour.

Hearing that I was a writer, they assumed I was indescribably rich but incurably innocent. Over table tennis, at the baths, in dirty bars, harmless as gorillas wrestling, they asked equivocal questions. 'Mate, was Shakespeare left-handed?' 'Did Jesus wear masks? Didn't 'e go on a secret mission, into the East? And weren't they not allowed to torture 'im?' This was interesting, because of an actual tradition that Jesus had indeed been ugly, even hunchbacked, with eyebrows meeting, as a precaution against mere sex appeal.

Their questions, however trivial, often seemed to mean something else. Did I remember the war? Was I sorry that the Germans had lost? I told them of the neat, affable Himmler, who confessed that if Hitler ever ordered him to hang himself, he would do so, yes, at once, the Führer always had his reasons. They stared, awed, admiring. Had Germany won, England would have had to learn. Learn what? 'Oh, like them Scouts.' The Nazi camps intrigued rather than shocked many, even Jews. 'Everythin' was upside down, wasn't it?' A view vaguely biblical, suggesting the last being first, the rich being sent empty away. Photographs of Bacon's paintings likewise stirred them, pricking nerves that responded to horror movies, prehistoric monsters, inarticulate fears. The atom bomb did not much concern them, save that it 'did in the Japs'.

Occasionally, they allowed me to read to them, but the effect was probably negligible. Salinger's Holden Caulfield had no supporters here. Girls disliked his attitude to his parents, some envying him for actually possessing parents; boys resented his swanky home, his pocketful of bucks. For them, America was Eldorado, Caulfield himself as phoney as those he despised, merely a rich kid biting the hands that fed him, a middle-class idler with money, taxis, girls, his seat at the table. Only one of his remarks did they applaud: 'I'm the most terrific liar you ever saw in your life.' Malraux and T. E. Lawrence they would have respected for the same reason.

There was challenge here, too, in the Fifties East End – incautiously I once spoke of 'slums' at which anger flared; what were slums, where were they? – where lively ignorance confronted all that I had learnt to respect and cherish. Political indifference was more refreshing than the fervour of Chinese children already intoning, 'Chairman Mao is dearer to us than our own parents.' My lot were interested in the Christie murders at 10 Rillington Place, fought for a sight of the gold-plated Daimler of Sir Bernard Docker and his flamboyant wife – soon banned from Monaco for insulting the princely flag. Executions fascinated them, but they ignored radio and TV pundits. They were ready to steal, seduce, fight and lie, but remained suspicious of charity, worthy intentions and power, mainly wishing to be left alone, to enjoy sensation. They had rituals without beliefs, wits sharpened by needs, hands poised for the main chance. They lived not in years or months, but by the minute, making an art of the short-cut, particularly in shops. A few did amiably rebuke me, in the name of the Young Communist League but, had I addressed them as 'proletariat' I would have at once lost them. They were independent.

'Dad' was frequently off-stage – in prison, chasing a girl – or a slightly sinister loafer. Sometimes he was unknown, occasionally 'in Korea', distant and nebulous as Orinoco or Samarkand had been at Burgess Hill, and imagined as vaguely occupied by Errol Flynn. One mum kept her husband's corpse beside her in bed for three weeks, wary of reporting his death to 'them'. Care of the elderly and the role of grandparents still existed, the family not yet divided by rehousing schemes, with front doors tightly locked, high-rise ghettos, and no pets allowed. I would sit with all generations in one room, impoverished but cleaner than Burgess Hill, munching buns, listening to gossip, rumour, accusation, black-market news. There was no generalized racial bias, though anger and violence might be directed at individuals. I felt their rank suspicion that they were continually being 'got at' by strangers. I began to be proud, grateful for their friendship.

Drugs were offered by bright-eyed children. 'It'll spice you up . . . sell those books of yours . . .' I realized Kipling's truth: 'All the earth is full of tales to him who does not drive away the poor from his door. The poor are the best of story-tellers, for they must lay their ear to the ground.' Again, Fifties London throughout confirmed Talleyrand's belief that Man is given speech in order to conceal his thought. I could seldom see where their teasing ended. 'Mozart ... 'e loved sums, teacher said. Dead, ain't 'e?' I had to understand by what was left unsaid, or said obliquely or in jest. As at Burgess Hill, it was best to pretend an ignorance even more substantial than it really was: young men and girls loved to explain, with patience and tedious detail, the workings of a gadget, the techniques of a gang, the rounds of a boxing match, the plot of some film. They needed a role, to be noticed, not only by would-be lovers.

Elder brothers, jealous of family favouritism, would inveigle younger ones into petty theft, to dislodge it. Some appeared anxious to disguise homosexual tendencies by fighting. Some, of high and obvious intelligence, were too shy, or disdainful, to ask a teacher's help, remaining illiterate, and drifting to crime as compensation. Few were resigned to the environment of neglect, grime, touts, tarts, swindles: a prison sentence or a fall of manna would be accepted with equal cynical cheeriness.

Once accepted, I was always welcome, sometimes as a butt. An old man, usually silent, suddenly pointed at me and, in a fake-Oxford drawl, said, 'The butler showed us in. His sec told us 'e was not at 'ome.'

'Can', he once asked, though retreating from a reply, 'your hands do things when you've told them not to?'

In time, they plied me with half-finished stories, expecting instant publication. The stories themselves were usually codes, messages, diaries, occasional warnings; often single sentences or disconnected paragraphs: 'Immense cunning lay over the streets like a cloud.' 'Many lived underground, undergoing considerable and voluptuous thoughts of big arches, colossal skyscrapers and islands all light but without traffic lights.' Some would surreptitiously leave writings on the floor, under a cup, impossible for me not to see: 'The child of a wandering step-mother grew up to adhere to strict frugality. Her ideas were capricious, her days too prolix, lustful to the last degree. A Pak fell for her, she regarded his love as coxcomb pathos and he was soon infamous to her, so he became profligate and diabolical, a laughing man but too fat.'

One youth exclaimed on a bright spring morning: 'I heard the sun today.' This was Len, aloof, older than the others, short, lean, scarred on face and hands, living in a hostel; adopted at 10, dishonourably discharged from the army at 19, tending to refer to himself in the third person. 'He's going out.' 'He's bored with you.' He would stand for long periods with his finger in a hole in the wall, but avoided girls and physical contact. I once found him beating a row of books. He would steal a tie, a box, make some tiny mark on them, thus convincing himself that they were his. He hated paying for a coffee, not, I realized, from meanness, but from inability to calculate the price and fear of being jeered at. He liked being with me, but on the unspoken condition that I did not talk. I often sat with people for hours, listening to them in unbroken silence, and, finally departing, they would thank me for my advice.

Len did once become friendly with a waitress, speaking little of her, but once muttering that she never laughed at him. He enjoyed hearing of cruelty to animals. 'There are too many of them. Always plenty more.' I encouraged him to write, and a week before he vanished, never again surfacing, he handed me, with unusual self-assurance, this: 'I am thinking of God. The reflection is of a face with eyes and mouth curiously like my own and yet not. The face moved in all directions from the ripples as the water drifted slowly down past the large white house in the fields. I looked to see whether it was somebody looking over me, but no, it wasn't. Yet it couldn't be my face because mine was reflected a bit below it. This worried me a lot. Then, sitting on grass, I wondered if I was mad as they say. They talked about this thing called God, whose face in the water was wiser but more cruel than mine. After sitting there, five minutes, or five months I realised that I had made a marvellous discovery, one face was lower than the other yet each was part of the other. This made me free. I would make people understand. I promised myself to be above pity or being sorry, which would only hold up my mission.'

Often I walked back, very late, past the broken cemeteries, ravaged docks, bombed churches and synagogues, finding tiny glimpses of the London of Sherlock Holmes and Jack the Ripper in a brazier, a patch of river mist, a bollard, a dray, a dim, lurching shape, and, from area stairs or basements, a growling snatch of patois, 'e's so dumb that 'e can't grow a nasturtium out of 'is sister's ear-'ole.' 'Your wife's run out on you, your gal 'as cattle-rash, your son-in-law's gone bust, your best pal 'ides 'is wallet and you're not too sure of your dog, and a voice comes down from bluddy 'eaven and something bangs you on the shoulder, and you 'ear "Never Mind".'

The Fifties were moving further from the war, Marshall Aid, Stalin, the Empire. Outside schools and youth clubs, patterns were later traced by journalists, though they were mostly unseen by me, intent on my private worlds. Vague fears and oppressions could coalesce in 'Ban the Bomb' being chalked everywhere, yelled by youth leaders, squawked by babies. Fear of the Bomb could add distance to the 'Generation Gap', an excuse to belabour the super-powers, an excuse to shirk work or responsibility, in a fatalistic trance. All were doomed, only instant pleasure was left. The Albemarle Report instanced adolescents' unease at the Russian-American policy of the balance of nuclear terror, and at the decline of Britain, once so great.

Liberal optimism had assumed that more education and freedom would release exceptional talents within almost everyone. This failed to happen. Education could provide enlightenment, but also discontent. Teachers, psychological tracts and advertisements fostered a belief that every child was exceptional. Extremist political parties excited young passions, but without obligation towards intelligence, and this produced results ever lamer. Considerable listlessness, disillusion, the resentments of 'mixed-up kids', were crystallized by James Dean's performance in the movie, *Rebel Without a Cause* (1955). The Century of the Common Man was threatening to become too commonplace for thousands still submerged. The Russells and Schweitzers, Einsteins and Eliots, Churchills and Attlees, Oliviers and Gielguds were far, far away, like Orion's Belt. Cities swarmed with the young who claimed that traditional ways of escape – from routine, mediocrity, adult authority, material deprivations accentuated by television displays of opulence – were being blocked. 'Everyone's against us.'

Other ways of escape were more easily available than volunteering for famine relief, agriculture, tree planting, canal restoration, nursing in distant lands. Violence, drugs, music, movies, dancing, television, science fiction, pornography, sex, idolatry and wishful thinking were ready outlets. Also glumness, suicide, retreat from reason. Much was disguised as 'anti-materialism' and 'protest' and had been anticipated by Aldous Huxley's doctrines of Eastern non-attachment, and by Maugham's novel, *The Razor's Edge*, though he himself was no promoter of austerity and spirituality, but of social and financial advance, civilized exchanges and hard work.

Jazz, pop songs and dancing helped one leap free of the earth. Clubs abounded, where Eddie Linden, North Country writer, could watch girlish boys and boyish girls, in 'the gyros, hydras, wheel-balances and wheatfields of dance'. Elvis Presley's early film, *Loving You*, convulsed millions. One admirer soon hailed him 'as the next best thing to God'. A black man, however, complained that to talk to Presley about coloured people was like talking to Hitler about Jews.

Like pop art, pop music incorporated itself with commerce, instant sensation, immediate comprehension, its crushing beat eliminating thought. Devotees claimed that visual and aural muscles, long flabby, were being revived: too many shapes and rhythms had been too long overlooked. By removing the implicit, the symbolic and the mysterious from vision and sound, the new cults rendered themselves more democratic, more communal, particularly helpful to those at odds with their parents. But the parents found the pop music rallies, transfixing vast audiences in emotional slavery, too close to Hitler's Nuremberg. Bill Haley's music, in *The Blackboard Jungle* (1955), set youth literally dancing in the aisles, their elders fleeing. Colin MacInnes rejoiced at intimations of a new culture, world harmony, even a rival administration. 'I'll report you to Elvis,' a youth threatened an old man who had remonstrated at his urinating on his doorstep. Haley himself, good-humoured, individualistic, arrived in London in 1957, greeted by massed banners and posters in a secular Ascension Day. He himself underwent some psychedelic sensations when being mistaken by an interviewer for Sir William Haley, ex-director of the BBC and Editor of *The Times*.

For many young, science fiction, 'Cleavage from Outer Space', as my pupil Arthur put it, was the only relevant literature; relevant to adventure, progress, technology, physics; hostile to domesticity, stuffiness, dead patriotism. Though usually lacking in wit, humour and scientific insight, and too often involving narrow stereotypes and implausible futuristic descriptions, it seemed also to contribute to imaginative speculation, and to the wide-eyed excitements, the wonder, alarm and unearthly colours too often enjoyed only by youth. I had a friend who was a sci-fi writer, prolific, though unreadable. He very generously gave me his novels, several a year, which guaranteed me a small unearned income at the local bookshop. Our friendship ceased in 1955 when, again, a thick expensive book arrived. I read a page, decided that it was not a novel, then hastened to the bookshop. Next week, he and his wife invited me to dinner, and I rashly congratulated him on his autobiography. 'Malcolm . . . it rang so absolutely true . . . honesty . . . self-revelation . . . so much that I've always suspected . . .' The atmosphere changed to frost, a look of hatred from the wife, a bright scarlet flush upon Malcolm. With a muttered excuse, I slunk into his study and opened the book. It was not an autobiography, nor indeed Science Fiction, but a novel about an impotent man.

Expectations generated by sci-fi seemed to climax in the first Russian sputnik in 1957, the year of British H-Bomb tests on Christmas Island. 'The Old World has been put to flight,' Ben, a Burgess Hill pupil assured me, with an expression of pity, for myself, for America, for the aged. Only the Dean was pessimistic. 'The last time they did it they caused the Gobi Desert.'

As early as 1959, thousands of adolescents were buying posters of Che Guevara, Castro's lieutenant in the successful invasion of that year, making a dramatic turn on a motorcycle as he sped on his crusade for freedom at whatever cost. 'That', a girl told me, 'is what Christ should have been.' Castro and Guevara had all that appealed to active youth: they were anti-American, anti-imperialist, anti-ordinary; in battle-dress, with his gun and cigar, his beret, his fearless smile, Che was a call to revolt, but also a rejection of Chesterton's belief that it is common sense that is always revolutionary. That he had been a boy gang-leader, smashing street lamps in sympathy with an electricians' strike, was an excellent credential. He called himself 'the New Man', no longer victimized by old ideas of existence, class, art, dedicated to the enslaved, the poor. 'The true revolutionary', he wrote, 'is guided by strong feelings of love.' Fighting brutal monopolists, destined to martyrdom, trained as a doctor, explorer and polemicist, he was an avatar from a Tolkien novel, a saviour clubbing down evil giants and malicious dwarfs. The world over, the young could be Lazarus or perhaps the sleeping princess awaiting the transforming touch.

Cuba needs Robespierres, wrote Fidel Castro, much admired by Graham Greene and young middle-class British enthusiasts, in 1954. Kenneth Minogue wrote of Guevara, after his death in Bolivia, in 1967: 'Here is a major exponent of communism outflanking the appeal of capitalism on its own individualistic ground.' This would not have appealed to the Beats – Burroughs, Ginsberg, Kerouac – whose jazz, rambling verse, unexacting versions of Zen Buddhism, communal pleasures, rejected bourgeois routine and security for the improvized life. Jack Kerouac's novel, *On the Road*, was a potted saga of hitching and driving across America, a headlong romance of the freedoms of speed, danger, space, drugs, jazz, new sights, new people. Oddly, this fervid laureate of the open road could not himself drive, and later died of drink in his mother's suburban home, supporting the Vietnam war.

In a widely read essay, 'The White Negro' (1958), Norman Mailer classified the Beats as hipsters, rejecting order, continuity, unambiguous language, and demanding the immediate thrill, affirmation of the barbarian within us. All this was for youth a welcome change from the values of their elders, from the outlook that allowed the *Sunday Times* in 1949 to greet Mailer's novel, *The Naked and the Dead*, in an idiom mouldy as rot. 'No decent man could leave it lying about in the house, or know without shame that his women folk are reading it.'

In the New Towns and universities, in suburbs, on the tube, at bars, the young and would-be young ostentatiously carried Allen Ginsberg's poem *Howl*, and William Burroughs's *Junkie* (1953) and *The Naked Lunch* (1959), celebrating drug-addiction, with homosexuality added. The latter novel sounded an enthralling overthrow of barriers, though some barriers were only imagined: 'The only people for me are the mad ones, the ones who are mad to live, mad to talk, mad to be saved, desirous of everything at the same time, the ones who never yawn or say a commonplace thing, but burn, burn, burn like fabulous yellow roman candles, exploding like spiders across the stars.'

A Stepney youth muttered, beside me, 'There's the fun . . . the risk of being jumped, being pounced on . . . a sort of speed in the waiting, in all of it.' Dons recalled Webster: 'I glory that I call this act my own.' And Nietzsche: 'Whoever has a *Why* to live for can endure almost any *How*.' Forerunning 'doing your own thing' was 'for kicks', the gratuitous act, replacing things that were 'not done'; self-expression, the separation of Being from Nothing, currently being discussed more academically abroad, by Sartre and Camus. In Paris in 1962, high-school teenagers, from secure and comfortable homes, placed a plastic bomb in the flat of André Malraux, and blinded a 4-year-old girl. They had no political interest, no coherent excuse. On Yorkshire moors, Myra Hindley and Ian Brady, asserting their own will and superiority, murdered two children and a youth, of whom they knew nothing, in whom they had no personal concern.

12

Questions

THE HALF-CENTURY HAD been a gruesome gathering of unreason, savagery, organized ignorance and methodical exterminations, as though time was being reversed. In Shakespeare's *Julius Caesar*, Cinna the poet is mistaken by the vengeful mob for the Cinna who helped murder Caesar. He protests, but the mob no longer cares for truth and justice. 'Kill him for his bad verses.' In the 1934 Night of the Long Knives, the Munich SS, hunting the anti-Nazi Dr Ludwig Schmidt, found only Dr Wilhelm Schmidt, a philosopher, whom they nevertheless dragged off to Dachau and eventually killed.

Revelations were still seeping through into the Fifties that would have startled much-despised Victorian or Habsburg statesmen into bemused incredulity. Hitler had promised 'a fairy tale' and grotesquely succeeded, with the usual premises reversed. Primo Levi, gifted chemist and writer, whilst a prisoner at Ravensbruck, saw women spending their days shovelling sand from dunes under a scorching sun. They worked in a circle, each slave forced to move sand from her pile to that of her right-hand neighbour, a torture totally meaningless, as all sand returned to its original place. After the war, Levi offended a German lady who asked him where he had learnt his fluent German. 'At Auschwitz!'

Marguerite Duras's husband, Robert Antelme, published in 1957 his memories of Buchenwald where he confronted skeletal figures and expected them to chirp or low: 'a vast triangle of striped rags, crooked arms, sharp elbows, purple hands, huge feet; open mouths aimed at the ceiling, closed eyes in bony faces covered with blackened skin, death-like skulls, each shape endlessly resembling every other, inert and as if laid out in the slime of a shallow pond'.

Behaviour, even amongst the SS, and the guards and executioners, often volunteers from the prisoners themselves, was unpredictable. Here too was the terrible truth that religion, art, scholarship, philosophy and professed political convictions seldom availed in the clawing search for survival, or often concealed continuing political conflicts far worse than anything animal. Love, stoicism and selflessness were shown by unlikely people, balanced by more who displayed the vilest contempt for their fellows. 'We knew that without budging we could watch a friend being beaten to the ground, and that along with the desire to smash the beater's face, teeth, nose, under our feet, we could also feel, voiceless and deep within us, our own body's luck. "It's not me who's getting it"' – a confirmation of what Shaw had told Virginia Woolf, in 1940: 'I am fond of saying that twelve hours hunger will reduce any saint, artist or philosopher to the level of a highwayman.'

Throughout the Fifties, war, and its even more hideous offshoots, were being debated; traced to male vanity and sexual aggression, to capitalism's emasculation of sexual vitality, to old men's jealousy of the young, to wobbling trade cycles and economic imperialism, to traumatic memories, to disappointment with religion and science, to 'nature', to the frustration of those better educated but ill-employed or not employed at all, to the demons, sin, or an imperfect balance within the human brain and nervous system. Much was confused and contradictory. I met socialists who were anti-Black and devotees of Napoleon, conservatives who loathed Churchill and deplored the Empire, marvellous writers who were foul-mouthed racialists.

Inevitably, beliefs and institutions, some established under the Roman Empire, some originating even earlier, now seemed at risk. Arnold Toynbee reiterated that civilizations collapsed not, essentially, through war and politics, but through suicide, loss of spiritual morale. Where, people were debating in 1950, was God in the death camps? In those camps, and under Nazi occupation, no church or political party had sustained consistent resistance, no dogma had been strengthened; the Resistance had largely emerged from brave individuals, miscellaneous though dedicated groups, and those needing brute revenge for old scores. After the war, over 40,000 people were killed or jailed by the French Resistance, few with proper trials, a number approximate to that of the victims of the French Revolution. Those who did resist, of course, could awe the rest of us. We read of Dietrich Bonhöffer, Christian pastor and German patriot, who, after agonizing moral doubts, agreed to join the July 1944 plot to murder Hitler, for which he was hanged. He wrote: 'It happened that an entire nation followed a buffoon, and yet Adolf Hitler was obeyed and his praises sung right up to the catastrophe. Therefore it can happen again.' Thousands, well-educated, attractive and amiable, had, like Beckett's tramps Vladimir and Estragon, wondered 'What shall we do now?' But, in crisis, myopic, susceptible to spurious charisma, or fearful, they dithered, heedless of a Bonhöffer; 'Freedom comes only through action, not through words taking wing.'

It had become inescapable to me that while human behaviour changes with circumstances – ferocious Vikings and Swiss transform to peaceful neighbours and sedate bankers – human nature had remained unchanged, at least since the Ice Age, and an Ibsen, or Dürrenmatt in his play *The Visit*, could starkly expose the ferocities, vindictiveness, destructive boredom or greed lurking within the peaceful and sedate. In the camps, though raised in civilized peace, Dutch and Norwegians could behave as badly or, less often, as well as anyone else: Pope Pius XII was to be arraigned in Rolf Hochhuth's play *The Representative* for indifference to Jewish sufferings; a Jew, Josef Franck, had led the Croatian anti-Semitic party of the Pure Right; Father Krunoslaw Draganovic, the Croatian scholar and a Red Cross official praised by Pius XII, had supported Catholic persecution of orthodox Serbs, though his fellow-countryman, the Catholic Bishop Strossmayer, was tolerant, wise, and courageous. A devout Catholic, Richard Korherr, was Himmler's Inspector of Statistics. From Münster Cathedral, Bishop von Galen denounced the Gestapo as murderers. Cardinal Gerlier of Lyon sheltered the French Grand Rabbi from the SS and publicly urged help for the Jews; the SS General Werner Best allowed scores of Danish Jews to escape to Sweden and, in Ruthenia, the Nazi General Krube saved many Russian Jews. Count Stauffenberg, Catholic anti-Hitler martyr, had once hailed the Night of the Long Knives as 'the lancing of a boil'.

If sinners clearly outnumbered saints, the latter had existed, by no means all of them Christian. In Camus' novel, *The Plague* (1947), Tarrou asks, 'Can one be a saint without God? – that's the problem, in fact the only problem I'm up against.' He complicates what is actually simple. Dr Rieux replies that heroism and sanctity do not really attract him. In language very much of the Fifties, he explains, 'What interests me is – being a man.' Tarrou admits that this is actually more ambitious than striving for sainthood. Modern saints, few of us recognized until the Fifties. I heard George Macleod, founder of the Iona Community, 'an uncomfortable socialist and a reluctant pacifist', preach in 1954 about Elizabeth Pilenko, in a sermon more dramatic than any current play. She had been imprisoned under Tsardom for protesting against intolerance; released by Lenin's regime in 1918, she was jailed again, for the same protest. Years later, in Occupied France, as 'Sister Marie', she sheltered French Jews in her home until she was arrested and sent to Ravensbruck, where her conduct as healer and comforter won respect even from the SS. One day, seeing a young woman, a stranger, weeping bitterly in the death queue, she swiftly rescued her by changing places, and finally met her end.

More controversial, more publicized, was Simone Weil who, in an essay on Homer, argued that in his world, as in today's, force was central to a world of horror, transforming people into things, vulnerable only to chance, with retribution its penalty. Europe, she felt, had produced nothing to match the simple, epic genius of the *Iliad*: people might rediscover that genius 'when they learn that there is no refuge from fate, and learn not to admire force, not to hate the enemy, nor to scorn the unfortunate'. Men, for all their brutality and excess, are morally superior to the gods who, purposeless, capricious and malicious, lack souls. Man, striving to overcome necessity, in rare luminous moments awakens his own soul, and through love, hospitality and courage against hopeless odds transcends force and horror; the gods are more guilty than humanity.

She believed passionately in freedom, freedom from class, falsehood, the dogmatic State, though for long she was politically gullible, admiring the Paris Commune as 'socialist', and Stalin's Russia as 'the workers' State'. Concern for her fellow-creatures, in her work in factories identifying herself with them ever more closely, had secured her sanctity in the Fifties, though her death in London in 1943 could have benefited none. She starved herself, her doctor, Henrietta Broderick, attesting: 'She was slightly mentally unbalanced ... the reason she gave for not eating was that she could not eat when she thought of the French starving in France.' Fifties saints also existed: Vinobha Bhave, who tramped India to induce landowners to surrender land to the poor; Danilo Dolci, dedicated to the Sicilian dispossessed. Their religion I do not know.

Arthur Koestler's *The Yogi and the Commissar* (1945) was still widely read in 1950. Given to me by David Sylvester to improve my understanding, it posed the historical duel between those striving to improve the world by individual transformation and regeneration, and those who support mass compulsion. Neither was impeccable. The Yogi could ignore bayoneting and rape, septic childbirth, villages without sewage, trachoma – holding spiritual blindness far worse than physical blindness. He and the Commissar had more in common than my own mentors – Shaw, Russell, Nansen, Chekhov – had suggested. 'No honest socialist', Koestler wrote in 1952, 'can write a survey of the left's defeats without accounting for the irrational factor in mass-psychology.' He developed Ernst Jünger's 'anti-capitalist nostalgia of the masses': 'It is idiosyncratic against the rationalism, the shallow optimism, the ruthless logic, the arrogant self-assurance, the Promethean attitudes of the Nineteenth Century; it is attracted by mysticism, romanticism, the irrational ethical values, the medieval twilight.'

Vast atrocities questioned the future of the churches, perhaps Christianity itself, though the religious instinct remained powerful. 'The most beautiful and deepest experience a person can have is the sense of the mysterious. It is the underlying principle of religion as well as of all serious endeavour in art and science. He who has never had this experience seems to me, if not dead, then at least blind.' Einstein, outside all dogma, concluded that he was religious in this sense. Bergman's films showed passionate yearnings, often religious, if scarcely denominational, though he was the son of a pastor. Many agnostics probably agreed. Certainly, ancient dogmas needed revision, reinterpretation, re-translation, often rejection. It could be plausibly maintained that nine-tenths of the Gospels was hearsay, repetition of legend, later interpolations, verbal ambiguity (Virgin could also mean 'young woman', Carpenter, 'scholar'), fantasy, and purloining of the best of contemporary teaching, usually Pharisaical.

Religion, in 1950, was as vigorously discussed as it had been in 1939, when the squat brown volumes of the Rationalist Press – Renan, T. H. Huxley, Russell, Wells, Llewellyn Powys, Winwood Reed, ex-Father Joseph McCabe – and the theological antics of Bishop Barnes of Birmingham, Conrad Noel, Marxist Vicar of Thaxted, and Hewlett Johnson, Dean of Canterbury, had readily convinced me that Christianity would be dead within five years. Religion could be no more than the romanticizing of survival tactics, with its convictions of an immortal soul, personal immortality and salvation.

Holden Caulfield spoke for many of his contemporaries: 'I'm a sort of atheist. I like Jesus and all, but I don't care too much for most of the other stuff in the Bible. Take the Disciples, for instance. They annoy the hell out of me, if you want to know the truth. They were all right after Jesus was dead and all, but while He was alive, they were about as much use to Him as a hole in the head.'

We had at best to scrutinize fundamentals. The Reformation had missed the chance of transforming God from *He* to *It*: defined by Augustine as a darkness, deep and dazzling. A personal God, all-powerful, all-good, all-loving, was now less credible than an imperfect, ceaseless experimenter, Shaw's Life Force, apt to make mistakes, dedicated to creation, opposed by some blindly destructive element. Salvation might be in assisting this creativity. St John's Gospel appeared to speak best for the Fifties: 'No man has seen God, ever. If we love one another, God dwells in us, and his love is perfected in us.' Possibly, *by* us. God could be the result, not the cause, of creation, a 'Son of God' the life force at its fullest. It remained easier to find reasons for belief in immortality than evidence for it. Personal eternal life could be revised into an impersonal life eternal, continued through the genes and in the effort of each individual against destruction. 'Whoever heeds my words and trusts in he who sent me has grasped Eternal Life – has already passed from death to life.'

This could be in the mystical and Mystery tradition of illumination, spiritual rebirth, permanent enrichment, leading to 'heaven', what W. B. Yeats called 'an improvement of the spirit', a gloss on the text of St Francis of the Desert, 'whoever knows himself, knows God'. Original sin, Newman's 'terrible aboriginal tragedy', was more easy to credit after the war than before. The Sermon on the Mount could be seen as a handbook for survival until the rapidly approaching end of the world, which did not occur. In the continuing world of Beria and Himmler, 'Respect strangers' was more helpful than 'Love your enemies'. Jesus could be seen, along with Socrates, Alexander, Virgil, and Marcus Aurelius, as stages of consciousness, reborn daily, latent in everyone. Sacraments seemed to be losing validity, though prayer, purposeful and concentrated thought, could still effect change. Rare moments of love, rapture and understanding might be prolonged into a further dimension, the Kingdom here upon earth. Prayer could be changed from petition or wheedling to vigorous technique. In one apocryphal gospel there is a passage: 'His disciples said to Him, "When will the Kingdom come?" Jesus said: "It will not come by expectations: none will say "See here" or "See there". But the Father's Kingdom is spread throughout the world and none sees it.'

The Jesuit Teilhard de Chardin discovered a personal mine of religious vitality, displayed in *The Phenomenon of Man*, attempting to unite an evolving universe, explicable or otherwise, by such concepts as 'Noogenesis' and 'Christogenesis', the supernatural merging with the scientific, astrology and numerology not disdained. The effort was much praised by Julian Huxley and, less surprisingly, by Philip Toynbee who found 'wonderful' the notion of an evolutionary God, a cosmic Great Presence, Supreme Consciousness, a Centre of Centres which the universe reaches by gradual stages. Love, Teilhard explained, is at the start of evolution, originating in the unity of atom and molecule. 'Love in all its subtleties is nothing more and nothing less, than the more or less direct trace marked on the heart of the element by the psychical convergence of the universe upon itself.' Exactly. This, however, was castigated by the Nobel prizewinner for medicine (1960), Sir Peter Medawar, in his *The Art of the Soluble*. 'Instead of wringing our hands over the Human Predicament, we should attend to those bits of it which are wholly remarkable, above all to the gullibility which makes it possible for people to be taken in by such a bag of tricks as this.'

A creative residue of traditional belief pervaded T. S. Eliot's *Four Quartets*, published between 1935 and 1942, and gratifying a mood widespread after the Second World War, which, like the poetry of St John of the Cross, transcended both narrow sectarianism and Modernism. Eliot fused East and West, Catholicism and Anglicanism, paradox and mysticism, the everyday and the scientific, epochs and moments, in a plea for renewal of spiritual appetite, the chance of grace, the flashes of illumination, coalescing in its perennial images of water, fire, rose, yew, with injunctions to prayer, observance, discipline, thought and action, marks of stability in a confused society, and a sense of illumination running throughout history:

> ... Not the intense moment
> Isolated, with no before and after,
> But a lifetime burning in every moment
> And not the lifetime of one man only
> But of old stones that cannot be deciphered.
>
> (from *East Coker*)

Ancient themes were restated through a modern sensibility, in cycles of complexity and simplicity, cross-references of suffering and ecstasy, garden and Blitz, lonely chapel and the London Underground, making a map of the soul in which Krishna and Buddha, Dante and Julian of Norwich, Milton and Eliot himself are all contemporaries; music is more vibrant for being unheard, stillness more graphic than movement, the invisible as vivid as the observed, and metaphors reveal further metaphors as the self achieves further transcendences.

More exclusive oriental mysticism was propagated by some of the Fifties young, seldom tested very rigorously. Correct breath-control, right posture, concentrated meditation, would induce right thought, leading to illumination, salvation, higher consciousness, though historians and travellers with Eastern experience were often sceptical.

Official Christianity remained, not greatly impaired by the discovery of the Dead Sea Scrolls and other antique documents in Jordan, Palestine and Egypt, these still provoking quarrels. Some gritty Christians must have applauded the Lutheran pastor who refused Communion to Hermann Göring on his last night in the condemned cell. Some retained a powerful sense of guidance by a personal God. Having retired from his job as British executioner in 1956, Albert Pierrepoint affirmed, in traditional style, 'my firm belief that I was chosen by a higher power for the task which I took up, that I was put on earth especially to do it, and that this same higher power, after protecting me through my career, influenced and governed me'. When a humanist, Margaret Knight, gave a short and mild radio talk on her reasons for atheism, thousands reacted in fury.

Christianity had consoled the Mandelstams during their dark agonies, as it had the French engineer, Colonel Michel Hollard, whose wartime espionage in France transmitting reports of the V1 rocket, General Sir Brian Horrocks claimed 'literally saved London'. Captured by the Gestapo in 1944, he was beaten, tortured and starved, but survived. Russell, Sartre and Ayer might tell him his beliefs were superstitious nonsense but, for him, argument was unnecessary. Whatever Belloc, Waugh and Greene might have thought, much of the Catholic world, oppressed by wartime guilts, suspicions and attacks, and still threatened by Stalin's battalions, must have been relieved by Pius XII's pronouncement of the Immaculate Conception of the Virgin Mary in 1950.

Jung still remained vigorous, and was postulating that the Christian Trinity was a proposition not yet completed. To project wholeness, integration, it needed the extra elements not only of the female but also of evil, to represent fully the divine within Man. Indeed, in an ancient tradition, God had a wife, Anath, eliminated from memory by jealous priests, like party hacks expunging a Trotsky; furthermore, Lucifer, son of morning, had been God's favourite. Jung had outlived Ellis and Jones, Freud and Adler, and some of his own beliefs. He had earlier held, like Thomas Mann, that Nazi 'Wotanism' had represented psychic rebirth, collaboration with natural instincts, archetypal myth, primeval elements of harvest, fire, leaders, purposeful comradeship, that healed and motivated humanity. He distinguished between the 'Aryan' and the Jewish unconscious, and saw Nazis as an inevitable and healthy reaction to blighted cities, polluted forests and maltreated animals. 'Yes,' he admitted later, 'I slipped up.' His analytical psychology and theory of the 'collective unconscious' had a considerable following in Fifties Britain, was cited by Arnold Toynbee, more often by J. B. Priestley who thought him a successor to William Blake;

Herbert Read's firm produced an edition of his writings. His theory of Psychological Types was a relief from dogmas of the tyranny of class, race, sect and gender. His reputation as a guru was surprisingly little sullied by reports of having seduced his young patient, Sabine Spielrein, promising her mother to desist once her bill had been paid. In 1952, he was addressing a young priest in terms reassuring to much of the British public, ignoring Wotan, repressed sexuality and the death-wish. Some years later, he repeated the gist: 'I find all my thoughts circle around God like the planets around the sun, and are as irresistibly attracted by Him. I would feel it to be the grossest sin to oppose any resistance to this thought.'

He claimed to possess a spirit guide, Philemon, who helped him contact the dead. In *Flying Saucers* (1959), he considered them as mandalas projected from the unconscious, the image of the eternal elements in the psyche united in completeness, a visible expression in an age of anxiety, fear, frustration and disillusion amongst people hitherto lacking integration. Scholars had traced UFOs back to primitive drawings and stone circles, but in the Fifties they were being consistently reported, sometimes logged, by airforces, studied not least in the White House and the Pentagon. Power is always concerned with superstition, much of it being itself superstition. Four space aliens reputedly landed in Texas from a machine whose prototype had been described by the prophet Ezekiel. Lord Dowding, victor of the Battle of Britain, believed that invisible and deathless spirits had landed from outer space.

Jung had taken seriously medieval 'psychic astrology' and alchemy as symbolic evaluations of personality and literal techniques of spiritual ascent, usually disguised from the authorities as magical hocus-pocus. He described his ominous dreams before friends' deaths. Before his mother's, he dreamed of a gigantic bloodstained wolf – Wolf of the Wild Hunter, of Wotan, gatherer of the dead, Wolf who devoured Wotan himself. In 1946, he republished his essay on Wotan, an apologia for Teutonic paganism, a revival of the gods, the immemorial and eternal regenerative instincts. He had rebelled against Freud's conviction of the domination of sex, but retained many Freudian teachings: 'By evaluating dreams as the most important source of information concerning the unconscious process, Freud returned to humanity a tool that had seemed lost forever.' He claimed to have seen the Wild Hunt and procession of the dead, over Bollingen. Freud himself, in 1911, had accepted honorary membership of the Society of Psychical Research and once said that, had he another life, he would have concentrated on this. Aldous Huxley belonged to the Ghost Club of Great Britain.

Freud's erstwhile associate, Wilhelm Reich, went further, believing that space-beings assisted him in controlling wind and weather. Reich had been expelled by Freud from his inner circle, by the Communist Party from all its circles, and later believed himself a spatial prophet. His 'orgone box', allegedly transmitting electro-chemical energies to cure human diseases, helped destroy charming but credulous Neville Bewley, who had taught Peregrine Worsthorne at one school, myself at another.

Koestler had stated that faith was wondrous, not only capable of moving mountains but of making one believe that a herring is a race horse. Increasingly concerned with the paranormal, he eventually endowed a university research Chair for this. The war, if anything, had strengthened, if not formal Christianity, at least astrology, spiritualism, clairvoyance, reincarnation and telepathy, all flourishing during the Fifties, inciting many questions. 'Life After Death Proved' was a frequent poster on the London Underground, advertising the medium Ronald Strong. Nehru and Peron (and later Nancy Reagan) consulted astrologers; atheist regimes in Moscow and in Prague had begun spending lavishly on astrological computers and paranormal research; independent Ghana in 1955 forbade the use of magic in elections. The American clairvoyant Jeanne Dixon foretold the fate of the Kennedy brothers, and clairvoyance was used in extremity by the CID. Julian Huxley, humanist rationalist, was now urging that all clues, like ESP, to untapped human possibility should be explored. In crisis, Winston Churchill, Charles Lindbergh, John Masefield and Robert Graves all felt they had received paranormal aid. Graves would confide that he made important decisions only under a full moon and that he had twice reached heaven: first when supposed dead in the Great War, and later when helped by the Mexican mushroom drug, he met the Mexican Dionysus and Semele. In Britain and France, witchcraft was reported as increasing, particularly in wealthier suburbs.

One instance crystallized a mood which I think was then widely felt, the mood which responds to traditional icons and images, feeling them beyond sectarian beliefs, like Jung's archetypes. Thus the Crucifixion affected Francis Bacon, a non-believer, who told David Sylvester that he had always been very much moved by pictures about slaughterhouses and meat, which directly related to the Crucifixion. 'There've been extraordinary photographs which have been done of animals just being taken up before they were slaughtered; and the smell of death. We don't know, of course, but it appears by these photographs that they're so aware of what is going to happen to them, they do anything to attempt to escape.'

Bacon suggested that the iconographic power was, in comprehensible human behaviour, the effect perhaps more compelling and urgent, more concerned with real compassion and possible redemption, an individual change of heart, than were grandiose theological notions about saving the world and conquering sin and death.

In the larger world there was an unexpected interpolation which gave some promise of combining antique theology with humane realism. A new Pope, John XXIII, began his pontificate in 1959 with a surprising demand. 'Let us open the windows'. Dialogues with other religious groupings began, not least, after two thousand years of intolerance, with Jewry. John's jovial, down-to-earth simplicity did not lack shrewdness. When asked how many people worked in the Vatican, he replied, 'About half.'

13

1956: A Change of Mood

LIKE ANY YEAR, one expected 1956 to show a mixture of the ignoble, the virtuous, the atrocious and the accidental; it gave no more promise than usual of actual crisis. However, early on I was told a story by an important member of the Foreign Office which gave me little confidence in the judgement or priorities of the place. His wife's brother had died. He had been worried because, the man being an impoverished nonentity, no one would attend the unnecessarily expensive funeral, so he had exerted pressure on grand friends to come to the wretched fellow's obsequies. But he and his wife had been astonished, then affronted, by a very large crowd of the poor and insignificant who had swamped St James's, Piccadilly, actually commandeering seats reserved for the grandees. 'How extraordinary. I couldn't help feeling that our family name had been tarnished by such people. They prayed too loud, they sang too fervently.'

President Eisenhower had five times rejected proposals to A-bomb China, though Americans were officially assisting the French against Vietnam Communists at Dien Bien Phu, where artillery bases were named after the French commander's mistresses. McCarthyism had passed its worst and an associate of McCarthy, Richard Nixon, repeated his promise of two years previously, that he was quitting politics. Britain seemed tolerably on course. The London American, Shirley Robin Letwin, whose essay *Against Tolerance* occasioned some heat, reflected: 'In a world accustomed to thinking that men must either submit or rebel, England has stood out as a country whose people did neither.' People around me appeared quietly complacent.

In China, despite Edward Heath vouching for Mao's 'delightful sense of humour', Fou Hsiao-t'ung, author of *Peasant Life in China*, was pleading for a chance of redemption, and had publicly to confess four-teen crimes. 'I have committed treason, gravest of crimes. But for the Party awakening me from madness, I cannot envisage what other crimes I might have done.' Two hundred and forty-two thousand had already fled from East Germany since the war. In Russia, Pasternak's *Dr Zhivago* was rejected for publication and the young poet Yevgeny Yevtushenko imagined, in 'Stalin's Heirs', the dictator in his coffin, not dead but dozing, contemplating a grim day of return. The poet urged:

> And I appeal now, at this instant
> to our rulers to double and treble
> the guards at Stalin's stone,
> that he may never rise again . . .

Alexander Solzhenitsyn, after eight years in a labour camp for criticizing Stalin, was working as a teacher, and preparing his massive indictment of the Gulag system.

In Britain, penalties for adult homosexuality were being relaxed, perhaps assisted by three widely read novels – Gore Vidal's *The City and the Pillar* (1948), Mary Renault's *The Charioteer* (1953), and James Baldwin's *Giovanni's Room* (1956) – treating homosexuality not as a corrupting perversion but as an unsensational matter of course. In 1957, the Wolfenden Report successfully advised the legalization of homo-sexual acts between consenting adults. Jean Genet was telling Sartre that homosexuality was a way of symbolically confronting death: 'Unable to consider Death rationally, I look at it symbolically by refus-ing to continue the world.' Less sententious is a story I have acquired from Ted Morgan who, in his biography of Somerset Maugham, reports that Churchill told Maugham that he had once gone to bed with a man – Ivor Novello – 'to see what it was like'. 'What was it like?' 'Musical!'

Thousands of childhoods had been affected by Walter de la Mare, who died in 1956. Eliot had written of his whispered incantations which allowed free passage to the phantoms of the mind. De la Mare's visions of lonely travellers, the quiet steeps of dreamland, the mad prince and the haunted garden seemed at odds with Auden's dictum: 'Poetry is not magic. Insofar as poetry or any of the arts can be said to have an ulterior purpose, it is by telling the truth, to disenchant and disintoxicate.' De la Mare's 'Napoleon' may have satisfied this.

> What is the world, soldiers?
> It is I;

I, this incessant snow,
This northern sky;
Soldiers, this solitude through which we go
Is I.

Auden himself subsequently compiled a selection of de la Mare's verse.

The Dean continued his researches into the Auric Egg, the Etheric Double, the debt of the Third Reich to the planet Pluto. In St James's Park, the inevitable stranger, swarthy, bearded, saw me with my notebook and at once introduced himself, his accent thick as the Dean's vision of Mussolini's aura: 'I am Somerset Maugham.' At my badly concealed surprise, he explained, a little warily, as if to an inquisitive child: 'The real one is an imposter. Vile man.'

The year 1956 was lively for the arts. Giraudoux, Hochhuth, Coward and Priestley had plays staged in London, which Brecht's Berliner Ensemble visited, Brecht himself dying that year, a Communist millionaire in worker's uniform, his riches slyly secured in capitalist Switzerland. Bergman's *The Seventh Seal*, Kagan's *Baby Doll* and Vidor's *War and Peace* were in the cinemas; Lampedusa's *The Leopard*, W. H. Whyte's *The Organisation Man*, and Angus Wilson's *Anglo-Saxon Attitudes* were in the bookshops. Ben Nicholson won the Guggenheim International painting award. At the Whitechapel Art Gallery, Richard Hamilton presented an exhibition, 'This is To-morrow', a miscellany of serious and Pop art, juke-box fantasies, science fiction, novel domestic gadgetry, shapes and designs dazzling with their futuristic possibilities. Lawrence Alloway wrote that it was dedicated to the concept of design as a human activity, devoted to the possibility of collaboration between architects, painters and sculptors hitherto obstructed by socio-psychological and aesthetic disunities. The spectator had the responsibility of ejecting conditioned reflexes. He had to discard such concepts as The English Way of Life, the Teachings of Christ, One's Duty, Industrial Art, Fine Furniture and Good Taste . . . in favour of Confusion, Fog, Disregard for the Ordinary Decencies, Luck, Organized Chaos and a crucial Blow Below the Belt. The catalogue exhorted: 'Remember this is the language of vision. When the foreigner speaks you do not say "I do not understand, therefore it is nonsense." You learn the language, you must open your eyes and see . . . The man whose taste stops at the Twentieth Century hides in the shelter of convention.'

Much of this, even the delicately observed nuances of class, speech and taste in the English Novel, leant towards what Rilke felt was the world of Reality, in contrast to the world of News. The latter, however, crushed almost all else when, in March, Nikita Khrushchev blew open the sky at the Twentieth Soviet Communist Party Conference, sensationally indicting Stalin for the pre-war Party purges, frame-ups and executions, the thousands of senior officers shot, the mass terror directed not only at the remnants of 'the defeated exploiting classes' – 'Many thousands of honest and innocent Communists have died from this monstrous falsification of such cases.' Of the 139 members and candidates of the Seventeenth Conference in 1934, 70 per cent were killed. Stalin had sanctioned 'the most brutal violation of socialist legality, and torture and oppression'. Khrushchev revealed Lenin's last letter to Stalin, rebuking him for gross rudeness to his wife, and querying whether their personal relations could endure. He detailed crass wartime mistakes, the mass deportations, the self-glorification, with Stalin becoming even more capricious, irritable and brutal, his persecution mania reaching unbelievable proportions, cleverly exploited by Beria. This secret speech was leaked to the American State Department by a Party source, probably Polish. It lit fuses throughout Eastern Europe, and Russian troops invaded Poland and East Germany to crush strikes and incipient revolt.

Khrushchev himself was no Tennysonian knight. He had long toadied to Stalin; with the secret police boss, Yezhov, and Molotov, he supervised the 1936 purge in the Ukraine where, having liquidated his predecessor, he became governor. He purged 163 of the 166 members of the Ukraine Central Committee. 'By lifting their hands against Comrade Stalin they lifted their hands against the very best that mankind possesses. For Stalin is hope, he is expectation; he is the beacon to guide all progressive humanity.' Here, in anti-Semitic territory, he intervened to pardon natives who had collaborated with Nazis in massacring Jews; he connived with Stalin in killing Jews, writers and nationalists. In Poland in 1956, his own grinning anti-Semitism was blatant: 'Too many Abrahamovitches in here.'

He and Bulganin visited England that year, the first such occasion since the arrival of Tsar Alexander I, victorious ally against Napoleon. Their reception was more amiable than rapturous, though at a dinner given them by the Labour National Executive, Khrushchev laid at Britain's door responsibility for Hitler's invasion of Russia. George Brown, rude, callous and alcoholic, no respecter of persons, particularly of his own wife and his colleagues, reminded him that, but for the Ribbentrop-Molotov Pact, Britain would not have had to fight Germany alone. He was supported by an infuriated Bevan. Nevertheless, Khrushchev's bumptious, peasant joviality, less predictable than Stalin's terrorist will, suggested that, in a haggling, cunning way, business could be done with him. There would be less killings.

Later in the year, serious doubts were cast. The anti-Stalinist reaction started by Khrushchev had spread to Hungary where a general rebellion under the moderate Communists Imre Nagy and Pal Maleta demolished the Stalinist regime and removed Hungary from the 'Camp of Socialism'. Within a week Khrushchev sent seven Russian divisions into Hungary. Europe and America heard an agonized voice from Budapest radio, 'For the sake of ... Help Hungary ...' then the silence of 3,000 Russian dead, 7,000 Hungarian. Nagy and Pal Maleta surrendered on the promise of a safe-conduct, and were later executed; this, Camus said, was the anti-Communist case in a nutshell. Khrushchev told a literary group that a few executions of writers could have averted the crisis. Picasso signed a French protest letter, while remaining a Communist and later accepting a Lenin Peace Prize. But British Communists defected in thousands, their party never fully recovering. They were casting away emotional and political props that had sustained them for years and now, finally disillusioned, confronted a fearful psychological void.

In Arnold Wesker's play, *Chicken Soup with Barley* (1958), Charmian Eyre's performance as Sarah, obdurate Communist, was as agitating as any I had ever seen: 'You think it doesn't hurt me – the news about Hungary? You think I know what happened and what didn't happen? Do any of us know? Who do I know who to trust now – God, who are our friends now? But all my life I've fought with your father and the rotten system that couldn't help him. All my life I worked with a party that meant glory and freedom and brotherhood. You want me to move to Hendon and forget who I am ... Socialism is my light, can you understand that?'

At the Wednesday Club, one member's prestige was doubled by introducing a genuine young Hungarian refugee. There he was, actually amongst us, eating, eating well, drinking double brandies and, save for demanding refills, saying little. His sufferings, his anguish, would excuse this. Meanwhile, we covertly discussed his plight. 'Do you think he'll accept a cheque?' 'I can find room for him at the Manor ...' 'He won't be offended by gifts. My wife's fur coat ...'

He at last looked up, sitting back satisfied, surveying us with slightly regretful goodwill. 'Of course ... I am leaving for New York. That is where the action is.' Cheque books were unobtrusively replaced, prospects of wife's goods going for auction receded. He said pleasantly: 'Of course, Hungary's only had one good government since 1919.' Our silence was inquiring. He winked. 'Hitler, of course. He knew what to do about the Jews.' His host's prestige lapsed. Over the last drink, my neighbour remarked that the situation was tragic, adding, 'There's no country in Europe that more admires my poetry.'

Hungary was overshadowed that November when, across the Suez Canal, Anthony Eden and Gamal Abdel Nasser faced each other like cowboys outside the saloon at sundown. Nasser's nationalization of the Canal, his deal with Stalinist Prague over arms and his success with Russia over building the Aswan Dam provoked anger, threats and finally the Anglo-French-Israeli invasion of Egypt. Gaitskell, the Labour leader, first denounced Nasser as a Hitler or Mussolini, then changed course and charged Eden as a militant aggressor. The Foreign Office role in the affair was not widely esteemed. It seemed generally ill-informed, indecisive, indulgent to enemies and suspect in its anxiety to preserve peace or achieve compromise. Churchill had called it a cowardly lot of scuffling shufflers though the then Foreign Secretary, Selwyn Lloyd, had been placed in the FO by himself, after a dialogue Shavian in its address: 'But, sir, I've never been to a foreign country, I don't speak any foreign languages, I don't like foreigners.' 'Young man, these all seem positive advantages.'

The role of the individual in history was depreciated by many intellectuals, but over Suez, individual powers and prejudices appeared substantial. Eden was uneasily aware of his monumental predecessor, and had never fully recovered from a 1953 botched gall bladder operation. Tense, at times hysterical, medically over-drugged, he allegedly shouted at the Foreign Office Minister Anthony Nutting, soon to resign in protest, 'I want him [Nasser] destroyed, don't you understand? . . . And I don't care if there's anarchy and chaos in Egypt.'

This seemed just as likely in Britain, still in hock to America, and where the invasion of Egypt provoked uncontrolled extremes from angry crowds. Tribal indignation was rife against Wogs and Gyppoes, not least among ex-servicemen, who also doubted Egyptian competence to manage the Canal. Many, including myself, exaggerated the importance of the Canal itself, envisaging catastrophic oil shortages. Britain was execrated by America and the British Left for refusing the offices and rejecting the strictures of the United Nations, though that body had been compared by Elie Kedourie to the Circumlocution Office; and Eden, foregoing his earlier enthusiasm, catalogued the many occasions when UN decisions had been ignored by other nations or vetoed by Russia. For those who still regarded Britain as a first-class moral and military power, the test was vital. The lion should roar, to pronounced effect. Others saw Nasser as a socialist dedicated to the poor, the emergent nations, to anti-imperialism, and at last found praise for Eisenhower and Dulles, now refusing financial aid to their old ally, whose bombs were falling on Alexandria. Eisenhower, with re-election ahead, refused a telephone call from Eden. The Queen, Lord Mountbatten, First Sea Lord, Sir Gerald Templer and Sir Dermot Boyle, heads of the Army and Royal Air Force, were rumoured to be opposing the use of force.

Crowds and anger grew. 'Eden Out!' resounded everywhere, then 'Wogs Out!' Quarrels blazed on the street. 'Eden's a Jew.' 'Eden is not a Jew.' 'Eden's no Jew ... Not *now!*'

Some liberals and Jews were divided between affection or loyalty towards Israel and a conviction that Arabs were being grievously wronged. Not since Munich had the country been so riven. I thought of Dreyfus, and cautiously watched my neighbours. Amongst them, the Dean, on abstruse evidence, revealed that Nasser had cast a spell over Eden, enflaming him to clinical madness. He fancied he had once witnessed a similar phenomenon; in 1637. More significantly, Khrushchev was threatening London and Paris with bombs.

Three hundred thousand British troops were being deployed and three hundred ships, together with bombers and tankers. Youths screamed 'murderers' as the bombers flew east over London, and were at once set upon by furious patriots. But millions of the fair-minded were confessing to shame at their own country's behaviour. David Astor wrote in an *Observer* editorial, 'We had not realized that our Government was capable of such folly and crookedness.' Aneurin Bevan addressed huge crowds and orated in the Commons. 'If the Prime Minister was as sincere as I think he is, then he is too silly to be Prime Minister ... We say that Britain has always stood for civilized principles and for humanity. How do we answer now when we drop bombs on helpless people?' Some days later, with the Allied attack visibly failing, under American pressure and UN censure, and with Budapest silenced, he added that Khrushchev was as stupid as Eden, and that Hungarian non-cooperation would render him as helpless as Eden, a judgement worthy of the Dean, not quite at his best.

The Wednesday Club seethed with righteous indignation. There were rumours, subsequently substantiated, of deceptions within the Cabinet, with Eden telling Nigel Nicolson that half-truths were 'necessary'. Nigel, Ben's brother, was Conservative MP for Bournemouth, co-publisher of *Lolita*, opponent of capital punishment, supporter of homosexual law reform: risky in such a town. He opposed the Government and eventually lost his seat to a very Far Right Tory group. He was told by my friend Lewis Lyne, former GOC of the British Zone in Berlin and at the time chairman of the United Nations Association, that he had asked Harold Macmillan whether Anglo-French intervention was a genuine attempt to get the Arab-Israeli fighting halted, or a chance to retrieve the Canal. Macmillan had replied with a broad wink, which Nicolson, in his diary, said he considered the most cynical thing any British government had ever done. At the Club, Nigel Nicolson was, of course, hero of the hour, Eden was damned beyond redemption, the American government, for once, much applauded for its condemnation of Britain. At the Fortieth Anniversary Lunch in 1993, John Bury reminded us: 'At the height of the crisis, in November '56, Stephen Spender returned to England from a lecture tour in America and was invited to tell us what the people on the other side of the Atlantic thought about our Suez adventure. Spender told us that after a very well attended lecture he had given in New York, numerous members of the audience had come up to tell him how much they agreed with our invasion of Egypt and how ashamed they were of their Secretary of State, Foster Dulles, for failing to support us. This unexpected news made Jocelyn Baines so furious that, frustrated beyond endurance, he stood up and delivered a vituperative personal attack on Spender, as if the American opinions were Spender's own, which they certainly were not – a classic case of shooting the messenger.'

At the next lunch, a guest, Paul Bloomfield, courteous and benevolent, who judged a book by the expression it left on a reader's face, mildly ventured his view that some of the loudest anti-British voices at the UN had vehemently supported the Russians in Hungary, that Foster Dulles was not the epitome of human sanctity, and that Arab nationalism might prove more dangerous than Franco-British imperialism. Philip Toynbee was exasperated: 'Really, Paul, this is intolerable. Neo-imperialist, fascist rubbish of the very worst sort. What do you think you are? I will tell you, you are absolutely . . . hideous! And ignorant. You seem not to have the slightest inkling of what the Second World War was all about . . .'

He continued for many minutes, in the tradition of Burke assailing Warren Hastings, the waitress glancing uneasily at the knives gleaming on the table. He was Liberal Britain stirred, if not to action, at least to oratory, Paul listening with the patient concern he might have awarded a reading from Henry James delivered in imperfect English with a slight stutter. When the oration subsided, Paul Bloomfield sighed, he glanced seriously round the hushed, crowded table, he refilled his glass, he refilled Bernard Wall's glass, then smiled as if at some distant but cherished reminder of happy days: 'I don't know whether this will interest you, Philip, but I have just come across a book written by Curtius, Robert Curtius, Ernst Robert Curtius, an account of a tenth-century German poet, Hucbald, who wrote, for King Charles the Bald, a poem of one hundred and forty-six lines, entitled "On Baldness", each word beginning with a T.'

Danger was dispersed by laughter. I did not care to mention my own story, one which might have been thought discreditable. My wife and I had been invited to dinner by an influential friend, who died the following week, in remote, opulent Dulwich, where he owned a Rembrandt, doubtless stolen. To win favour, we brought a bottle of liqueur, beyond our means. This was accepted with some grace, and a promise to open it afterwards. Within seconds, Suez exploded amongst us, and I was soon thundering clichés worthy of Toynbee, indeed of Eden himself: 'Monstrous ... disgraceful ... people like yourselves ... beastly arrogance ... Never darken your doors again ...' Grabbing my wife, I stormed out. Up the garden path we went, only to halt at the gate, sharing a single image – the bottle of liqueur. Back we went. The door was opened, rather timidly. 'Well ... there may be something in what you say ...'

That November twenty thousand packed Trafalgar Square, banners and cut-outs floating above. 'Britain Out': 'Law Not War': 'Eden Must Go'. MPs, trades-union leaders, students, show-bizzers, and nebulous celebrities blazed and stamped, prosecutors for the World. Fireworks were hurled at mounted police. I was immersed in one of Canetti's mobs, in the Thirties news reels, in the ready-made language of boyhood fiction. Veins stood out like knotted cords, veins throbbed above eyebrows, veins threatened to burst. A voice screamed, 'You hound'; nerves snapped, eyes glinted, gimlet-like, teeth were bared, fangs gleamed; faces were mottled, fiery, crazed like madmen. The mob bayed, stamped like thunder. Kenneth Tynan was seen remonstrating with a mounted policeman: 'This horse is *still* on my foot!'

Orators were outlined against the sky, their postures apeing the imperial statues around them. Mounted police were about to charge, tear gas to be used. 'Eden Out.' 'Life without consciousness,' Brodsky said of him, and was promptly kicked. I could not wholly believe that such jungaloid uproar and hatred meant only love and compassion for Arabs; on all sides figures, gladiatorial, Dionysiac, were bawling their hatred of war and of cruelty, yet the passion of these savage faces was impure, as the bombing of Alexandria was also impure, debased by language which proclaimed it as Punishing the Guilty, Asserting Our Dues, Saving the West, Exercising Our Rights. Opponents retorted with, Repetition of the Worst Nazi Atrocities, Unique Barbarity of

Oil Imperialism, Action Unparalleled in Our History. In myself had been no purity: I had been horribly afraid. Safely back home, I pondered the turmoil, and the make-believe mystique not only of crowds but also of individuals. I remembered early nineteenth-century Russian crowds howling for 'Constantine and Constitution', imagining them man and wife; Roman crowds, murdering the Gracchi who yearned to help them; Franco's soldiers bawling 'Long Live Death'.

In 1950, a close friend, a German Jewish exile, had astounded me by defending dictatorship as the only power that could have created a drama so elemental and titanic as the siege of Stalingrad. I read Ernst Junger on the Great War: 'It was horrible but also had something tremendous about it. I did not want to miss it at any price. You have to see what human nature really is.' I wondered how those ardent, demented faces in Trafalgar Square related to an observation of Kierkegaard, himself much discussed in the Fifties: 'When Truth conquers with the help of ten thousand yelling men – even supposing that the victory is a truth – then, with the form and manner of the victory a far greater untruth is victorious.' Perhaps unfairly, I repeated Dr Johnson: that much, perhaps most human activity is due merely to the need to fill up time. And that there is always that need to damn or injure, harboured by most of us, as a terrifying squatter, or welcome, amusing guest.

A fortnight, or a single shrieking afternoon, had sufficed to implement the message of Buchan and Greene, that civilization was a fragile crust. Great art, major science and profound wisdom had for most of us shrivelled to irrelevance. From Khrushchev's threats, Hungarian killings, American sneers, raving streets, I, and those about me, found no refuge in Tippett and Britten, Sutherland and Moore, *The Confidential Clerk*, *On the Waterfront* or *Smiles of a Summer Night*. Under threat from the sky, from riot, from a run on the banks, better assist the wounded than contemplate a Vermeer. Huxley's mescalin patterns, once enviable for their pure uselessness, were now futile and irresponsible.

Such a feeling soon ceased. Eden himself faded away, reviving later, in the English way, as Lord Avon. The storm cone was hauled down, deck-chairs re-opened, but perhaps a longish summer had ended. A. L. Rowse supplies an aside about the silent Churchill. 'He was indeed lucky to have been out before Suez, which would never have occurred if shrewd Clem Attlee had been there. Almost the last thing, he went into 10 Downing Street and said: "Now, Anthony, no getting caught out on a limb with the French." This was exactly what happened.'

Commentators held inquests. The *Manchester Guardian* said that Suez had stripped off tinsel that had garnished a decade of economic failure.

Eden himself, shortly before his resignation, wrote that Suez had announced that Britain's future was no longer as a world power, but only as a part of Europe, competing with her associates and thus needing to be better educated, and more aware of the expenses of welfare and defence, and of the disadvantages of high taxation. The *Financial Times* judged: 'The effort to maintain swanky appearances had bankrupted many a proud family of ancient traditions. First the lands are mortgaged, then servants go, and finally the roof falls in. Britain now stands somewhere between the second and third stage.' At parties, in The *New Statesman*, at the Wednesday Club, Malcolm Muggeridge was in full throttle: 'In the twilight of expiring imperial systems, deluded figures like Sir Anthony are liable to rush frenziedly into the centre of the stage and begin declaiming lines belonging to a play on which the curtain has already fallen.'

George Lichtheim, a journalist of much sparkle and some deep interior grief, who, accepting 'a quick drink' would talk for three hours without expecting interruption, considered, in the quarterly *Midstream*, that neither Labour nor the Tories had any real answer to the seizure of the Canal by a hostile dictatorship. The Left clung to appeasement, disregarding Nasser's semi-fascist regime and its intention of destroying all British Middle East interests; the Right banked on gunboat diplomacy, indifferent to the threat of Russian intervention and trusting to luck to dodge American obstruction. Hugh Thomas, rising intellectual, thought Suez just beat the Burgess-Maclean scandal as the crisis that most preoccupied society, as an obvious defeat rather than part of the retreat from Empire, usually disguised with some skill as the transformation from Empire (bad) to Commonwealth (good).

As the Fifties recede, I realize how subjective my view is. As I write, Sir Peter Hall, on television, is castigating 'the miserable Fifties', dominated by class and public school, the Theatre still wilting under censorship, society oppressed by sexual obscurantism, all primed for the joyous liberations of the Sixties. Some weeks later, Daniel Johnson, reviewing Peregrine Worsthorne's autobiography in *The Times*, mentions 'the sheer nastiness of 1950s Britain, a lace-curtain-twitching society compared to which New York and Washington must have seemed liberal in the best sense of the word'. R. D. Laing, a rising guru, representative of the mentally distressed, agreed.

My recollections are different, but I did, or thought I did, sense a change, in the streets, at bars, in homes and in 'the media' after Suez. 'Disenchantment' is probably too emphatic – few, surely, had been

enchanted in my lifetime – more a pervasive sourness. Britain had lost
Great Power status, unquestioned since Oliver Cromwell. The foundation of the European Common Market was a fateful challenge, or
signal opportunity, for her to find a new role within complex post-
imperial relationships, yet on the streets it was largely observed with
scepticism, indifference or resigned pessimism as it went ahead without
Britain's participation.

I read in 1957 of the Kingdom of Kush. Apparently, after China and
Rome, it had been the largest and most productive society. Where
was it now? I could not even find it on the map. Still brooding over
Trafalgar Square, I encountered Baudelaire's description of himself
within a Paris revolution: 'My frenzy of 1848. What was its nature?
Desire for vengeance. Natural bent for destruction. Literary fanaticism,
recollection of things read . . . Or honest, decent anger at things ill-
done?'

Philip Larkin was, in private letters, referring to 'the successive
gangs of socialist robbers who have ruled us since the war', and to
'rampaging hordes of blacks'. His tone could perhaps be more jocular
than vicious; his sentiments would have disconcerted his growing
number of admirers but probably have been applauded by that majority
who either disliked poetry or disapproved of poets.

John Raymond felt Osborne's *The Entertainer* (1957) 'a grotesque cry
of rage and pain at the bad hand history was dealing out to what was
once the largest, most prosperous empire in the world'. Here, the
decaying music-hall comedian Archie Rice, 'his face held open by a
grin, and dead behind the eyes', sings:

> We're all out for good old number one,
> Number one's the only one for me,
> Good old England, you're my cup of tea,
> But I don't want no drab equality.
> Don't let your feelings roam
> But remember that charity begins at home.
> For Britons shall be free.

Sterling Crisis, Balance of Payments Crisis, Berlin Crisis, Conver-
tibility Crisis and Devaluation Crisis had been surmounted, yet high
hopes had perceptibly lowered, amply assisted by Budapest and Suez.
Again, what should have happened, frequently did not. Stafford Cripps
denied all intentions of devaluing the pound, before doing so. Bevin
felt about Russia that 'Left can speak to Left in comradeship.' He was

wrong. Promises of peace and prosperity were followed by bombs on Alexandria. Support for Israel, the underdog, was less heady. We more often forgot the Jewish contention that a state cannot be built on logic or clemency but on justice. This, together with a controversial Biblical claim, tended to remind us of Ben-Gurion's remark, uttered in whatever tone: 'They have land: we want it.' Orators had proclaimed that nationalization would prevent public-service strikes: 'the People does not strike against itself'. But miners struck some fifteen hundred times in 1947–8. Harry Hopkins, in his book *The New Look*, showed the human factor persisting beneath modernization: 'In Grimethorpe in the old days under the coal owners, it had been the custom in some pits that if the men could finish their "stint" in five hours, they could pack up and go home. In the bright new world of the National Coal Board that sort of "rule of thumb" was out. In the old days, "rag-outs" were often settled in rough-and-ready fashion with the Boss on the spot. Now the slightest squabble might all too easily become a matter for a complicated, impersonal, nation-wide, conciliation machine; one of the Grimethorpe strikers' bitterest complaints had been that the union representatives who assessed their stint were not *Yorkshire* miners!'

Traditions, legends and impulses were often found unaffected by sensible legislation. Dockers, against whom Attlee had three times to dispatch troops and who, despite being impeccably proletarian, were to march against West Indian immigration, had long worked under haphazard, strong-arm conditions, in a 'liberty' promoting squalor and favouritism. By the Fifties, new conditions were in motion, under the National Dock Labour Board, but Hopkins felt, 'deep down in this great inarticulate mass of men smouldered a resentful suspicion that the new "Equality" was being bought at too high a price.'

New Towns, slum clearances and better sanitation meant also a new respectability, a loss of colourful street drama, gossip and social casualness; the tight front door, locked garden gate, separation from grandparents, dwindling loyalties. Looking back to a vanished East End, decades later, Lord Snowdon reflected to Daniel Farson: 'The high-rise buildings destroyed the chat over the garden wall and the importance of the milkman . . . If [the bottle of milk is] not taken in, the neighbours know there's something wrong.' Much of this had not occurred in 1957, but the drift was obvious. And, as Empire dwindled and conscription ended, masculine energies suffered diminishing outlets.

It was a relief to watch the quicksilver elegance of Audrey Hepburn and Fred Astaire coalescing with Gershwin's tunes in *Funny Face*

(1957), set largely in a tourists' Paris of fashion models, with a mock-Sartrean café philosopher and his witless acolytes, solemn chanteuses, romantic streets and bridges. A less attractive revelation of popular taste was the spectacle of Epstein's giant nude, *Jacob and the Angel*, being trundled round as a salacious show-piece billed as 'Too hot for Blackpool'.

As Coronation euphoria was superseded by the new mood, there were scoffs at the monarchy not readily imaginable under George VI. John Osborne's diatribes gibe at it as 'The National Swill' and 'the gold filling in a mouthful of decay'. The new Elizabethan Age was failing to register, and Royal mystique was scarcely enhanced by Miss Crawford, former governess to the royal sisters, who published best-selling trivia about them until debasing their questionable value by a meticulously written description of the Queen's dignity and the admiring crowds at two events which, due to last-minute strikes, had not occurred. Less hilariously, Lord Altrincham condemned the court as socially exclusive, the Queen's personality that of a priggish school-girl with a voice which was 'frankly a pain in the neck'. Malcolm Muggeridge sneered at the 'ersatz religion', dubbing it 'pure show', 'a sort of royal soap-opera' that generated snobbishness and sycophancy, in which even duchesses – he did not name them – found the monarch 'dowdy, frumpy and banal'.

More momentous was the mounting debate about nuclear disarmament which, like religion, race, sex and pacifism, blurred party divides. Officially, after Russia had become an atomic super-power, Labour and Conservative co-operated in the Anglo-American Balance of Terror policy. Lord Altrincham had defined the A-Bomb as the main shield and buckler of freedom, but unofficial dissent against this view was loud and important, assisted by vigorous anti-Americanism, agitating against racial and educational segregation, impingement on general human rights, dollar imperialism, the Pentagon, the CIA, the FBI, and much else. If Britain were to lead the world towards peace with unilateral nuclear disarmament she would free herself from American entanglements, restore moral prestige lost at Suez, and doubtless influence the Russians, though Khrushchev, like Brezhnev after him, sneered at this as 'inspired lunacy'.

Some distinguished soldiers and rather more eminent scientists supported the Campaign for Nuclear Disarmament (CND) though its appeal was, in large, more emotional than technical. The old saw about politics being too important to be entrusted to politicians was illuminated by resounding amateurs taking a hand in the game. In 1955, Russell's anti-Bomb Pugwash Manifesto was co-signed by Einstein,

Max Born and J. F. Joliot-Curie on behalf of 'a biological species which has had a remarkable history and whose disappearance none of us can desire ... Shall we put an end to the human race: or shall mankind renounce war?' Fifty-two Nobel Laureates appealed for the renunciation of force, though Field Marshal Montgomery declared that the Bomb would be used by Britain if attacked, and that he himself would bypass politicians in ordering its use. Anglicans were perhaps reassured by the Archbishop of Canterbury, Geoffrey Fisher: 'The very worst [the Bomb] could do would be to sweep a vast number of people at one moment from this world into the other and more vital world, into which anyhow they must all pass at one time.'

J. B. Priestley published a letter in the *New Statesman*: 'We might break the wicked spell that all but a few uncertified lunatics desperately wish to be broken. We could begin to restore the world to sanity and lift this nation from its recent ignominy to its former grandeur ...' His view carried weight, given his vast, built-in, middle-of-the-road audience. The letter was reprinted as a pamphlet, and was followed by one from Russell. In Russia in 1958, the physicist and H-Bomb specialist, Andrei Sakharov, vainly appealed to Khrushchev for nuclear disarmament; while Linus Pauling, American Nobel chemist, presented the UN Secretary-General, Dag Hammerskjöld, with an apocalyptic assessment of the results to be expected from continued nuclear-testing.

Stirred by these exhortations, the Campaign for Nuclear Disarmament, under the presidency of Russell, gathered itself around writers, scientists, politicians, churchmen and entertainers: Priestley, Jacquetta Hawkes, Rose Macaulay, A. J. P. Taylor, Doris Lessing, Michael Foot, Kenneth Tynan, James Cameron, Kingsley Martin, Ritchie Calder. One leader was John Collins, founder of Christian Action, Canon of St Paul's, stalwart fighter with his wife Diana against capital punishment and apartheid, raising, with her, thousands of pounds for black prisoners, secretly meeting Russian agents to give information to help a proposed raid on the notorious South African convict camp on Robben Island. (Detractors to this day maintain that Russia supplied funds to CND and that CND itself supplied gifts to Castro.) Another supporter, a secular saint to match Elizabeth Pilenko and his old associates Fridtjof Nansen and Lord Robert Cecil, was the former Labour Cabinet Minister, Philip Noel-Baker, veteran pioneer of the League of Nations, with J. C. Smuts and with his fellow-socialist Arthur Henderson.

For CND, the future Poet Laureate, Cecil Day-Lewis, wrote 'Requiem for the Loving', with music by Donald Swann. The CND protest marches to the Atomic Energy Research Establishment at Aldermaston, the first in 1958, numbering some 50,000, became annual rituals, with steel bands, jivers, trades union and party banners, posters with quotations from Einstein, babies in prams doubtless drooling 'Ban the Bomb'. Like medieval pilgrimages, the marches flourished on mixed motives, and left-wing support was not unanimous. Communists at first opposed them, but, finding that the movement denounced only America, never Russia, then supported them. The egalitarian republican Anthony Wedgwood Benn, in 1958, analysed unilateralism as typically British self-deception, while professing incredulity about the eventual use of nuclear weapons. Denis Healey, ex-Communist sympathizer, felt they should be retained 'as the ultimate weapon, if other methods failed to halt the Red Army' and this could well have represented majority national opinion.

One marcher was Eddie Linden with experiences by no means exceptional. A working-class Glaswegian, porter in a hospital, old people's home, railway station, former Communist, founder-editor of the literary magazine *Aquarius*, founder of Catholic CND and author of a CND protest letter to de Gaulle – whose response was negligible – Eddie marched both with fidelity to his beliefs and in the hope of a sexual encounter. 'The sensation of physical flesh was overwhelming, and I suppose it got to me. I noticed dozens of others of both sexes cruising around, but the fact that we were there on a march held sway and I never saw any open degeneracy.' This was encouraging: a single-minded crusade would have been a recipe for fanatical excess.

Kenneth Minogue commented on the marches in *The Twentieth Century* (1960): 'Inevitably the Aldermaston affairs became part of the fantasy world of moral gestures; they became a vehicle of righteousness, allowing their older supporters the moral arrogance of feeling that, in the midst of a sea of apathy, they were "doing something about the Bomb" . . . There is a great mass of opinion, heavy with sympathy, and remote from responsibility, which is led by journalists and intellectuals into these stunts. Politics for them is not merely a way of maintaining social life; it is a succession of emotional causes with names like Apartheid, Little Rock, Hola, Cyprus, Suez, Nyasaland . . . names that produce a delicious shiver of indignation.' What was consistently astonishing was that though, by a ukase of 1935, the death penalty in Russia had been lowered to reach 12-year-olds, this stayed virtually unnoticed amongst the heavily pro-Russian Aldermaston contingents.

My wife marched with CND. I did not. I was surfeited with idealistic, rich and impractical Burgess Hill parents, with their socialist cocktail parties, H-Bomb committees, anti-American resolutions, compassion for the poor, sent by post. I could more easily identify with young Tony, in Doris Lessing's play, *Each His Own Wilderness* (1958), who is as typical as any in the later Fifties, wedged between the idealistic and the brutal or cynical or merely stupid: 'Rosemary, listen – never in the whole history of the world have people made a battle-cry out of being ordinary. Never. Supposing we all said to the politicians – we refuse to be heroic. We refuse to be brave. We are bored with all the noble gestures – what then, Rosemary?' She answers, 'Yes. Ordinary and safe,' and the play ends with Tony's response: 'Leave us alone, we'll say. Leave us alone to live. Just leave us alone.'

14

Existentialist Answers

'WHY', CECIL DAY-LEWIS once asked, 'do we all, seeing a Communist, feel small?' Not all of us did, but he could have cited ignorance, conviction, a misuse of language. In 1920, Lenin had proclaimed, 'To speak the truth is a petty-bourgeois prejudice.' Human credulity produces too many myths, abstractions lose meaning and become cheap music. F. M. C. Fourier, the nineteenth-century socialist and co-operatist, who had once catalogued forty-nine varieties of cuckold, eagerly declared that *socialism* could even transform the sea to lemonade. Harold Laski had compared Stalin's henchman, Andrei Vyshinsky, to Jeremy Bentham. Iris Murdoch briefly joined the Communists – for which she was refused entry to America on a post-graduate scholarship; likewise Kingsley Amis, who had thought that Communism was all about 'compassion' before discovering that it was all about 'compulsion'. Pasternak's Dr Zhivago reflected, during the Revolution, that the start of all future evil was when people lost faith in individuality, in the value of personal opinions. 'And there arose the power of the glittering phrase, first Tsarist and then Revolutionary.'

Post-war events invited powerful dissent. In 1950 appeared *The God that Failed,* edited by R. H. S. Crossman, which gained a large readership. It contained essays by ex-Communists and ex-sympathizers, a record of common idealism followed, reluctantly, sadly, by disillusion and disgust with Party cruelty, cynicism, intrigues, betrayals, stupidity and narrowness. Here was the worst of the Christian tradition of intolerance, purges, heresy hunts, conducted in the name of human brotherhood and accelerated by technology. Koestler spoke for his associate writers: 'At no time, in no country, have more revolutionaries been killed or reduced to slaves, than in Soviet Russia.' For seven years, Koestler admitted, he had excused all this. 'How our voices boomed with righteous indignation, denouncing flaws in the procedure of justice in our comfortable democracies; and how silent we were when our comrades, without trial and conviction, were liquidated in the Socialist Sixth of the World.'

In post-war Moscow, a former woman secretary of Lenin's had told Isaiah Berlin: 'We are a scientifically governed society and if there is no room for free thinking in physics – a man who questions the laws of motion is obviously ignorant or mad – why should we Marxists, who have discovered the laws of history and society, permit free thinking in the social sphere?' A. J. P. Taylor liked to cite J. P. Plamenatz's critique, that Marxist historicism could be proved only by statistics unavailable to Marx or anyone else. Evelyn Waugh disbelieved that a writer could be a genuine Marxist, 'for a writer's materials must be the individual soul (which is the preoccupation of Christendom), while the Marxist can only think in classes and categories, and even in classes abhors variety'.

During the later Fifties, left-wing hopes descended on Mao Tse-tung in China, who had consistently ignored advice from Stalin, and who was to prove as publicity-conscious, womanizing, callous and dedicated as Louis XIV. His personal physician once excused his tyrannical addiction to young girls as his rightful perquisite, 'splendid and natural for the God and Supreme Lord'.

Mao, discussing politics with Nehru in 1957, and the prospects of a revolutionary war, said afterwards: 'I told him that if half mankind were destroyed, the other half would still remain. But in return, imperialism would be completely destroyed and only socialism would still remain in the world, and, within fifty years or a hundred, the population would again increase by even more than fifty per cent.' This was a reminder of the French Revolutionary leader, Barère: 'True humanity consists in exterminating one's enemies.'

In Mao's China, Beethoven's Sonata for Piano and Horn was castigated for expressing 'the vile nature of the Bourgeoisie'. His 'Great Leap Forward' policy, initiated in 1958, suggested a gigantic effort towards the next century, but actually, like Stalin's war against his peasants, brought economic chaos, mass starvation, shootings and labour camp atrocities.

Much displayed in London coffee bars and at Sunday lunches, Mao's Little Red Book gained him a parrot reputation as a thinker, with such unremarkable saws as, 'In History it was always those with little learning who overthrew those with too much.' This was impressively saluted by a Tientsin textile worker who confessed that from Chairman Mao's philosophic thought he had learnt to analyse the complexities of woollen yarn snapping on warping frames. Malraux met Mao and was deeply sympathetic, though, as Jeffrey Meyers has reminded us, Mao had obliterated the ancient Chinese culture of which Malraux was a connoisseur. In his memoirs, Khrushchev reflected: 'Like Stalin, Mao never recognised his comrades as his equals. He treated those around him like bits of furniture, useful for an appointed time but then to be discarded.'

Jean-Paul Sartre had written in 1950 that he and his friends were not Party members so had no obligation to discuss Soviet labour camps, and were 'free to remain aloof from the quarrel over the nature of this system, provided there were no events of sociological significance'. Whether a minimum of fifteen million deaths by execution, slavery, deportation and starvation possessed such significance remained undiscussed, though 'To keep a living hope, we must, despite all mistakes, horrors and crimes, recognise the obvious superiority of the socialist camp.' However, his independent spirit, particularly in his plays, made his relations with French and Russian Communists frequently uneasy. Their press, though often quoting his gibes at Marshall Aid, McCarthyism and segregation, disliked his recognition of the ends-means dilemma – for an obedient Communist there is no dilemma. While exploiting his name, as they did Picasso's, they periodically reviled him as a decadent, bourgeois Trotsky, a Fascist hyena, a slimy rat, a lubricious viper, and used claques to disrupt such telling plays as *Les Mains sales*.

Competing with Maoism and post-Stalinism, Sartre and Camus dominated fashionable Existentialism, which held that existence, like the universe, was 'absurd', lacking meaning and purpose unless endowed with them by resolute human will. From Nothing, the individual could achieve Being, by choice, choosing not to acknowledge the determinist baggage of God, history, genetics, the unconscious, capitalism, the State and inherited moral values. To be rejected were indifference, moral neutrality, charismatic flourishes, mere fashion, all of which could corrupt and betray the human will. 'By their fruits you will know them', and indeed know ourselves.

This, despite Sartre's support of the Russian State and loathing of America, sounded an exciting chance for a restart, a dumping of history, and, encouraged by readings or reports of books by the two Frenchmen, we began convincing ourselves of our personal freedom by making some spontaneous and otherwise motiveless action divorced

from the past, genetics, fate, tradition and the rest, like a Puritan seeking
evidence of Grace. We would make ourselves, find identity through
action. We are what we do. For back-up, we accepted Malraux's
dictum that humanity's assertion against fate is best fought through art.

Existentialism – self-assertion, the struggle against the hell of other
people, manifest will – could be used as an excuse even by waiters
grown rich on bad service, by pretty girls who arrived late or not at
all, even, J. M. Richards told me, by Vera Cunningham's parrot, as an
exercise of will, an escape from Kenneth Clark. Girls and boys imitated
Juliette Greco's listless hair, smudgy clothes and glum smile, and
intoned her lugubrious songs, with a tunelessness that indicated not
lack of talent but a break from convention. I myself, glad of history
and tradition, though not, I hoped, enslaved by either, was relieved
when my schoolfriend Alan Ross shrugged off Existentialism in 1950
as a convenient philosophical loophole, an emergency exit for an intelligentsia that no longer found politics fashionable: 'a misunderstood,
vaguely fatalistic absolution from ethics, that, for a long time, with its
echoes of vice and sexual licence, jazz, and unkemptness exercised a
fascination over the intellectually unfledged.'

It was not new. Philosophers quickly referred to Kierkegaard,
through Jaspers and Heidegger: useful names in the espresso bars and
bomb-sites, though it would not have surprised the fifth-century
Welsh monk Pelagius, let alone Maugham, or indeed Thomas Hardy.
The hero of the average Western movie was an existentialist without
knowing it. Thomas Hardy wrote, in 'A Young Man's Epigram on
Existence' (1866):

> A senseless school, where we must give,
> Our lives that we may learn to live!
> A dolt is he who memorizes
> Lessons that leave no time for prizes.

The absurdity of existence both Macbeth and Lear came to recognize;
also Kipling, with his sense of man fortified only from within himself against hostile nature and a chilling universe, expecting nothing,
receiving little, striving, but without illusion that his work will endure.

> Ah! What avails the classic bent
> And what the cultured word,
> Against the undoctored incident
> That actually occurred?

Much of this was probably how most sensible Europeans had long
lived, for six days of the week, and was curtly expressed by the Belgian

painter Guillaume Hooritz: 'If I am not myself, who will be?' J. B. S. Haldane told A. J. Ayer that the literary source of Sartre's *Le Néant* was in Schiller's *Die Jungfrau von Orleans* – 'And the only profit we carry away from the battle of life is the insight into nothingness.' In 1929, long before Sartre's *La Nausée* and Camus' *L'Étranger*, Alberto Moravia had published his pessimistic anti-bourgeois, anti-mediocrity novel, *Gli Indifferente* (*The Time of Indifference*). He later concluded that the only difference between himself and the Frenchmen was that in 1929 he was unaware of the word Existentialism.

Albert Camus, from North Africa, had co-edited with Sartre the left-wing *Combat*. He had had the more impressive Resistance record, untainted by suspicions of socializing with the invaders. He had been a Communist, but later renounced the Party and deserted Sartre. 'Politics is not a religion; if it becomes one it becomes an Inquisition.' He too was an atheist, found life and the universe absurd, unless the self-fulfilling individual acted beyond his habitual self. One should, he considered, refuse to be a god, in order to be a man. He accepted the Nobel Prize for Literature in 1957, which Sartre refused, and during the Fifties his novel *La Peste* (1947) was widely read in Britain. Here, Oran is abruptly smitten with plague and, as in war, or the Occupation, or internal personal travail, extreme crisis provokes extremes of behaviour, exposing the individual essence – in earlier terminology, the soul. Each person is a bundle of possibilities, nothing is guaranteed; civic departments and medical services are only as strong as those who man them. Action itself cannot promise survival, only moral impetus and identity; religion is proved neither a source nor an impediment to social cohesion, nor is it necessary for personal virtue. Like tyranny, like existence itself, the plague is arbitrary, amoral, meaningless, inflicting death on some, ignoring others. To revolt against it is at least a form of rebirth.

Of all the characters, Dr Rieux perhaps best expresses post-war values, the Fifties spirit – unromantic, stoical, unsensational, responsible, decent, working not for reward but because the job has to be done; sceptical, without ideals, rhetoric or show. At the end, his friend Tarrou dies, he survives. Tarrou had 'lost the match' as he put it. But what had he, Rieux, won? No more than the experience of having known plague and remembering it, of having known friendship and remembering it, of knowing affection and being destined one day to remember it. So all a man could win in the conflict between plague and life was knowledge and memories. But Tarrou, perhaps, would have called that winning the match. Something of the existentialist's loneliness is shared in Jean Rice's outburst, in John Osborne's *The*

Entertainer: 'Here we are. We're alone in the universe, there's no God, it just seems that it all began by something as simple as sunlight striking on a piece of rock. And here we are. We've only got ourselves. Somehow, we've just got to make a go of it. *We've only got ourselves.*'

For Rieux, doubtless for Camus himself, life is not a burden – it carries a warm southern sensuality and sunlit hedonism – but he insists on the individual's obligation, direct, inescapable, to respect courage, honesty and seriousness; to work and to heal, to encourage and to console others. Few, in all periods, escape some form of plague, but even if it is fatal, it can induce us to live life more fiercely, help others more abundantly. Whether Life has ultimate purpose is unimportant. Opportunities abound to render our own life purposeful.

Camus' narrator has the quiet, tolerant, Forsterish tone I heard so often in the Fifties, without wholly accepting it. 'The evil in the world [the narrator says] always comes from ignorance.' Socrates, Buddha, perhaps Jesus, often taught this. It was hard to believe it. Richelieu and his amoral mentor Father Joseph, de Sade, the exterminators of Red Indians, the planners of the Final Solution, none were ignorant. Nevertheless, I could return to Rieux and learn from him. He was 'a man who was sick and tired of the world he lived in – though he had much liking for his fellow men – and had resolved . . . to have no truck with injustice and compromises with the truth.' Fate might possibly exist but should nevertheless be resisted; one should not cringe in the face of death, to other people, to abstractions. To overcome plague, 'the thing to do was to do your job as it should be done'. Camus' own death, in a meaningless car accident, seemed symbolic, though he might have agreed with Dickens: 'But the journey is ever onward, and we must pursue it or we are worthy of no place here.'

The Plague, like other of Camus' works, was part of the growing scepticism of general laws and dogma. 'It's only in bad novels', Lara remarks to Pasternak's Zhivago, 'that people are divided into two camps and have nothing to do with each other – in real life everything is mixed up.' I remembered General Gordon – Lytton Strachey's butt – remarking, 'I have not two but a hundred natures, none thinking alike and all wanting to rule.' I also returned to Dr Johnson: 'All theory is against the freedom of the will, all experience for it.'

British existentialism emerged from an unexpected quarter, a sleeping bag on Hampstead Heath, the home of someone calling himself a socialist supporter of world government. Colin Wilson had earlier joined the Syndicalist Workers Association, after a brief flirtation with Anarchism. He had sold books, been a hospital porter, worked in a laundry, in a provincial department store, as a bottle-washer and navvy.

More a prodigious reader than an original prodigy, he gravitated, without knowledge of German or Russian, towards the 'cultural, metaphysical mid-European', to Hesse, Thomas Mann, to Ouspensky, Gurdjieff, Dostoevsky, to Camus. 'I recreated a religious attitude out of bits of Nietzsche, Eliot, Shaw, Dante, and the Bhagavad Gita.' Obsessed with genius, including T. E. Lawrence under this heading, he was very much the ambitious, serious post-war youth who, despite the United Nations and World Health Organization and Unesco, felt a vital element missing or not catered for, in politics, in intelligence, in social life. He crystallized his dissatisfactions and remedies in a single image: 'A man without ideas has nothing to do but contemplate himself and the stock of mental images drawn from his experiences. People can do better, the Outsider does better.'

In Paris he sold magazine subscriptions, subsisting on chocolates; on Mahler, Bruckner, Bartok, Beethoven, on Dostoevsky, absorbed in 'the metaphysical nature of freedom'. He was addicted to Joyce and Faulkner, though his own prose, unremarkable, showed no trace of either which, granted his material, was convenient. Back in London, he attended 'The Bridge', a group dedicated to international unity through tolerance, individualism, freedom and an aversion to authoritarian dogma. He reiterated Nietzsche's creed, not Freedom *from* but Freedom *for*. 'Before the talk about freedom begins,' he wrote in *Encounter*, restating his beliefs from a position of unexpected celebrity, 'we ought to consider the question of who is to be free. If we are talking about a crowd of fools, this freedom might do more harm than good.' It implied an intellectual aristocracy, despite his dislike of leadership cults and patronizing élites, though it was in the tradition of Shaw and Wells, that the common man should cease to be common. His self-disclosures would have contented both: 'The whole Outsider thing sprang from the fact that I was born into a working-class environment, was too clever for it and wanted to escape. I felt an outsider.' Wilson desired the tapping of 'the enormous power-house that underlies consciousness'. His book *The Outsider*, published in 1956 and dedicated to the ever-generous and helpful Angus Wilson, was a further addition to the gospel query, 'What shall a man do to be saved?' The answer followed that of the ancient Mysteries. Dissatisfied with the ordinary, the initiate seeks rebirth by self-discipline, patience, concentration, right knowledge and, for Wilson, a sustained, sometimes agonizing intellectual effort.

The Outsider convulsed reviewers and was a swift best-seller. The title gave to many a sense of self-importance, self-understanding, difference, in which their very deficiencies seemed proof of status, though prolonged and agonizing intellectual effort had limited appeal. Brodsky swiftly gave an over-stacked party, 'from an Outsider for Outsiders', at which, excited by the existentialist possibilities offered by the white jacket of the poet Nicholas Moore, someone emptied a bottle of ink over it, and a girl removed a chair just before an elderly sculptor sat down. For others, outsidership was a licence to throw racialist taunts, Mosleyite slogans. Altogether, this, like 'the Bomb', was an excuse for failure in a philistine world, for rant, for resembling that ancient Greek philosopher who wore a peacock feather in the Agora, to attract attention.

Wilson's photograph, smiling, bespectacled, in polo-necked sweater, appeared throughout the land, the Outsider in person, standing for truth, penetrating others' secret desires, smart hypocrisies, the unreality of bourgeois existence, the irrationality of social structures, exuding 'a sense of strangeness, of unreality', but reinforcing Christ's message, to 'Live more abundantly', his need being 'To discover how to lend a hand to the forces inside him, to disrupt conventional comforts and stabilities.' Also literary reputations too long accepted on trust needed deflating; Wilson, over the radio, declared the invalidity of Shakespeare's. His personal life was suitably dramatic, his girlfriend's father threatening to horse-whip him for reasons non-literary, and in language splendidly remote from Faulkner and Hesse, Sartre, Camus, Hemingway: 'The game is up, Wilson! We know what's in your filthy diary'.

At the ICA, he lectured on 'The Outsider' undeterred by disrespect from Richard Hamilton and oafish applause from the Dean. The message was reiterated. Man's enemies are herd-values, triviality, the weight of mental inertia, stale ideas and irrelevant history; escape is in self-realization, self-mastery, to expand luminous moments of vision and insight into authentic freedom. Freedom is no social or political programme. The Outsider, like Camus' Meursault in the condemned cell, can be more free than an unheroic bourgeois plagued by greed, complacency and ignorance in a well-serviced Garden City. The Outsider's credo was Shaw's: 'Let them dread above all things stagnation.' It was that sentence in Camus' *L'Étranger*, 'Freedom is release from unreality.' It was Sartre's 'Freedom is not simply being allowed to do what you like; it is intensity of will, and it appears under any circumstances that limit man and arouses his will to more life.' This could, of course, have been written by Mussolini, and indeed frequently had been. Wilson considered Sartre and Camus taught too much nihilistic pessimism. He quoted Shaw, 'I don't want to be happy, I want to be alive and active.' He quoted Nijinsky's diary, 'The static personality is a prison,' and exhibited visions of moral and intellectual fluidity, 'soul energy', spiritual intensity. Like Carlyle, Robespierre and Nietzsche, he insisted not only that people could be galvanized but that they damn well should be, to enter freedom, freshness, wholeness, freed from the Outsider's greatest enemy, triviality.

Afterwards, he invited questions. A woman, all pearls and frills, stood up: 'Mr Wilson, I am puzzled, so please do tell me. I do not consider myself an intellectual, I have never been called an outsider. I have a beautiful home and a well-kept garden, a loving husband and two friendly and well-behaved boys. We have saved and made sacrifices to afford them an excellent education. We enjoy simple things, and go abroad to see places of historical interest. So please tell me, in all seriousness, where I have gone wrong.'

Freed from triviality, Colin Wilson rose in his pomp, a man of wrath. His words I recall more or less exactly, though I now trust to his generosity of spirit if my recollection is not word-perfect: 'You . . . you're the worst of the lot! Unspeakable! A mainstream criminal! Of course you enjoy simple things, you're incapable of anything else. Your house is garbage, your garden a midden and swamp, your husband is Gordon FitzHomo and your children are dung. Their school should be prosecuted. You're the dregs of the country, barely conceivable in your enormity and it's appalling that you ever were conceived. When you nerve yourself to go abroad, black flags are run up and the port authorities hold their noses.'

Off-stage, Colin was amiable, helpful, amused by notoriety though, like Bernard Shaw, recognizing the need for a serious writer, in a society uninterested in ideas, to adopt an unmistakable persona, to be news.

Intellectuals' reactions to *The Outsider* were varied. Philip Toynbee and Cyril Connolly rhapsodized over it, Philip finding the book 'truly astounding, luminously intelligent'. He praised its escape from parochialism, its fluency with Continental ideas, its range of reference, from mystic saints to Van Gogh, Ouspensky to Hemingway. Others were more critical. For Dwight Macdonald, 'The book is, for all its highbrow décor, an inspirational how-to treatise – be glad you're an outsider; face up to life; achieve peace of mind; develop your hidden asset, will-power!' There were jeers at 'Pop philosophy'.

In conversation, Ayer approved Wilson's industry but later wrote that the book was 'mainly a tissue of not always very accurate quotations from such philosophers as Nietzsche and contemporary existentialists . . . I believe that what originally led reviewers like Connolly and Toynbee astray was their unfamiliarity with abstract ideas combined with a middle-class sense of guilt when confronted by the work of an autodidact.'

Indeed, for Wilson's next book, *Religion and the Rebel* (1957), though a second course of the same meal, Connolly and Toynbee reversed their opinion and lost considerable respect. 'A deplorable rubbish-bin,' Philip wrote, seconded by the *New York Times Book Review*, who assessed Wilson in general as brash, conceited, pretentious, presumptuous, prolix, boring, unsound, unoriginal and totally without intellectual subtlety, wit and literary style. This warmed me towards the author and I read my wife's copy of *The Outsider*, soon stimulated by this annotation by a man much younger than myself, of writers and activists I had barely heard of – Barbusse, William James, Novalis, Ramakrishna, Berdyaev – to read further works and ponder them. While not consistently rating myself as a Hollow Man, I thought Wilson more bracing than the elegant Connolly who, in *The Unquiet Grave*, had asserted that the goal of all cultures is to decay through over-civilization: 'the factors of decadence – luxury, scepticism, wariness and superstition – are constant. The civilization of one epoch becomes the manure of the next.' This might be true, but it was more interesting to behave as if it were not. Momentarily, Colin Wilson offered the young, particularly the unpublished, a prospective leader, lonely, romantic, slightly menacing, capable of a coup, exciting by being indefinable.

In 1910, Boris Pasternak had stood with his father Leonid, the painter, at Atapova station, where Tolstoy lay dying, a wrinkled old man: 'Four slanting sheaves of light reached across the room and threw over the corner where the body lay the sign of the big shadow of the crosspiece of the window and the small childish crosses of the shadows of the firs.'

I probably first heard of Pasternak through Beatrice Scott, translator, with Robert Payne, of his *Collected Prose* (1945). Subsequently, she translated his *Safe Conduct*, and her version was much admired by V. S. Pritchett. Then, in 1952, Maurice Bowra, in *The Creative Experiment*, examined Pasternak's poetry at length. Hugh MacDiarmid considered that, in stature, Pasternak had succeeded Yeats, Rilke, Valéry. John Strachey had met him before the war, and wrote in *Encounter*, 'I have never forgotten the sense of incomparable aliveness in the man. He was possessed with immortality in his sense of "only a stronger word for life". Of his survival through the darkest times of all in the nineteen-thirties little is, I think, known. There is one anecdote. In one of the very worst years an English visitor to Moscow is said to have somehow got hold of his telephone number and rung him up. Pasternak replied:

"Oh, but my dear fellow, didn't you know? I died some years ago." '

He never sought heroic martyrdom. Isaiah Berlin met him in 1945 and 1956. 'He felt he had something to say to the rulers of Russia which only he could say, although what this was – he spoke of it often – seemed dark and incoherent to me. This may well have been due to lack of understanding on my part – although Anna Akhmatova told me that when he spoke in this prophetic strain, she too failed to understand him.' In the latter year, Pasternak submitted *Dr Zhivago* to the editors of *Novy Mir*, who rejected it. He thought it his finest work, the poetic acknowledgement that mankind is not master of life but its guest, but realized that he would have to publish it abroad, so Berlin smuggled it out of Russia. Pasternak's wife, to safeguard the children, tried to dissuade him from this, but capitulated under his anger. *Dr Zhivago*, first published in Italy in 1957, was in Britain and America the literary sensation of 1958, leading towards his aborted reward of the Nobel Prize, though for this and for publishing the book abroad, Pasternak was expelled from the all-powerful, monopolistic Writers' Union. What was its offence? The editors explained. 'The spirit of your novel rejects the Socialist Revolution, it claims that it gave the people only suffering and destroyed the Russian intelligentsia.' Worse, it not so much rejected the Revolution as seemed indifferent to it, the mortal sin of orthodox religion and politics alike. Actually, the novel was religious, concerned with rebirth on earth, physical matters being less important than spiritual illumination, poetic insight. Poetic unawareness damns, love can redeem, in the perennial myth in which defeat is the means for recovery and ascension.

To a totalitarian atheist bureaucracy this was anti-rational, anti-People, a moral vacuum, in which two adulterers reject political obedience and even full loyalty to their own work and relationship. The Stalinist cultural boss, Zhdanov, had ordained in 1946: 'The job of Soviet literature is to assist the State in educating youth correctly, to answer its needs, to raise the next generation to be strong, believing in its cause, fearing no obstacle, ready to overcome all difficulty.'

No more than Lucky Jim did Yuri Zhivago subscribe to this. He believed in no cause that the Party would have recognized or even understood. Personal dignity, expression and survival were what mattered, together with sexual freedom, always hated by a dictatorship as escaping its control, thumbing a nose at orthodoxy. Pasternak exactly represented Graham Greene's demand that a writer should be the grit wedged into the machine. Back in 1935, Pasternak had been ordered to attend the Paris Anti-Fascist Conference, graced by Aragon, Gide, Rosamund Lehmann, Spender, Auden, Dreiser, Malraux and Babel.

He told Isaiah Berlin that he had spoken unwillingly, beginning: 'I understand that this is a meeting of writers to organize resistance to Fascism. I have only one thing to say to you about that. Do not organize. Organization kills art.'

Art, he later affirmed, has two constant, unending preoccupations; it is always meditating upon death and is always creating life. Creation is the novel's core, not that of the Perfect State, but of love and charity without humbug. Zhivago is no saint, indeed is flawed, inconsistent in his loyalties and affections, at times selfish or apathetic and the more convincing because of it. As a doctor he helps people, but Society, State and People he can see only as abstracts, crushing the individual genius and oddity which make bearable the human lot.

Zhivago compares a man who complacently describes how prison re-educated and matured him, to a circus horse describing how he broke himself in. Everywhere he sees energetic people zealous for 'The Revolution', which has slumped into an all-purpose slogan, justifying cruelty and flunkeyism. Their obsequiousness is so mindless that it destroys their reasons for living, and leads them to applaud their own executions. 'And in order to do good to others he would have needed, beside the principles which filled his mind, an unprincipled heart – the kind of heart that knows no general cases but only particular ones, and which has the greatness of small actions.'

This was just what infuriated Party spokesmen, officials, the tyrannical and the sanctimonious: a refusal or inability to see life as 'either-or', a ruthless premise which blights revolution, deforms promise, literally deforms life. Robespierre and Saint-Just had discovered this too late, and it was a lesson that the Russian rejected. There is also the matter of his greatest love, not his mistress Lara, but poetry, demanding complex, often selfish dedication: 'After one or two stanzas and several images by which he was himself astonished, his work took possession of him and he experienced the approach of what is called inspiration. At such moments the correlation of the forces controlling the artist is, as it were, stood on its head. The ascendancy is no longer with the artist or the state of mind which he is trying to express, but with language, his instrument of expression. Language, the home and dwelling of beauty and meaning, itself begins to think or speak for man and turns wholly into music, not in the sense of outward, audible sounds, but by virtue of the power and momentum of its inward flow. Then, like the current of a mighty river polishing stones and turning wheels by its very movement, the flow of speech creates in passing, by the force of its own laws, rhyme and rhythm and countless other forms and formations, still more important and until now undiscovered, unconsidered and unnamed.

'At such moments, Yuri felt that the main part of his work was not being done by him but by something which was above him and controlling him; the thought and poetry of the world as it was at that moment and as it would be in the future. He was controlled by the next step it was to take in the order of its historical development; and he felt himself to be only the pretext and the pivot setting it in motion.'

This was a declaration of independence from one who, in Party terms, was a blackleg, a religious lazybones; it was also flying in the face of a growing French philosophical distrust of language, that, with its ability to discriminate, order and classify, was, as Roland Barthes was to complain, 'quite simply, fascistic'.

Philip Toynbee refused to rate *Dr Zhivago* a work of genius. Pasternak admired Tolstoy, Rilke, Proust and Joyce, but was unconcerned with Modernist fragmentations and kinetic gadgetries. He found Sartre's *La Nausée* unreadable, telling Isaiah Berlin that he worried lest, after four centuries, France could no longer produce literature. *Dr Zhivago*, Philip judged, was a residue of the classic, straightforward nineteenth-century novel, a formula quite played out, archaic in this century, an old-fashioned, even a reactionary return to linear narrative, clumsy plotting, melodramatic episodes of innocent virgins, rich seducers, improbable coincidences and artificial interventions, and waved aside V. S. Pritchett's argument that, as a plea for private life and integrity, the novel should not be so judged.

Philip was in America in 1959, where he met Edmund Wilson. There followed an exchange:

Toynbee, rather nervously: 'Mr Wilson, you know, I didn't altogether agree with your view of *Dr Zhivago* ...'

Wilson, heartily: 'Ah! Good! It's an unexpected pleasure and indeed considerable reassurance to meet a British author who knows Russian, and can thus appreciate the infinite nuances of such an apparently simple word as *garden*, or the multiple associations of, say *yellow* or *red*. It's possible the Russian manuscript I worked from may differ in a few slight respects from Pasternak's preferred original. Nevertheless ...'

Toynbee, uneasy: 'Well, it wasn't actually a Russian edition that I reviewed. You see ...'

Wilson, even more heartily: 'You would have perused the Italian version, and there are certainly some very good things there. In one respect, indeed ... You will be in a position to enlighten me ...'

Toynbee, miserably: 'I'm afraid not. The English translation ...'

Wilson, in the tone of an American Lady Bracknell: 'The English *translation* ... !'

*   *   *

In 1957 appeared *Voss*, by the Australian novelist Patrick White, which at least one critic compared to Tolstoy's *War and Peace*. This too, though for me a titanic work hewn out of harsh landscape, savage history, the barely controllable rasps in human personality, did not wholly conform to Philip's demands and those of a young 'experimental' novelist, B. S. Johnson, who was already proclaiming: 'A writer is obliged to discover what is new. Only a stubborn adherence to obsolete techniques places the novel in the position of a minor art.' White, who had written plays and experienced the fires and bombs of wartime London, had wandered amongst many classes in a dozen countries, knew as much about fragmentations, time-shifts and multiplicities within the ego as any Fifties writer in any continent, was as susceptible to the techniques of painting and sculpture as most critics, and as knowledgeable about the discoveries of physics, medicine, geology, the vital interconnections, as most academics. Sylvia Lawson, writing in 1991, saw 'extended Cubist sequences' within his descriptions: 'Wall, skies, furniture, fences, ways of sitting and feeling are juxtaposed; various pasts into the present,' but for many of us, White discovered the new, not in the formal techniques but in language. In an 1958 essay, 'The Prodigal Son', he wrote: 'Writing, which had meant the practice of an art by a polished mind in civilised surroundings, became a struggle to create completely fresh forms out of the rocks and sticks of words. I began to see things for the first time. Even the boredom and frustration presented avenues for endless exploration; even the ugliness, the bags and iron of Australian life, acquired a meaning.' From *The Aunt's Story* (1948), his novels exposed the skull beneath the skin, the raw being beneath civilized decorum, rituals and values – as, beyond the Australia of brilliant lights, clear-cut architecture and pulsating communities, lurk deserts, mysteries, cliffs and boulders, torrid suns and fierce winds; beings primitive yet sophisticated, sensuous, bound to lost worlds and live memories, while, in the cities, the ladies and gentlemen are closer than they imagine to legends, spirits, violence, legal piracy, gallows-talk; to nakedness. Some New Australians, furthermore, had known the Nazi camps. Setting *The Aunt's Story* alongside a novel with a comparable theme, Angus Wilson's *Late Call*, I saw a work of genius alongside one of a very intelligent and compassionate talent.

Voss, more hero than role model, struggles to cross the continent, with tangled motives, confronting brute physical challenge which threatens to rip the guts from conventional history and culture, with the same tenacity and pain with which White explores the geography of language, the gritty depths within the brilliant or worn-out surfaces of words. His scope, for me, reduced the 'New' French novelists Robbe-Grillet and Michel Butor to pedantic cleverness, in the Second Eleven; and he had the vividness of perception of D. H. Lawrence, without the preaching.

White's pen, in all his novels, was continuously at flash-point, intensifying the prose more fiercely than Virginia Woolf, heightening his observation as minutely as Robbe-Grillet, finding vocabulary for German refugees, middle-aged spinsters, an ambitious colonial painter, Australian suburbanites, those accustomed to fumble for words. He was determined 'to find the extraordinary behind the ordinary'. His sentences, like his readers, were made to work; literature should not be lulling or comfortable, but exploration as taxing as Voss's struggles through desert and scrub, past fissures and larva, dead trees and dim, ominous, brooding shapes. Endless pronouncements, stimulating or infuriating, make for slow reading, useful for myself, who read too hastily: 'The past is a miracle of minor saints.' 'The soul remains anchored. It is a balloon tied to a bunch of bones. Still, it will tug nobly.' A woman in a later novel 'held her head graciously when she could have let loose a whole string of the yawns she was suppressing. From feeling them swell inside her throat, he saw them as a continuum of soft unlaid eggs in the innards of a slaughtered hen.'

Personality, like class, even gender, is fractured, its bits and pieces colliding in and out of childhood, the present and the future, though White himself remained craggy, bad-tempered and alarming, no poetic recluse but angrily campaigning for aboriginal rights and republicanism; against tyrannical multinationals, nuclear tests, the Vietnam war, uranium mining, American pressures; joining in the quarrels over the Sydney Opera House. Also, giving his Nobel Prize money to benefit Australian writers less well rewarded.

A century ago, Richard Wagner, who had hailed his own *Ring* libretto as the greatest poem ever written, had stated: 'The genuine art form cannot at present be created but only prepared for, yes, by revolutionary means, by destroying, by crushing all that deserves to be crushed.' In the Fifties, this undesirable prophecy seemed just possible in music, abstract art and amongst writers striving to shed the past, to strip language of classical and stale associations, discover genuine truths about people and society without the stock properties – stable, homogeneous personalities, final endings, logic, nuclear families – that, by seeking to entertain, merely distorted, shirking new vision and new human types. Writers could be visitants in a strange land, where rivers, mountains and forests waited to be named. Marshall McLuhan was now arguing that literacy had weakened perceptions and awareness, dismembering the unity of the senses and general vitality. By preferring the coarse, undiscriminating reading eye to the more delicately attuned ear, civilization softened its reactions to nature and the organic: in the global village, literature would become unnecessary and obsolete, replaced by the visual and auditory media.

White and Pasternak had used the resources of a vast hoard of words and imagery, but at the ICA, in *Observer* columns, there was increasing mention of Samuel Beckett, hitherto unknown to many, though he was soon to be reckoned, in *The Times Literary Supplement*, one of the greatest prose writers of the century. Reacting against the Durrells and Leigh Fermors, critics approved his belief that language should reduce itself and the world to nothingness; he complained to Richard Coe that he was afraid of English, 'because you can't help writing poetry in it'. Poetry too was hostile to truth. He had written, in German, to Axel Kaun that, for him, English was failing to reach 'the Nothingness'; that grammar and style were as irrelevant as a Victorian bathing suit. 'Let us hope that the time will come, thank God that in certain circles it has already come, when language is most efficiently used when it is most efficiently misused. As we cannot eliminate language all at once, we should at least leave nothing undone that might contribute to it falling into disrepute. To bore one hole after another in it until what lurks behind it – be it something or nothing – begins to seep through it; I cannot imagine a higher goal for a writer today.'

Writers, Beckett thought, should seek a new form to accommodate 'the mess of contemporary life', a world empty of God, design, meaning, order, choice; a world of accidents, of the unfinished and unproven, where the real is, at best, unreal.

Suspecting that minimalism was not the sole guardian of truth, despite its refutation of entertainment, preferring the organic to the revolutionary and novel, I found this unprepossessing. Language, from an Orwell, a Karl Kraus, a Dickens, an Ibsen, was man's keenest weapon against monstrosity. However, Beckett himself, living in Paris, seemed from this distance austere, courageous, remarkable. He had assisted James Joyce, he had worked for the French Resistance and had had to hide from the Gestapo. He had also written an unpublished novel, in which he scorned Balzac's 'chloroform fiction' which pared people down to 'clockwork cabbages', though Cousine Bette, Vautrin and César Birotteau have more vitality than many of Beckett's characters, 'shredded breath', as he called them. He prided himself on 'emancipating' them 'from identity', imagining this an improvement on the wretched Balzac, Tolstoy, Dostoevsky, Mann or Bellow.

Beckett had an advance guard of critics proclaiming his genius, though doing so with noticeable care for grammar and style, and elaborate use of words, as though the Victorian bathing suit retained practical advantages. I also heard that he had, unlikely though it seemed, appeared in first-class cricket. I turned him up; yes. 'Matches, 2 : Innings, 4 : Runs, 55 : Catches, 2 : Bowling, 0 for 64.' The only other writer of stature who had played at this level was Conan Doyle, whose figures were: 'Matches, 10 : Innings, 18 : Runs, 43 : Catches, 1 : Bowling, 0 for 10.'

Unwilling to welcome a literature of nothingness, a theatre of silence, I was unprepared for the power of *Waiting for Godot*, the theatrical explosion of 1955, which left people arguing about the identity of Godot, the play's meaning, as they once argued about Hamlet's madness or Orson Welles's 'Rosebud'. Beckett himself, when invited to explain the play, would reply, 'Exactly what it says,' though once he expanded to a critic, 'If I knew, I would have said so in the play.' I was less concerned with its meaning than with its force. Never gifted with critical acumen, and already stupified by the chatter, I watched and waited. Only to those who need instant answers, snap judgements, Christmas cracker mottos, was the play any more 'difficult' than most serious work, which cannot find existence well-made and orderly, but more often, more truthfully, knows it to be muddled, painful, inconclusive, mysterious, often despairing, with people's utterances often opposed to their thoughts, often a means only to avoid mutual understanding.

In Vladimir and Estragon, Beckett fused two immemorial archetypes, tramp and clown, with echoes of Lear's Fool, of Sancho Panza, perhaps Thersites. They were two Laurels without a Hardy, with further echoes of Chaplin and Keaton, with their training in music-hall and vaudeville: masters of mime, improvization, graceful inanity, manipulating laughter or shock – the shock of the strange – by a lift of the shoulder or eyebrow, shattering one moment and creating another by an unexpected dance, a languid *non sequitur*. Beckett's pair began yielding me a sense of dignified futility, the genuine stature of human independence, an almost overwhelming sympathy for humanity's plight. Life flickered from embers that might never revive, sustained less by hope of Godot than by memory, obstinacy, the spice of repartee. Bound together by inexorable webs of existence, the two, perhaps most of us, are divided only by trivialities, lost in waste, revolving like dead planets round a sun, perhaps illusory but certainly dying; enduring pain, trudging towards nowhere, awaiting a sign from 'the great cold, the great dark, the air and the earth abode of stones in the great cold alas alas'. I remembered suddenly a line from some Reformation agony: 'We are in the desert, on a wild heath under the bare heavens.'

Here, and later, Beckett was creating a world, a universe, far from my own, akin to a phenomenon dreaded by our Northern forebears, the periodic *Fimbul* Winter, desolate, world-bound, lasting three years but with forebodings of universal destruction, which hones human purposes down to brute survival, within a degree of loneliness seldom encountered in prose literature and seldom, I hope without conviction, in life. People, in *Fimbul*, hang on – just; possessions are worthless, relationships wither to claw and tooth; blood and mind starve. It is Jesus's Time of Troubles, prelude to Judgement; existence with its colours, variety, impetus, its dazzling interconnectedness, is reduced to a grey, imprisoning monotony redeemed only by courage and wry humour. When Molloy, in *Molloy* (1951), mentions that he is still alive, he adds, 'that may come in useful'.

In this light, the light of Homer's twittering Hades, or Newgate's condemned cell, I found very convincing some information in Martin Esslin's *The Theatre of the Absurd* (1961): in San Quentin gaol in 1957, fourteen hundred American prisoners sat in total concentrated silence through *Godot*, shaking as they left the theatre. The local newspaper commented that the play demanded that each watcher 'draw his own conclusions, make his own errors. It asked nothing in point, it forced no dramatised moral on the viewer, it held out no specific hope. We're still waiting for Godot, and shall continue to do so.'

It was a salutary tonic against glib optimism and shallow expectations, though Beckett's definition of art seemed expressive only of his own art: 'the expression that there is nothing to express, nothing with which to express, nothing from which to express, together with the obligation to express'. His vision and techniques were continually refined so that in the play *Breath*, lasting thirty seconds, Beckett used no words, to 'encompass human life between the cry of a newborn child and the last gasp of a dying man'. To those raised on Shakespeare, Shaw and Chekhov, it might not have presented a full evening's entertainment or revelation. One of the minor pleasures of life, after all, is coping with life: the spirited wrestle, at some length, with the brutal and the unfair, the plain wrong and the inhuman good.

A much younger writer from the Fifties, John Wain, was later to write that Beckett had a very minor talent. 'His reputation will come to be seen, in retrospect, one of those interesting collective lapses in taste like the Victorian admiration for Martin Tupper.' Beckett, he continued, was a connoisseur of hopelessness, for whom 'the capital crime is simply to be alive; that is the stupidity, the evil, the appalling meta-physical gaffe for which we are to be snubbed and punished for ever'.

However, Beckett had spoken to Harold Hobson, the drama critic of the *Sunday Times*, in a way that, I think, qualifies Wain's strictures: 'I am interested in the shape of ideas even if I do not believe in them. There is a wonderful sentence in Augustine . . . "Do not despair; one of the thieves was saved. Do not presume; one of the thieves was damned." That sentence has a wonderful shape. It is the shape that matters.'

Vladimir and Estragon conveyed more than shape, and, that night in 1955, briefly expelled from my imagination another image, from a writer whom Beckett and his addicts probably despised: Jean Cocteau. It was from *Les Enfants terribles* and had lain in me like a seed pod deposited by the wind: 'The world owes its enchantment to the curious creatures and their fancies; but its multiple complicity rejects them. Thistledown spirits, heartrending in their evanescence, they must go blowing headlong to perdition. And yet, all started harmlessly, in childish games and laughter.'

Throughout the Fifties, Isaiah Berlin was acquiring repute as a historian of ideas, a philosopher, an authority on Russian history. Born in Riga, from 1957 he held at Oxford the Chichele Chair, for social and political theory. Wartime service in the British Embassy, Washington, had involved him in an incident now celebrated. His regular reports on American conditions were scrutinized by the Cabinet and particularly attracted Churchill, who professed a wish to meet 'Berlin'. Lady Churchill obediently arranged a luncheon, at which the composer of 'Alexander's Ragtime Band', after a sequence of unprofessional answers to expertly composed questions, was left baffled by the great man's obvious disillusion and increasing grumpiness.

Whenever I heard Isaiah Berlin, I was reassured about the richness of life – an escape from Beckett's desolation, the hard dicta of Sartre. I sensed dedicated men and women, the poets and thinkers and political leaders, working on, despite war, persecution, poverty and folly; masterpieces being created and scrutinized, humour bubbling from unexpected places; the fallibility of the great who do not thereby lose greatness; the inescapable pre-war Russian Terror, genius eliminated by mediocrity, a few guilty perishing amongst innocent millions; Berlin's own humane belief in fellow-men, his admiration for heroes and heroines, unperturbed by cynicism, disillusion and moral fatigue. He spread about him an atmosphere of history being made, not by remote automatons but live, breathing people.

I once heard Berlin in a lecture describe Tolstoy, in his village school, instructing peasants that art must induce morality. Alas, Tolstoy himself was addicted to Mozart and Maupassant, whose moral didacticism was faint. However, he could not resist playing the one and reading aloud from the other, assuaging his conscience by rebuking his pupils if they enjoyed it. I could imagine Berlin's smile, at Flaubert's visiting the Church of the Holy Sepulchre in Jerusalem, and immediately encountering a life-sized portrait of Louis-Philippe.

Sir Isaiah's 1956 essay on the nineteenth-century Russian thinker Alexander Herzen affected me intellectually as deeply as Pasternak, Beckett and White had emotionally, though of course the two strands intermingled. Here again was the humane, unpriggish, liberal spirit cutting through the dogmatic abstractions which had destroyed Robespierre and Saint-Just, as well as large numbers of their fellow-countrymen, and their international successors. For Herzen, 'One of the deepest of modern disasters is to be caught up in abstractions instead of realities.' He spoke of 'the despotism of formulae'.

Or, 'If only people, instead of wanting to liberate Humanity wanted to liberate themselves, they would do a very great deal for human freedom.' Or, 'Who will finish us off? The senile barbarism of the sceptre or the wild barbarism of Communism ... Communism will sweep across the world in a violent tempest – dreadful, bloody, unjust, swift.'

Sir Isaiah made successive comments which I noted and have repeatedly re-read: 'Herzen's political and social views were arrestingly original, if only because he was among the very few thinkers of his time who in principle rejected all general solutions, and grasped, as very few thinkers have ever done, the crucial distinction between words that are about words, and words that are about persons or things in the real world.'

Particularly useful for post-war disappointments and Fifties dilemmas were Berlin's human signposts, for a number of us more appetizing than the toxic freedoms of Kerouac and Burroughs, the theoretical deductions of Sartre and Heidegger: 'The heart of his [Herzen's] thought is the notion that the basic problems are perhaps not soluble at all, that all one can do is to try and solve them but that there is no guarantee either in socialist nostrums or in any other human construction, no guarantee that happiness or a rational life can be attained, in idealism and scepticism – not unlike, for all his vehemence, the outlook of Erasmus, Montaigne, Montesquieu ... Herzen says in effect: "Organized hooliganism can solve nothing. Unless civilization – the recognition of the difference between good and bad, noble and ignoble, worthy and unworthy – is preserved, unless there are people who are both fastidious and fearless, and are free to say what they want to say, and do not sacrifice their lives upon some large, nameless altar and sink themselves into a vast, impersonal, grey mass of barbarians marching destroying . . . what is the point of the revolution?

'For Herzen, one of the greatest of sins that any human being can perpetuate is to seek to transfer moral responsibility from his own shoulders to those of an unpredictable future order, and, in the name of something which may never happen, perpetrate crimes today which no one would deny to be monstrous if they were performed for some egoistic purpose, and do not seem to be so only because they are sanctified by faith in some remote and intangible Utopia.'

Bismarck believed that politics is not a science that could be taught. By 1956, I was learning that, like marriage, like teaching, like acting, it is an art compounded by experiment, guile, intrigue, insights, observation and bluff, a balance between cliques, crowds and personal convictions, absorbing as a novel not quite of the finest quality. Amid reluctance to risk 'value judgements', the Burgess Hill suspicion of leadership, the hippies' contempt for common sense, the mods' and rockers' intoxication through violence, the language of Sir Isaiah Berlin had an effect like opening windows after a cigarette-fumed, ill-tempered bridge party. Once, after a Berlin lecture, a man of villainous appearance and mouldy breath, in an overcoat coloured like a map of Wales, turned to me: 'That Berliner . . . he sure does talk, he sure does make jaw, he sure does *know!*'

15

Theatricals

REVIEWING TERENCE RATTIGAN'S play, *Adventure Story*, in 1949 in the *Spectator*, James Pope-Hennessy used a language about to become obsolete. 'What a relief it is to find a play which is such excellent theatre, and makes no intellectual and very few emotional pretensions or demands.' This was an attitude against which Ibsen and Shaw had raged years before, which Brecht condemned and Beckett had disowned. In England it was to be challenged most flamboyantly by Kenneth Tynan, advocate of the new dramatists, John Osborne and Arnold Wesker. Tynan preferred the raw, demotic, aggressive 'Kitchen Sink' to what he considered the etiolated verse-plays of T. S. Eliot, Ronald Duncan and Christopher Fry.

From whatever internal pressures Tynan, like the Regency dandy Beau Brummell, needed to be noticed, to astonish. 'Shock is the denial of what is expected.' He could follow Brummell in dress, deportment and insolence, and Oscar Wilde by possessing, if not genius, then considerable talent reinforced by unexpected turns of fancy and repartee. 'My views on corporal punishment are pronounced: I believe with Mr Coward, that women should be beaten regularly, like gongs.' By adroit play-acting, clutching an imaginary collapsed hip, he escaped menacing Oxford bullies. The journalist Alan Brien wondered: 'What could a Beardsley from a middle-class Birmingham home do – except decide to be a genius or a freak?' Kathleen Tynan records: 'During his first term [at Oxford] he had made to order a purple doeskin suit, waisted over the hips, which he wore with gold satin shirts.' He told Ralph Glasser, 'Oxford's only use is to give you a stage to strut on and promote yourself. And that's what I'm good at.'

Little of Tynan's showy exoticism suggested security. Yet for a man who was dead at 53, his passage, with its plumage, glittering swoops, starry anecdotes, its startling ascent and slow decline, was a Fifties show-piece. Baudelaire called the Dandy an unemployed Hercules, though Tynan was neither. After Oxford he was briefly in the West End as an actor. His performance, as First Player in *Hamlet*, was, if Beverley Baxter, drama critic of the *Evening Standard*, is to be believed, of excruciating badness. He wrote smart journalism and scripted Donald Mackenzie's novel *Nowhere to Go* for Maggie Smith's first film, but it was as a critic and, later, as adviser to Olivier at the National Theatre that he achieved final influence. He promoted what seemed new, audacious, international: Brecht, Genet, Beckett. His dramatic criticism was not dandified or pretentious, and was seldom arrogant. In contemporary work he would discern the inner play so often stamped out by outsize performances. He wrote of Tennessee Williams's plays having the static quality of a dream rather than the dynamic quality of fact. Whereas Arthur Miller's plays were 'hard, "patrist", athletic, concerned mostly with men, Williams's are soft, "matrist", sickly, concerned mostly with women. What links them is their love of the bruised individual soul, and its life of "quiet desperation".'

Tynan saw John Osborne's *Look Back in Anger* (1956) as a 'minor miracle', a smash hit against the tyranny of good taste, uniting class war and sex war in a revelation of 'post-war youth as it really is', though his credentials as an authority on youth were not of the highest. It focused on the crude, rhetorical, unstoppable Jimmy Porter, no product of Oxbridge, articulating the contempt and resentment of those who, despite the Century of the Common Man, could see privileges still earned by lack of talent, philistine pretentiousness sold as culture by Sunday papers, Old Boy controls rampant in an England of meaningless work, joylessness, cheapened vocabularies, mindless catchwords, with property developers and hypocritical scoundrels rampant, threatened only by the A-Bomb. His speeches declaimed the misgivings, the grievances and the impatience of almost everyone who resented the power and corruption of parents. Also of wives.

Porter became controversial overnight. J. B. Priestley deplored him, Colin Wilson thought he needed kicking. Osborne himself said that he had wanted to make people feel, to give them lessons in feeling. Noël Coward found the play 'electrifying'. Tynan pronounced Jimmy Porter 'already a central figure in contemporary mythology'.

'Nobody thinks,' Porter raged, 'nobody cares. No beliefs, no convictions, and no enthusiasms. Just another Sunday evening?' Earlier excitements – the Festival of Britain, the New Elizabethan Age, growing European unity, the Welfare State, new universities – all dissolved in dismissive rant, which, despite Tynan's rapture, was more theatrical than factual. Porter complained: 'I suppose people of our generation aren't able to die for good causes any longer. We all had that done for us, in the thirties when we were still kids. There aren't any good brave causes left. If the big bang does come and we all get killed off, it won't be in aid of the old-fashioned, grand design. It'll just be for the Brave New – nothing-very-much thank you. About as pointless and inglorious as stepping in front of a bus.'

There was considerable reading of Sunday papers in the play, which, in 1956, would have been crowded with dynamic causes at home and abroad. Let the oafish Porter, I felt, join anti-slavers in Libya or the Gulf, resistance groups in Estonia, Nazi-hunters in South America, volunteer for social service in Africa, in Israel, in India, and much else. He was in no way part of that tiresome commodity, 'the human predicament', but only displayed the Porter predicament, with corrosive rancour, stupendous laziness and galling lack of talent.

Admittedly, I watched the play in unsympathetic circumstances. My companions were a Polish Jewish girl, tragically orphaned, a Gaullist Resistance officer, and an English colonial administrator who had, at 19, led troops into Belsen, and I reacted more through them than myself. The men were courteous but perplexed, the girl was furious with Porter's submissive women and Porter himself. All had known torment, atrocities, criminals in power, and were unable to understand, for they were profoundly grateful for England's war effort, for her part in the Berlin Airlift, her generosity to themselves. Each was working hard in useful, humanitarian causes. Afterwards the Frenchman quoted Epictetus, of whom I had never heard, though, snobbishly, I nodded and grinned as though I had. He had been a crippled slave, admired by Marcus Aurelius, and at a few words from him the squalls of Jimmy Porter dwindled to squeaks: 'I must die. But must I die groaning? I must be imprisoned. But must I also whine? Can anyone prevent me departing without a smile, with good courage, at peace with myself? My leg you can chain, certainly, but not my will. Even to Zeus himself, that is immune.'

Porter seemed, that week, irredeemably trivial, and I imagined the shrugs of Malraux or of Arthur Miller. I remembered a news-reel shot of Louis and Edwina Mountbatten in India, dressed as if for a Viceregal reception, calmly walking hand in hand into a riotous mob, emerging unscathed and triumphant, then de Gaulle in Paris in 1944, striding towards Notre-Dame, German bullets falling around him, which he did not appear to notice.

Porter howled: 'I knew more about – love ... betrayal ... and death, when I was ten years old than you will probably ever know all your life.' My Polish friend shifted uneasily. At 10, she and her family had been rounded up by the Gestapo. Half the audience must have known battle, terror, blitz, many of them were Jewish. The play was intolerably provincial, another 'Look at me' fantasy. An elderly woman behind us quavered: 'That poor young man. To think that no one gets him to the doctor!'

Too much history is a search for someone to blame: class, wives, school, parents. Also, Maurice Cranston wrote, in 1957, that behind Porter's attacks on the upper classes could be detected a deep desire to have been born one of them, to share their privileges. Later, I read the play quite alone; stage directions revealed nuances and meanings I had missed, some of them obscured by the sheer noise and onrush of performance. Porter gained poignancy: the lost jazz band, the lost madeleine. Alison's words were moving, in this quietness: 'It isn't easy to explain. It's what he would call a question of allegiances, and he expects you to be pretty literal about them. Not only about himself and all the things he believes in, his present and his future, but his past as well. All the people he admires and loves and has loved. The friend he used to know, people I've never even known – and probably wouldn't have liked. His father, who died years ago. Even the other women he's loved. Do you understand?'

Yes. Common enough, but not banal. Like those he condemned, he was mostly 'Looking forward to the past'.

Osborne's effect was blasting. A number of 'posh' West End actors – Denholm Elliot was one – lost ground. The West End accents and drawing-rooms, the aphorisms, the cocktails appeared irretrievably doomed, along with refined restraint, stiff upper lips, Home Counties comedy, sexual understatements, and the last of the pre-Suez, wartime values.

Even the Fifties Ballet was affected, through Kenneth MacMillan, youthful admirer of Fred Astaire, pupil in a girls' tap-dancing school, who had forged his father's signature to win a Sadler's Wells scholarship. His *Somnambulism* (1952) and *House of Birds* (1955) led on to *Romeo and Juliet, Song of the Earth, Checkpoint, Mayerling* and *Prince of the Pagodas*, and angered those who sought ballet for romance or escape, and had been bored or repulsed by Kurt Joos's pre-war *The Green Table*, a bitter, anti-war satire, with robot-like figures emptily gesticulating round a green baize conference table, while Death prowled, blowing where he listed. MacMillan tore away nursery illusions and pretty decorations, and drew his dancers deep into the century. Rape, suicide, sexual repressions, cruelty and terror had their place in dance drama, as in life.

Neither Coward nor Rattigan went meekly to ground after 1956. For Coward, though not Shaw and Brecht, the theatre was 'a house of strange enchantment, a temple of dreams'. That clear, clipped voice remained unmistakeable: 'What it most emphatically is not and never will be is a scruffy, ill-lit drill-hall serving as a temporary soap box for political propaganda.' The remainder of the Fifties and all the Sixties apparently refuted him but he remained unabashed. 'Twice as long as the real thing and just as loud,' he said of Lionel Bart's *Blitz*. Though Sheridan Morley has revealed that Coward helped finance Pinter's *The Caretaker*, he continued to berate 'the scratch and mumble' acting in 'dust-bin drama'. He complained, against the puritan drama centred upon the Royal Court Theatre: 'We must all just sit and wait for death, or hurry it on, according to how we feel. To my mind, one of the most efficacious ways of hurrying it on is to sit in a theatre watching a verbose, humourless, ill-constructed play, acted with turgid intensity, which has received rave notices and is closing on Saturday.' As against Stanislavsky, and Lee Strasberg's 'method' schools of acting, he advised actors to speak clearly, not to bump into each other, and 'if you must have motivation, think of your pay packet on Friday'.

Osborne's next play, *The Entertainer*, found an image in the broken comedian, Archie Rice, an image both tragic and horrific. Here was a requiem for a great institution, symbol of a lost, pre-Suez Britain of ungrudging humour, relative unity, a vulgarity which lacked morbidity, listlessness and self-distrust, a sort of swaggering assurance, now gone. Archie despises his audience, but is concerned not to demolish or enrich society, merely to endure the day unscathed. Owing much to Olivier's bravura swagger and collapses, all the tricks of the trade, in a display that could have started the Northern Lights, it spoke directly to me, as had Orwell and Dickens, laureates of the unnoticed. Breaking through the beat-up hopelessness, pain, soiled and fake jocularity, Olivier dropped his words as if delicately, unhurriedly carving them, each to a slightly different weight. One passage particularly needed jotting down, as both of and beyond its time. Archie says to his daughter: 'Did I ever tell you the most moving thing that I ever heard? It was when I was in Canada ... I suppose you've never sat lonely and half-stewed in some bar among strangers a thousand miles from anything you think you understand. But if ever I saw any hope or strength in the human race, it was in the face of that old fat negress getting up to sing about Jesus or something like that ... I don't suppose we'll ever hear it again. There's nobody who can feel like that old black bitch with her fat cheeks, and sing. If I'd done one thing as good as that in my whole life, I'd have been all right. Better than all your getting on with the job without making a fuss and all that, all your rallies in Trafalgar Square.'

In the later Fifties, Colin MacInnes read me an article by the Jewish novelist and football critic, Brian Glanville, which showed pity for Jewish writers who had either abandoned rich, traditional subject matter without finding a better substitute, or remained absorbed with 'an East End world which no longer exists, presented in terms of a tradition which was built up and died in Eastern Europe'. Colin and I respected Glanville but were perplexed, already familiar with the younger Jewish writers around us who, if they were concerned with East London, were doing so in terms of the tragedy and comedy, not of a static and lost community, but one of change, movement, nostalgia and passion. One of Arnold Wesker's East Londoners joins the International Brigade in Spain. Emanuel Litvinoff remembered pre-war Whitechapel but his novel *The Lost Europeans* (1958) set devastated European Jewry against the busy glitter of post-war Berlin prospering from defeat: Dannie Abse, Frederick Raphael, Wolf Mankowitz, Mordecai Richler, Bernice Rubens, Harold Pinter, Rudolf Nassauer, Jon Silkin, Gerda Charles, Arnold Wesker, Glanville himself, all grappled with post-war, post-Holocaust themes, in a world still muddled, seeking outlets and new vocabularies where, far from the East End, a rich middle-aged man tied a cord across the garden path of a blind woman, having painted 'Filthy Jew' on her front door, and, at a mild tennis party, a youngish, almost beautiful German face turned to me as if in accusation and murmured: 'My troops fought well in Warsaw.'

Glanville had selected Bernard Kops as one writer still trapped in the tradition of the old East End, the culture of Israel Zangwill. MacInnes maintained that Glanville 'could not conceivably have done so more ineptly'. True, *The Hamlet of Stepney Green* was set in the East End, but unattached to a ghetto outlook. Loosely based on *Hamlet*, a theme many centuries older than Shakespeare, it displays a post-war youth straining to escape his own Denmark, the ghetto inheritance, and win freedom from today's tensions. His sister has already departed north and has married a Gentile Communist vegetarian. The play affectionately but decisively mocks the old Jewish world and traits enforced by transitory historical pressures, superannuated now that English Jews are rejoining mainstream international culture. Throughout it, there is the struggle, the fight, rebirth, the overthrow (sometimes painfully) of beliefs hallowed but archaic. It crackles with Fifties vitality, without Jimmy Porter's scowls and abuse. Kops can be as crude, but his Hamlet is determined to open a real gate in a dream world. 'Commit arson every day in your imagination, burn down the previous day's lies, have a little revolution now and again in your heart; try and help lonely people. People are lonely all over the world; lonely and lovely because they are animals with souls.

'Make the most of your life – because life is a holiday from the dark – make the most of the world – because it is your world.'

Wesker's name was often followed by the epithet 'Kitchen Sink', in varying tones of respect, though it also applied to the fashion in painting headed by John Bratby, an artist compared by some to Van Gogh, though David Sylvester thought his work 'an enthusiastic mess . . . it is as well to remember that the graveyard of artistic reputations is littered with the ruins of expressionistic painters whose youthful outpourings once took the world by storm'. 'Kitchen Sink' suggested virtuous simplicity, but watching Wesker's *The Kitchen* (1959) I sometimes felt myself watching a sophisticated ballet, expertly produced by John Dexter. Ronald Hayman noted: 'Wesker shows how the rhythm of a working routine can determine not only the rhythm of the relationships that are possible inside it but the rhythm of the characters' lives . . . John Dexter's decision to eliminate food had the effect of sharpening the focus on the cooks' miming movements, and they characterised themselves all the more clearly through the way they dished out non-existent fish or rolled out imaginary pastry.'

Wesker, a small, generous, affectionate young man, combative without rancour, had himself been a pastry cook in Paris. Like Wells and Gorky, he rose from obscurity to denounce and sympathize, to proclaim and refresh, and was constantly aware of young human plants blocked by lack of light, soil and water. He touched emotions, topical, but neglected in the West End, and, if inclined towards sentimentality, faced social facts, people's transient hopes and disillusions. In *Chicken Soup with Barley*, in a scene set in 1946, 15-year-old Ronnie Kahn enthuses for 'the beginning', envisaging 'Plans for town and country planning. New cities and schools and hospitals. Nationalisation! National health! Think of it, the whole country is going to be organised to co-operate instead of to tear at each other's throats.'

Government, however, is a sequence of disappointments, organized failure. Ronnie's eldest sister, once a militant against Mosley's Blackshirts, is by now disillusioned. A few scenes, and a few years later, she exclaims to her mother, who has never struck her socialist colours: 'Haven't you ever stopped, Mother – I mean stopped, and seen yourself standing with your arms open, and suddenly paused? Come to my bosom. Everyone come to my bosom. How can you possibly imagine that your arms are long enough, for God's sake? What audacity tells you you can harbour a billion people on a theory? What great, big, stupendous audacity? Tell me.'

Tested by the Holocaust, Hungary, Suez, CND, Israeli dispossession of Arabs and Arab attacks, such plays reminded us that politics are as much an emotional prop as an intellectual conviction. In Wesker's *Roots*, the young girl, Beattie, aspires to something better, a culture that does not fail working people, coarsen their standards, rob them of discrimination and individual minds. The big audience at the Royal Court in 1959, responding to Wesker's text and Joan Plowright's acting, seemed to repeat the exhilaration of the 1945 Labour electoral victory, and Tynan rated the last act as moving as any piece of native writing he had seen on a West End stage.

Beattie has returned from London to visit her family, part of the Norfolk labouring poor who, in relation to her cultural beliefs, resemble sleepwalkers under the Matterhorn. She is enthralled by her progressively minded city boyfriend, whose political and artistic ideas have opened superb possibilities to her which she yearns to communicate, if only through his voice. Here she produces a Bizet record and exhorts her bemused mother in a manner which extracted tears from a superior-looking girl in the most expensive row: 'I'll show you. Now sit you down gal and I'll show you. Don't start ironing or reading or nothing, just sit there and be prepared to learn something. You aren't too old, just you sit and listen. That's the trouble, you see, we ent ever prepared to learn anything, we close our minds the minute anything unfamiliar appears. *I* could never listen to music. I used to like some of it but then I'd lose patience, in the middle of a symphony, or my mind would wonder 'cos the music didn't mean anything to me, so I'd go to bed or start talking: "Christ almighty!" he'd say, "don't you know something's happening around you? Aren't you aware of something that's bigger 'n you? Sit back, woman," he'd say, "listen to it, let it happen to you and you'll grow as big as the music itself." An' sometimes he talk as though you didn't know where the moon or the stars was. Now listen. This is a simple piece of music, it's not highbrow but it's full of living. You want to dance to it. And that's what he say socialism is. "Christ," he say, "Socialism isn't talking all the time, it's living, it's singing, it's dancing, it's being interested in what go on around you, it's being concerned about people and the world!" Listen, Mother. Listen to it. It's simple, isn't it?'

Even further east than the old Jewish East End, Joan Littlewood and

Gerry Raffles had been using the Theatre Royal, Stratford, for their Theatre Workshop, encouraging, blasting, rewriting new plays by unknown writers – Brendan Behan's *The Quare Fellow*, Frank Norman's *Fings Ain't Wot They Used T'be*, Shelagh Delaney's *A Taste of Honey* – candid expressions of the unorthodox, the murky, the disreputable, the honest. There were unpretty, no-nonsense productions of Shakespeare too and Sunday night vaudeville with, in music-hall tradition, spirited exchanges between performers and audience, the latter sitting uncomfortably with rugs, shawls, hot-water bottles, thermoses and whisky, generating a rough, genial, outspoken atmosphere alien to the West End theatres where black-satined ladies of utmost gentility sold, with trained condescension, expensive chocolates and over-priced though uninformative programmes, and where, at matinées, trays of tea and biscuits provided a rattling accompaniment to the next act.

A minor though brief entertainment was a journalistic invention of the 'Angry Young Men', a disparate group which allegedly included both Colin Wilson and John Osborne. It was supposedly concocted by the press officer of the Royal Court Theatre to give a fillip to seat sales for *Look Back in Anger*. What they were angry about was never wholly clear, certainly not malnutrition, slavery, genocide, prison camps or arbitrary floggings. 'Materialism' was sometimes suggested, though they did not shrink from publicity, lucrative interviews and large royalties. None were Julian Sorels or Shigalevs, nor did they much resemble the original Angry Young Man, H. G. Wells: 'I came up from the poor in a state of flaming rebellion, most blasphemous and unsaintly.'

John Braine's Joe Lampton, in his novel *Room at the Top*, did not wish to demolish the heights but to establish squatters' rights. Geoffrey Gorer, in 1957, was noting the Fifties phenomenon of 'Hypergamy': ambitious young men ascending socially, through girls richer and better-connected than themselves. Braine, outwardly aggressive, hard-drinking, suspicious of others – though not of Priestley, of whom he wrote with discernment and admiration – yet often likeable, seemed wracked with uncertainties, and was to die years later in circumstances of some pathos. Colin Wilson wanted people to read more vigorously. Osborne tended to look back rather than forward. Kingsley Amis and John Wain produced lively, disrespectful novels with thumb-nosing anti-heroes; well-crafted, unspectacular poems; self-assured, rather insular criticism unaffected by the French 'flu and fashion, or by any need to 'experiment', Amis being disrespectful to Angus Wilson on the one hand, to Modernism on the other, while praising the very English, middle-class novels of Elizabeth Taylor. Often linked together like a music-hall turn, Amis and Wain did not actually possess much in common, and must have had rather less after Amis's memoirs were published. There he printed a grossly unfair letter from Philip Larkin, like himself a jazz-loving toreador of sacred cows, but also with no obligation towards new, if fashionable, reputations. 'Isn't England a marvellous free, open country? Take a fellow like old John Wain, now. No advantage of birth or position or wealth or energy or charm or looks or talent – nothing, and look where he is now! Where else but in England could such a thing happen?' Wain eventually became Oxford Professor of Poetry, and produced useful books on Shakespeare and Dr Johnson, an appreciative and just assessment of Arnold Bennett, many novels, and 'The Shape of Feng', an under-rated poem on *Hamlet* themes.

Amis's *Lucky Jim* (1954) had been decently satirical about the sitting ducks of a university senior common room. He issued a Labour pamphlet, though later adopting a right-wing stance and accepting a knighthood. A smiling, amiable figure, he always seemed pleased to see me, and was always, I suspected, even more pleased to see me go. I realized that he would read no work of mine unless paid to, which indeed he once was, his review written in terms which, I fancied, would put paid to me. I imagine him in the Fifties to have been a stimulating university teacher in Wales, with his lack of intellectual snobbery, his professional industry and no-nonsense acumen. He was far from the slow, stately figure who years later resigned from a West End club, having been sat next to a Lord Reigate. *Lord Reigate*. A story akin to that of Beau Brummell resigning his commission when the regiment was transferred to Manchester, 'Manchester, Your Royal Highness, *Manchester!*'

Lettice Cooper, novelist and biographer, in the *London Magazine* (1957) wrote of the novels of Braine and Amis: 'These ebullient social comedies have returned full cycle to the contrived happy ending of the last mid-century. For any sane industrialist to offer Lucky Jim a well-paid job in his firm is as cheerfully improbable as for Wilkins Micawber to have become a prosperous citizen in Australia.' Somerset Maugham took a much more bilious line in the *Sunday Times*: 'I am told that today rather more than sixty percent of the men who go to the universities go on a government grant. They are the white collar proletariat ... Charity, kindness, generosity are qualities which they hold in contempt. They are scum. Mr Amis is so talented, his observation is so keen, his sympathies are so evident that you can hardly fail to be convinced of the truth of what he tells.'

The Angry Young Men were never a movement that threatened what was soon beginning to be called 'The Establishment'. Other writers saluted the lack of stuffiness, or pretentiousness, or eloquent waffle of those who understood that originality is seldom a complete answer; an original work can easily be surpassed by those who build on it, as Shakespeare's historical plays surpass those of Bale. The AYM accepted the Novel as they found it, with ample scope for their distinctive individual talents, not striving to reform or destroy or reinvent the world. They solved no mysteries but gave entertainment, some of which has endured. They were no part of 'Kitchen Sink'. Wain's anti-hero in *Hurry on Down* (1953) is a university drop-out, whom Wesker's questing Beattie would have regarded with bewildered dismay. They had no roots in the vanishing Empire, no ambition to pronounce cultural ukases, though forward enough in declaring their serious leftish moral principles. They were joined by such talent as Malcolm Bradbury (*Eating People is Wrong*, 1959) and Keith Waterhouse (*Billy Liar*, 1959), with more lively projections of anti-heroic youth, discontented, small-scale, disenchanted, decent without piety or flag-waving, often comic, sometimes farcical, without very obvious literary influences, or indeed, noticeably interested in literature itself, despite sometimes teaching it. Honest, not given to adventurous techniques, they might have absorbed Tolstoy's words: 'I have never seen lips of coral, but I have seen them the colour of brick, nor turquoise eyes, but certainly the colour of blue used in laundries.' Alan Sillitoe's *Saturday Night and Sunday Morning* (1958) showed working-class situations from a genuine working-class viewpoint.

The Fifties anti-heroic stance was seldom anarchic or sterile and was doubtless a necessary reaction to war and dictatorship. Arthur Miller reflected, in his introduction to his *Collected Plays* (1958): 'To use the word hero today is anathema, because we're most interested in the sinister complications of people, the sinister contradictions that end up as anti-hero.' Sinister contradictions were inexplicit in most of these English novelists, many of whose characters could well have associated with Camus' Dr Rieux.

Probably most writers and readers unconcerned with literary theories would have agreed with Iris Murdoch's remark, many years later to Bryan Magee, that she knew who were the great writers of the past and would not surrender them to a theory, but rather considered the theory in their light. She herself, much encouraged by Canetti, an independent mind with a philosophic grounding unusual amongst English novelists, had reached a large public with her first novel, *Under the Net* (1954), and retained it through over twenty more. No writer in Britain was more sturdily free of movements, schools of literature and fashion.

Abroad, the *nouveau roman* was still treating experience as if under Huxley's mescalin. Robbe-Grillet was attempting to unfreeze imaginations by minute observation of objects, people and atmosphere, eschewing the untruths and deceiving or distracting associations of adjectives, comparisons and metaphors for exact description delivered as if from a photographer, a physicist, or an engineer. This befitted an age when Theodore Roseburg was gathering material for his treatise, *Life on Man*. Western imagination, trained by Verne and Wells for voyages in outer space, under the ocean, through the earth's crust, and enlarged again by the sputnik, tended to overlook the central fact of the individual human body, itself a continent of secret wars, alliances, combined operations, individual sorties, with microbes demolishing dead tissues, helping digestion, destroying malignancies and promoting disease. His descriptions parallel the French novelists' microscopic vision of emotions, relationships and physical texture.

For Robbe-Grillet, Michel Butor and Nathalie Sarraute, haphazard movements within the psyche were more significant in their turmoil than when stabilized into what older generations had mistakenly called 'character'. Plot itself falsified reality, the flux of existence, the new, more truthful novels beginning, so to speak, before and after nominal events. Stories contained opposites and could be related variously, the author's account perhaps the least reliable.

British critics were more concerned with such developments than actual novelists, despite commendations from Philip Toynbee, B. S. Johnson and Alan Burns. Of Sarraute's fiction, Robert Taubman wrote in the *New Statesman*: 'Apparently a pursuit of nuance, it opens up in fact a whole range of experience we don't often read about . . . Manners are again *interesting*, human contacts have a comparably rich and subtle texture.' While admiring her novels, particularly *The Golden Fruits*, economical, witty, acute and ironic, I could not discover much more in manners and contacts than that supplied by a close reading of Dickens, let alone Proust or, indeed, V. S. Pritchett, no fervid disciple of advanced Paris. However, Sarraute herself conceded that 'the traditional novel retains an eternal youthfulness: its generous and flexible form can still, without resorting to any major change, adapt itself to all the new stories and all the new conflicts which develop within successive societies.'

Alongside Iris Murdoch and Nathalie Sarraute, Sybille Bedford was another woman writer to captivate me in the Fifties. Her account, taut, authoritative, with an eye for the ludicrous or meretricious, of the Bodkin Adams trial, *The Best We Can Do*, appeared in 1958, and she was later to write on the Lady Chatterley prosecution, the indictment of Jack Ruby for the shooting of Lee Harvey Oswald and, in Frankfurt (1963), the trial of twenty-two Auschwitz officials who pleaded that the camp had been a protective asylum for re-education, that the 'gassings' were only disinfectants, that the officials were loyal and humane patriots. She reported some hundred trials in all. And in *The Face of Justice* (1961), she turned her attention to six Algerians accused of mass murder.

Earlier, in 1953, had appeared *The Sudden View: A Mexican Journey* (reissued as *A Visit to Don Otavio*), very sharp, very visual, strongly affected by history, place, the bogus, the incongruous, the tragic, by eccentrics and by comedy. Journeying to see a Mexican grandee, Don Otavio, she found more than the horrors, cruelties, melodramas and superstition so inescapable in Mexican politics, religion and everyday life. Her eye and ear for detail were as idiosyncratic and telling as those of Fedden and Leigh Fermor, and, indeed, E. M. Forster. She observed that in a kitchen doorway, 'a very old white-bearded man was improvising poetry – sometimes sentimental, sometimes heroic, sometimes obscene – to a huddled and enthralled audience all big hats, crimson blankets and beautiful eyes'. A busybody donkey, a hedonist who likes to count people's money, wanders into some mansion and insists that a servant straps her under-hooves. Much is stated or implied by unconventional dialogue: 'Hear you had quite a rumpus yesterday. Gardener killed his wife and two of the mozos, and wounded some of the housemaids. If I were Otavio, I'd make it an excuse to sack the man.' She never ignored the niceties and importance of food: 'Supper in the provinces is at nine, and a shorter meal – chicken broth, omelette, a hot vegetable course, beefsteak or cutlets, a salad, beans, fruit, breads and chocolates, perhaps an extra piece of cake for the children, but you may ask for many things that aren't on the menu.'

In her *French Provincial Cooking*, Elizabeth David eagerly cited *The Sudden View*, expressing not just a passing compliment but also artistic fellow-feeling. The book was an organic medley of poetic fictions, bizarre confrontations, local history, psychology without jargon, and 'mad, enchanting details in vast landscapes, vistas that ambushed and captivated'. This was interesting, for David's own books were early stirrings from wartime and post-war austerity, an escape from isolation from France and indeed the Continent, in the matter of serious attention to food.

Henceforward, I was alert for Sybille Bedford's travel pieces; about France, Switzerland, Italy, Denmark, Portugal, Yugoslavia, still written

with that particular historical and political awareness, sensory imme-
diacy, the pause for the odd or grotesque, the delight in the human
scale, contempt for the immoderate or vogueish. Panoramic Rome she
reduced to a place of individuals and cherished, out-of-the-way sites;
Florence to three tiny restaurants easily overlooked, always superb. She
conveyed pleasure in leisure, talk and friendship: 'We began with a
salmon fresh from the Loire, a coolness of pink and pale green'; in little
hotels like Monet paintings: the ease, friendliness, simplicity of Fifties
travel. 'And always friendly, always light: our progress abetted, smiled
at, waved on. When we were hungry, we ate; when we were tired,
we slept; when we were in doubt, we asked. There was always wine,
a room, a word.' She could also be tart. 'During the Occupation even
one-cow farmers grew to Cadillac riches from black-market butter; and
so in 1944 the populace threw stones at the advancing Allied soldiers
because liberation from the Germans put an end to that.'

Restrictions had lifted in the Fifties, foreign travel was easier, and
notes from such writers assisted my own small progresses. She observed
the aristocratic elegance of Danish buildings, then their affinity to the
domestic baroque of north Portugal, line and grace reaching even
cottages in a land which retains aristocrats but lacks beggars. Portugal
too provoked her admiration and amused affection: 'Portuguese stares
are blank and black, immovable as flies on a butcher's meat; you turn,
you whisk, you say something: they are still in front of you. The disturbing thing is that there is no curiosity. The faces do not see. No
flicker of interest of communication animates them. Speech effects no
break-through.' One passage, on Portuguese speech, is typical of her
approach; amused, knowledgeable, curious, precise yet with a burst of
fantasy: 'The general recipe for pronunciation is to forget everything
one has ever heard or learnt of Spanish or Italian, to top off final vowels
and as many others as laziness suggests, draw out the remaining ones,
change any consonant into one easier to say, replace all 's's with a
double shsh, aim at a nasal twang (a blend of Cockney with meridional
French will do), sing the whole like Welsh, explode it to sound Polish,
and do not forget a hint of Dutch. Begin with the name of the capital:
Leesh-bowah. The trouble is that the Portuguese will not even try to
listen to your efforts!'

They may not listen but they sometimes hear. At a Portuguese
literary salon I once attempted Sybille's instructions, but the result was
preposterous; a stout woman novelist gibbered, a tall critic snarled,
two vicious children applauded and a waiter carrying a tray of drinks
slipped and appeared to break his arm.

We were not, in 1959, very obviously edging towards the European super-state, but in instinctive defence-mechanism I was learning from literature and history the precious gifts of small communities: Welsh and Irish literature, and Icelandic, with its Socratic proverb, 'Middling wise should each man be, never wise in excess.' Scandinavian democratic education, Finnish music and architecture, Dutch painting, English literature, political democracy and the giant conception of legal opposition – worth a dozen Declarations of the Rights of Man – together with Edinburgh, Venice, Florence, Dresden, Dublin, Zurich. Of the Swiss, Martha Gellhorn remarked to Sybille Bedford, 'What a genius they have for the small change of freedom!'

Who was Sybille Bedford? I would ask. The name is deceptive, for she is the daughter of an Italian princess and a German nobleman, Maximilian von Schoenbeck. The couple latterly lived apart and, at her father's death, Sybille joined her mother in Rome, then London, 'for an education which did not take place'. In fact she learnt much from her father, a connoisseur of wines and of his relatives; from her lively, sophisticated but erratic mother she sensed the nature of life: marvellous plans, disappointments painful but fruitful, the delights of self-discovery and conversation, dramatic encounters, distant goals and ambiguous rewards. Travel galvanized a sensitivity tuned to human oddity, sceptical of the portentous and noisy, as did a lifelong friendship with Aldous and Maria Huxley, itself more valuable than a doctorate.

All this suggested, if not élitism, at least the significance of élites, and she did indeed look back to an old multi-lingual society of spas, salons, private trains, pleasure domes, with frontiers not geographical but social and cultural; flawed by arrogance, complacency, indifference to the future, often by lack of imagination despite familiarity with the arts and, though without special intimacy, with artists. As her masterpiece, *A Legacy* (1956) showed, her imagination prospered on élites, but she demanded that they accept responsibilities, and was outraged as much by those who from opportunism, greed, trashy ambition or cowardice, toadied to Fascism, as she was by new élites of politburos.

No Fifties writer played less to the gallery. She proved a stocky, resolute figure with very light-blue eyes, now edged and alert, now musing, sometimes impatient, especially bright when directed towards those fancying themselves unobserved or speaking too loudly, too boastfully. Often shy, she could yet produce memorable stories – about Thomas Mann grandly holding court, Cyril Connolly causing a flood which brought down Edith Wharton's ceiling by a furtive and ill-judged disposal of food, stories of Resistance leaders, international lawyers, famous wines ... tiny incidents sparkling in the margins of history, civilized oases within chaos. A clipped voice quickened at an ungenerous remark, or at deference to some well-publicized fraud, or at a report of an influential figure performing as a judge for a literary prize without having bothered to read the book submitted. From her I learnt further to treasure 'that sense of lighter heart, deep-grooved pleasures, daylight and proportion'.

In her garden I once spoke at more than necessary length about Cary Grant to a lady of impressive features and stylish clothes. When I paused, she said serenely: 'Some of what you say may, of course, be true. On the other hand, I was once married to Cary Grant, and . . .'.

Robert Conquest, introducing his poetry anthology, *New Lines* (1956), explained: 'if one had briefly to distinguish the poetry of the Fifties from its predecessors, I believe that the most important general point would be that it submits to no great systems of theoretical contrasts nor agglomerations of unconscious demands,' continuing that Orwell, 'with his principle of real rather than ideological honesty, exerted, even though indirectly, one of the major influences on modern poetry'. He concluded that the most glaring fault when the new period opened was the omission of the necessary intellectual component from poetry. Here was a reaction to the heaven-storming, barn-storming Dylan Thomas, closely followed by W. S. Graham, and Henry Treece, better remembered as a provocative historical novelist and writer for children, and some lesser planets. They had been championed by Herbert Read as neo-romantics, post-Modernists, post-Auden, aloof from cosmopolitan eclecticism; calling themselves the New Apocalypse, though called by Robert Nye a verbal glue-factory; glazing with colour, surging with verbal splendours but lushly over-spending themselves. They left poetry needing cleaner lines, more restrained emotions, clearer thought.

Conquest's contributors included Larkin, Amis, Donald Davie, Wain, D. J. Enright; their verse, delivered in neat, well-turned, intelligent, sometimes dryly witty packages, called by J. D. Scott, Literary Editor of the *Spectator*, 'The Movement', a title rather portentous for the poets' actual wry, polite tone. It produced no masterpiece and, save for Davie and Enright, its leaders became more famed elsewhere. Conquest, soft-voiced, with gentle charm, combined grinding historical research with controlled yet passionate indignation and became a foremost and disturbing authority on Communist Russia, detailing Stalinist atrocities in such books as *The Soviet Deportation of Nationalities*, *The Harvest of Sorrows* and *The Great Terror*. In the 1960s he was one of the few writers not to denounce America's involvement in Vietnam.

A. Alvarez, himself a poet, and poetry editor of the *Observer*, besides being a mountaineer, a squash-player and, like Robin Fedden, an expert on the motives and techniques of suicide, argued that these writers had little in common save a unity of flatness, 'little more than a negative determination to avoid bad principles', illustrating this with a composite poem of his own invention, twelve lines of quotes from eight of Conquest's poets, preserving a uniform accent and manner. He considered gentility the danger to British poetry, in an age of Holocaust and atomic explosions, when, as he put it, mass evil had been magnified to match the scale of mass society, so that horror films fitted contemporary anxiety more than most poems. Few British poets, in Alvarez's view, were breaking from insularity into a world of new frontiers, new methods of analysis, new vocabularies for transformed visions: 'The pieties of the Movement were as predictable as the politics of the Thirties' poets. They are summed up at the beginning of Philip Larkin's 'Church-going' . . . This, in concentrated form, is the image of post-war Welfare State Englishman: shabby and not concerned with his appearance; poor – he has a bike, not a car; gauche but full of agnostic piety; underfed, underpaid, overtaxed, hopeless, bored, wry.'

I do not recall much underfeeding in the Fifties but would subscribe to Alvarez's general image, reflected as it is in so many Fifties novels, not least in those of Amis and Wain.

16

The Decade Closes

POLITICS CONTINUED, DESPITE the contempt of Angry Young Men and Outsiders. The new Premier, Harold Macmillan, was no ostrich. An influential publisher, familiar with many writers, he had also endured the Great War trenches, had been haunted by northern England's mass unemployment, and had served in the wartime government. Sniffing 'the wind of change' in Africa, he cantered through the Late Fifties with a deliberate, even stagey insouciance that earned him the sobriquet 'Supermac', irony mingling with affection. Since the Suez fiasco, his tenure had appeared as a lively restorative, and he successfully appealed to the country at the 1959 Election. In 1957, famously, he had stated: 'Let us be frank about it. Most of our people have never had it so good. Go around the country, go to the industrial towns, go to the farms, and you will see a state of prosperity such as we have never had in my lifetime, nor indeed ever in the history of this country.' He was repeating similar claims made some years earlier by Sam Watson, a miners' leader. Another socialist, Anthony Crosland, did not now gainsay this, and mentioned the sociologist Robert Field, who had stated that since the war living standards, 'average consumption', had increased by 20 per cent.

Sceptical of such statistics and premises, higher souls rushed to lament these materialistic standards, to decry the shallow philistinism of *prosperity*, and all that gathered within admass, with powerful if unwholesome connotations anticipated long ago by H.G. Wells in *Tono-Bungay*. The word was invented by J. B. Priestley who, in *Journey Down a Rainbow* (with Jacquetta Hawkes, 1955), explained: 'This is my name for the whole system of an increasing productivity, plus inflation, plus a rising standard of material living, plus high-pressure advertising and salesmanship, plus mass-communications, plus cultural democracy and the creation of the mass-mind, the mass-man . . . It is better to live in admass than to have no job, no prospect of one, and see your wife and children getting hungrier and hungrier. But that is about all that can be said of it. All the rest is a swindle. You think everything is opening out when in fact it is narrowing down and closing in on you. Finally, you have to be half-witted or half-drunk all the time to endure it.'

A later graffito expressed it more succinctly: 'Advertising is Permanent Rape.'

Another word, 'subliminal', popularized by Vance Packard in *The Hidden Persuaders*, focused on the insidious exploitation by salesmen and politicians of the mass subconscious, directing a succession of brief images to lodge in the mind, associating pleasure, fulfilment, power and youth with their products. They were not always triumphant. A soup manufacturer gave away nylons for each can sold: people subconsciously associated soup with feet and were swiftly nauseated.

Anti-Americanism persisted, in line with William H. Whyte's *The Organisation Man* (1956) which showed how cartels, monopolies, trusts and conglomerations usurped the older American values of individualism, personal ambition and personal enterprise, replacing these with fealty to the vast, impersonal, amoral and ruthless. Consumerism was exploiting natural resources – oil, wood, soil, animals – with a feverish disregard of the future, a condition which provoked John Christopher's novel *The Death of Grass*, in which world famine overtakes the exhausted planet, the British government orders the destruction of Leeds by atomic power to reduce the population, and the island – like the rest of the world – reverts to anarchy, people clawing their way to agonized survival at whatever cost. An American, Fairfield Osborn, warned his countrymen in 1954 that in the last four decades they had used more world resources than the entire world had used in the four thousand years up to 1914.

Yet Fifties optimism was not quite exhausted. Philip Toynbee was excited because 'we now know more about each other than ever before', though the discoveries were not always wholesome. Despite a critic's conviction that colour television was a lunatic dream, 'the Box' was showing its mettle in such useful programmes as the current affairs *Tonight* (1957) and the arts survey, *Monitor* (1956). Feminism was stirring, promises abounded in infallible contraceptives, sexual utopias, schools yet more comprehensive built with yet more glass, and renewal of the fantasy and colour guaranteed by the Festival, already so long ago. Guarantees, however, eventually disappoint, and, forty years afterwards, glumly symptomatic, a Hampstead councillor queried financial aid for the Keats archive on grounds of élitism: also, 'for people to enjoy it, they would need the ability to read and write'. I myself scarcely bothered to calculate the implications of Britain's refusal to join the EEC from a position of advantage.

A debate began in 1959 between C. P. Snow and F. R. Leavis which, if it scarcely engrossed all Britain, certainly enlivened the weekly journals, injected as it was with acrimony, misinformation, personal prejudice and hilarious bad taste. It originated with a Cambridge lecture on 'The Two Cultures and the Scientific Revolution', by Snow, who had prevailed against my earlier strictures to his future wife and become a very popular 'serious' novelist. This, in Leavis's opinion, was a grave fault. He had also had considerable experience in practical and experimental science, 'privileged to have a ringside view of one of the most creative periods in all physics'. In his lecture he deplored the division between literature and the sciences, and seemed to apply to cultural aspirants a test, of being familiar with the Second Law of Thermodynamics, a test which I myself would not then have passed.

This was not new. Matthew Arnold and T. H. Huxley had debated the relations between science and literature. Seventy years previously, H. G. Wells had observed the gap between 'the superb and richly fruitful scientific investigations that are going on, and the general thought of the educated section of the community'. Shaw too mentioned to Virginia Woolf in 1940 that the neglect of the aesthetic factor in science had deprived it of its claim to be scientific. A. J. Ayer often lamented the disunity between science and philosophy, with such notable exceptions as Peter Medawar and Karl Popper, but admitted that he himself had done little to remedy it. In *Contact* (1946), V. S. Pritchett had extended the argument: 'hardly a writer in England knows what a factory is like, how a car is made or steel cast or ships built or cloth woven', while adding that literature concerning mines, shipyards, sidings, factories and mills has produced some of the dullest works of our time. Nevertheless, 'There is a divorce between life and literature, between life and popular culture. Where the imagination should dwell there is a vacuum, and the prospects of democratic culture, that famous, unborn babe, seem trivial. Man lives in a continual need for the description of his surroundings . . . That moment when the thousands burst out of the shipyard gates at five o'clock and blackened the streets; that other, when the waggons trickled over the lump in the marshalling yard, or when the hammer came down on the boiler end like some outrageous gong in an eastern temple: they called for print.'

In fact, such poets as Auden, Kathleen Raine, Peter Redgrove, Harry Kemp, Dannie Abse and Alex Comfort were scientifically equipped, and the new sculptors – Armitage, Butler, Paolozzi – seemed at home with technological processes, gadgetry, scientific impersonality. Wells, Russell, Whitehead and Ayer were not scientifically ignorant; even Virginia Woolf's fastidious *The Waves* has been interpreted as delineating not only prime elements within herself but also those analogous to the interplay of atoms natural to an intelligent contemporary of Rutherford, Jeans and Einstein. The cultural gap discerned by Pritchett was partially bridged by such novelists as Priestley, Jack Lindsay, A. J. Cronin, Nigel Balchin, William Cooper, Nevil Shute and Nicholas Mosley, and by young painters such as Josef Herman and Prunella Clough. A literary critic, Bernard Bergonzi, indifferent to Snow as a novelist, pursued this further: 'It could be argued that the art and literature of the modern movement reflect the deeply changed concept of reality that has been indicated, in its own way, by twentieth-century science. Cubist painting, and *Ulysses* and *The Waste Land* can be seen as products of a post-Newtonian model of the universe.'

There was some rift between science and literature but, for myself, the significant theme was the presence of a Third Culture, in which authoritarian technicians and amoral scientific experts could embrace the humanities with equal ease. The cruel and relentless Aztecs had been remarkable builders, sculptors and potters. Shlomo Aronson, biographer of the Nazi Gauleiter and terrorist Heydrich, attested that, as a violinist, he was 'mellow and delicate, his fingering first-rate and he showed outstanding feeling . . . and could be so moved by his own performance that he wept while playing'. Just so.

A substantial Fifties link between the worlds of Snow and of Leavis was the distinguished scientist Dr Jacob Bronowski, who also wrote radio plays and an opera, co-authored *The European Intellectual Tradition: from da Vinci to Hegel*, and wrote *The Common Sense of Science, Science and Human Values, The Poet's Defence*, and a study of William Blake. He enjoyed a mass television audience, in the BBC Brains Trust, alongside such thinkers as Julian Huxley, Marghanita Laski, A. J. Ayer and C. E. M. Joad.

My contact with this prodigy was at one remove, unexpected and, briefly, terrifying. I had been given tea in the office of a Midlands Director of Education. Afterwards, with a false smile, virtually a leer, he asked me if I would mind meeting a few interesting people. Politeness deterred me from reminding him that I had a train to catch, and that, though all people are of course interesting, too few give proof of it. 'Good!' He smiled again. 'Very good.' He then opened a green door, led me down a corridor, opened a brown door, and pushed rather than led me on to a stage, beneath which, seated in long curved rows, was an immense crowd of earnest men and women, a Teachers' Conference. My host, while I stood trapped, puzzled, near panic, then spoke words which still occasionally rattle through my dreams, clank through my waking hours.

> 'Dr Bronowski has been unable to turn up.'
> (Groans)
> 'Nevertheless, I am happy to introduce . . .'
> (Renewed and louder groans)

With that, the Director whisked away like the White Rabbit, leaving me to face the deprived multitude. After speaking I know not of what, I at least received Bronowski's cheque which, in my circumstances, was substantial.

F. R. Leavis was still insisting, if in prose sometimes rather tortured, that literature should relate to life, total existence, rather than to soulful trivialities and the escapades of ambitious careerists. Himself a powerful teacher, he thought that Snow's demand for more science at the expense of the humanities in education represented inorganic philistinism, having more in common with *Lucky Jim* than with Matthew Arnold and Ruskin. Literature meant access not to the corridors of power (Snow was to become Minister of Technology) but to the very springs of life, together with what Mrs Leavis liked to call delicacy of feeling. Snow, he continued, was uttering only specious clichés, and the 'society' depicted in his novels, with its hierarchies, titles, institutions, intrigues and rewards, was devoid of the full-blooded totality of Shakespeare, Blake, Dickens, D. H. Lawrence. One did not, of course, have to be Leavis's pupil to query Snow's suspect assertion that scientists were 'the soundest group of intellectuals we have', their culture on a 'higher conceptual level' than that of most literary folk by being more democratic, humane and socially respon-sible, freer from racialism and class-consciousness. Leavis, though he would have been displeased to hear it, was sharing Maugham's distaste for new, careerist universities. ('The white-collar proletariat', Maugham wrote, 'do not go to university to acquire culture but to get a job.') His acerbic personalizing of the issue added spice, even venom, to the dispute. First mentioning what he called really distinguished minds, deeply responsible to their age and thus illuminating, prophetic, influential, he added: 'Snow's relation to the age is of a different kind; it is characterised not by insight and spiritual energy, but by blindness, unconsciousness and automatism.' Snow, who resented personal criticism, made his own tart replies, largely in private, refusing Bernard

Miles's offer of the Mermaid Theatre for a counter-attack. Intellectuals, however, took sides, and correspondence columns briefly sagged beneath hefty names, to no very visible effect.

The Fifties, on the ebb, were leaving their beached memories: Brodsky reading Thom Gunn's poems to a bored peke, Jo Grimond's eloquent charm as he crusaded for the Common Market, Audrey Hepburn and George Peppard circling each other in *Breakfast at Tiffany's*, Joern Utzon's plans for the Sydney Opera House, Billy Graham's teeth and uplifted finger, Hitchcock's sinister *Strangers on a Train*, Castro reaching Havana, Eisenhower visiting Franco. Wurlitzer organs vanished into the depths forever, all lights blazing, like the *Titanic*. Tanks were on Paris streets in nervy 1958 when the French awaited a coup, expecting paratroops from the sky, until de Gaulle returned, saviour in classic style, to build the Fifth Republic. 'Little Willie' had died, also Arthur Schnabel, Eugene O'Neill, W. R. Hearst, Colette, and Thomas Mann. Bernard Berenson, whose secretary, Luisa Vertova, briefly married Benedict Nicolson, wrote in his diary for the last time before he too died, in 1959, aged 94: 'I remain sceptical about my personality. It really seems to have reached its present integration in the last twenty years, with the wide and far vision I now enjoy, with *tout comprendre c'est tout pardonner*, expecting little and trying to be grateful for that, the serenity for which I am now admired. But I keep hearing the Furies, and never forget them.'

In contrast to such dignified integration in Florence, in Rome there was shown Fellini's *La Dolce Vita* (1959), a glittering, acidulous revelation of shallow opulence, elegance concealing flesh and mind tettered as if with plague-spots. The film was rebuked by the Vatican as obscene, though it was scarcely being offered as a moral panacea, and caustically exposed the obscenity of prosperity.

Recalling these years, I have cited witnesses keener than myself. Another writer could have seen different things or seen the same things differently, and appealed to testimonies of wholly different persuasion. On the whole, I remember a pleasant enough decade, with the pitfalls and graces, atrocities and hopes inseparable from life in any period. More than once it made me mindful of Glubb Pasha's description, in *The Course of Empire* (1965), of eleventh-century Baghdad which, though in political and military decline, possessed, as he put it, a free medical service, new universities, disorderly youthful conduct, a five-day working week, with women flooding the learned professions, and much callow adoration of popular singers.

Bibliography and Acknowledgements

I MUST THANK all authors from whose work I have quoted. I enjoy sharing with readers the thoughts of my contemporaries and friends. There are a few poets whose full work I have been unable to trace in order to find its title. Complaints and demands should be addressed to me. In addition to books mentioned in the text, and journals, notably *Contact, Encounter, Twentieth Century, Horizon, World Review, London Magazine, Midstream, Adam* and *Nine*, I am grateful to the following authors, who have affected me in their various ways. All books were published in London unless otherwise stated.

Kenneth Allot (ed.), *The Penguin Book of Contemporary Verse*, Penguin, 1950
Lord Altrincham, *The National and English Review*, 1967
A. Alvarez (ed.), *The New Poetry*, Penguin, 1962
Robert Antelme, *L'Espèce Humaine*, Gallimard, 1957
Schlomo Aranson, *Heydrich*, Berlin, 1966
Alexandra Artley, *Murder in the Heart*, Hamish Hamilton, 1993
W. H. Auden, 'Letter to Lord Byron', 'As I Walked Out One Evening' and 'May',
    Collected Poems, edited by Edward Mendelson, Faber & Faber Ltd, 1976
A. J. Ayer, *Part of My Life*, Collins, 1977
Michael Ayrton, *A Matter of Pastiche*, Penguin New Writing, 1947
George Barker, *Eros in Dogma*, Faber & Faber 1944; and 'To Stephen Spender', *Collected
    Poems*, Faber & Faber Ltd, 1957
Sebastian Barker, *Who is Eddie Linden?* Landesmass, 1979
Cecil Beaton, *Diaries, 1948–55*, Weidenfeld & Nicolson, 1973
—— *Diaries, 1955–63*, Weidenfeld & Nicolson, 1976
Sybille Bedford, *As It Was*, Sinclair-Stevenson, 1991
Hilaire Belloc, *Places*, Cassell, 1942
—— *Stories, Essays and Poems*, Everyman's Library, 1938
—— *Selected Essays*, 1948
—— 'Lord Lucky', *More Peers*, 1911. © the estate of Hilaire Belloc. Reprinted by
    permission of Peters Fraser & Dunlop Ltd
Bernard Bergonzi, *The Situation of the Novel*, Macmillan, 1970
Isaiah Berlin, *Personal Impressions*, Hogarth Press, 1980

John Betjeman, *A Few Late Chrysanthemums*, John Murray, 1955

—— *John Piper*, Penguin, 1944

—— 'The Dear Old Village', *Collected Poems*. © John Betjeman 1958, 1962, 1970, 1979. Reprinted by permission of John Murray Publishers Ltd

Andrew Boyle, *No Passing Glory*, Collins, 1955

Edward Buca, *Vorkuta*, Constable, 1976

Alan Bullock, *Hitler and Stalin*, Harper Collins, 1991

Michael Burn, *Mr Lyward's Answer*, Hamish Hamilton, 1958

Elias Canetti, *The Torch in My Ear*, André Deutsch, 1989

David Caute, *Joseph Losey*, Faber & Faber, 1994

Anne Chisholm and Michael Davie, *Beaverbrook*, Hutchinson, 1992

Richard Coe, *Samuel Beckett*, Grove Press, 1964

Alex Comfort, 'Letter to an American Visitor', *Tribune*, 1943. Reprinted by permission of Dr Alex Comfort

Susan Cooper, *J. B. Priestley*, Heinemann, 1970

Noël Coward, *Future Indefinite*, Heinemann, 1954

Maurice Cranston, *Sartre*, Oliver & Boyd, 1962

R. H. S. Crossman, (ed.), *The God that Failed*, Hamish Hamilton, 1950

E. E. Cummings, 'anyone lived in a pretty how town', *Complete Poems 1904–1962*, edited by George J. Firmage. © 1940, 1968, 1991 by the Trustees for the E. E. Cummings Trust. Reprinted by permission of W. W. Norton & Company

Hugh Dalton, *Call Back Yesterday*, Muller, 1953

Walter de la Mare, 'Napoleon', *The Complete Poems of Walter de la Mare*, Faber & Faber Ltd, 1969. Reprinted by permission of the Literary Trustees of Walter de la Mare, and the Society of Authors as their representative

Michael De-la-Noy, *The Honours System*, Allison & Busby, 1985

Patric Dickinson, *The Good Minute*, Victor Gollancz, 1965

Milovan Djilas, *Conversations with Stalin*, Hart Davis, 1962

Charles Eade (ed.), *Churchill by His Contemporaries*, Hutchinson, 1953

T. S. Eliot, *Selected Essays*, Penguin, 1951

—— 'Choruses from 'The Rock IX', 'East Coker', 'Burnt Norton' and 'Burbank with a Baedecker: Bleistein with a Cigar', *Collected Poems 1909–1962*, Faber & Faber Ltd

Martin Esslin, *The Theatre of the Absurd*, New York, 1961

Daniel Farson, *Henry*, Michael Joseph, 1982

Leslie A. Fiedler, 'The Middle Against Both Ends,' in *Encounter*, 1955

G. S. Fraser, *Ezra Pound*, Oliver & Boyd, 1960

Donat Gallagher (ed.), *The Essays, Articles and Reviews of Evelyn Waugh*, Methuen, 1984

A. M. Gibbs (ed.), *Shaw: Interviews and Recollections*, Macmillan, 1990

Ralph Glasser, *Gorbals Boy at Oxford*, Chatto & Windus, 1988

Victoria Glendinning, *Rebecca West*, Weidenfeld & Nicolson, 1988

Margaret Gowing, *Independence and Deterrence: Britain and Atomic Energy 1945–52*

Kenneth Harris, *Attlee*, Weidenfeld & Nicolson, 1982

Ronald Hayman, *British Theatre Since 1955*, Oxford University Press, 1979

David Holbrook, *Llaregubb Revisited*, Bowes & Bowes, 1963

Michael Holroyd, *Lytton Strachey*, Heinemann, 1968

Harry Hopkins, *The New Look*, Secker & Warburg, 1964

Justine Hopkins, *Michael Ayrton*, André Deutsch, 1994

Aldous Huxley, *The Doors of Perception*, Chatto & Windus, 1954

—— *Heaven and Hell*, Chatto & Windus, 1956

C. G. Jung, *Memories, Dreams and Reflections*, Routledge, 1963

Nigel Jones, 'The Writer as Warrior: Ernst Jünger,' *London Magazine*, 1983

Anthony Kenny, *Thomas More*, Oxford University Press, 1983

John Kerr, *A Most Dangerous Method*, Sinclair-Stevenson, 1994

D. L. Kirkpatrick (ed.), *Contemporary Novelists*, St James's Press, 1986

Bernard Kops, in *The Financial Times*, 1992

George Lamming, *In the Castle of My Skin*, Michael Joseph, 1953

Philip Larkin, *The Less Deceived*, Marvell Press, 1955

—— *Required Writing*, Faber & Faber, 1983

Sylvia Lawson, 'Bags and Iron', *London Review of Books*, 1991

F. R. Leavis, *New Bearings in English Poetry*, Penguin, 1963

Peter Lewis, *The Fifties*, Herbert Press, 1989

Emanuel Litvinoff, *Notes for a Survivor*, Northern House, 1973

Elizabeth Longford, *The Pebbled Shore*, Weidenfeld & Nicolson, 1986

Nadezhda Mandelstam, *Hope Against Hope*, Collins Harvill, 1967

—— *Hope Abandoned*, Collins Harvill, 1974

John Masefield, 'An Epilogue', *Odtaa*, 1926. Reprinted by permission of the Society of Authors as literary representative of the Estate of John Masefield

Jeffrey Meyers, 'André Malraux: The Art of Action,' in *London Magazine*, 1975

Kenneth Minogue, 'Che Guevara': in Maurice Cranston (ed.), *The New Left*, Bodley Head, 1970

Caroline Moorehead, *Troublesome People*, Hamish Hamilton, 1987

Ted Morgan, *Somerset Maugham*, Jonathan Cape, 1980

Sheridan Morley, *A Talent to Amuse*, Pavilion Books and Michael Joseph, 1985

Nicholas Mosley, *Rules of the Game*, Weidenfeld & Nicolson, 1982

Norman Moss, *Klaus Fuchs*, Collins, 1987

Malcolm Muggeridge, 'On Suez', in *New Statesman*, 1956

A. S. Neill, *The Free School*, Herbert Jenkins, 1953

Nigel Nicolson, *Portrait of a Marriage*, Weidenfeld & Nicolson, 1970

Iris Orton, *The Dreamer and the Sheaves*, Oxford University Press, 1956

George Orwell, 'From One Combatant to Another', *Tribune*, 1943. © the Estate of the late Sonia Brownell Orwell. Reprinted by permission of A. M. Heath & Co Ltd

John Osborne, in *Declaration*, ed. T. Maschler, Jonathan Cape, 1957

—— 'The Entertainer', *The Entertainer and Other Plays*', Faber & Faber Ltd, 1956

Frances Partridge, *Other People*, Harper Collins, 1993

Boris Pasternak, *An Essay in Autobiography*, Collins Harvill, 1959

Albert Pierrepoint, *Executioner Pierrepoint*, Harrap, 1974

Ben Pimlott, *Hugh Dalton*, Jonathan Cape, 1985

Paul Potts, 'About Walt Whitman', in *New Road*, Grey Walls Press, 1949

—— 'Dante Called You Beatrice,' *Poetry London*, 1960

Ezra Pound, 'Lustra' sequence, *Selected Poems*, Faber & Faber Ltd, 1938

V. S. Pritchett, *A Cab at the Door*, Chatto & Windus, 1968

—— *Collected Essays*, Chatto & Windus, 1991

—— *London Perceived*, Chatto & Windus, with Heinemann, 1962

Frederic Prokosch, *Storm and Echo*, Faber & Faber, 1959

—— *Voices*, Faber & Faber, 1983

Maria Rivas, *Marlene Dietrich*, Bloomsbury, 1993

Theodore Roseburg, *Life on Man*, Secker & Warburg, 1970

Alan Ross, *The Forties*, Weidenfeld & Nicolson, 1950. Alan Ross is Editor of *London Magazine*, a valuable literary record of the post-war period.

—— 'To Stanley Matthews'. Reprinted by permission of Alan Ross

A. L. Rowse, *Memories of Men and Women*, Eyre Methuen, 1980

Bertrand Russell, *Autobiography*, Allen & Unwin, 1967–9

Siegfried Sassoon, 'Doggerel About Old Days', *Collected Poems 1957*. Reprinted by permission of George Sassoon

D. S. Savage, *The Personal Principle*, Routledge, 1944

Albert Schweitzer, *More From the Primeval Forest*, Allen & Unwin, 1931

—— *The Quest for the Historical Jesus*, Berlin, 1901

Ignazio Silone, *The Story of a Humble Christian*, Victor Gollancz, 1970

Robert Skidelsky, *Oswald Mosley*, Macmillan, 1975

Colin Smythe, *A Guide to Coole Park*, Smythe, 1983

Albert Speer, *The Secret Diaries*, Collins, 1976

Stephen Spender, *Eliot*, Fontana Collins, 1975

—— *World Within World*, Hamish Hamilton, 1951

Derek Stanford, *Inside the Forties*, Sidgwick & Jackson, 1977

Christopher Sykes, *Evelyn Waugh*, Collins, 1975

David Sylvester, *Interviews with Francis Bacon*, Thames and Hudson, 1975

A. J. P. Taylor, *English History, 1914–1945*, Oxford University Press, 1965

Dylan Thomas, 'Poem in October', *The Poems*, J. M. Dent, 1953. Reprinted by permission of David Higham Associates Ltd

Anthony Thwaite (ed.), *Selected Letters of Philip Larkin: 1940–85*, Faber & Faber, 1992

Arnold Toynbee, *Experiences*, Oxford University Press, 1969

Kathleen Tynan, *The Life of Kenneth Tynan*, Weidenfeld & Nicolson, 1987

Kenneth Tynan, *Tynan Right and Left*, Weidenfeld & Nicolson, 1967

Peter Vansittart, *Paths from a White Horse: A Writer's Memoir*, Quartet, 1985

John Wain, *A House for the Truth*, Macmillan, 1972

Simone Weil, 'The Iliad, or, the Poem of Force', in *The Mint*, 1948

Rebecca West, *Black Lamb, Grey Falcon*, Macmillan, 1941–2

Theresa Whistler, *Imagination of the Heart: the Life of Walter de la Mare*, Duckworth, 1993

John Whitehead, 'The Poetry of Frederic Prokosch', in *London Magazine*, 1990

Simon Wiesenthal, *The Murderers Amongst Us*, Heinemann, 1967

Richard Wilbur, 'Mind', *New and Collected Poems*, Faber & Faber Ltd, 1956

A. N. Wilson, *Hilaire Belloc*, Hamish Hamilton, 1984

Angus Wilson, *The Wild Garden*, Secker & Warburg, 1963

Stephen Winsten, *Days with Bernard Shaw*, Hutchinson, 1957

Leonard Woolf, *Beginning Again*, Hogarth Press, 1964

—— *Sowing*, Hogarth Press, 1960

—— *Growing*, Hogarth Press, 1961

—— *Downhill All the Way*, Hogarth Press, 1967

Peregrine Worsthorne, *Tricks of Memory*, Weidenfeld & Nicolson, 1993

James Wright, *The Branch Will Not Break*, Longman, 1963

Yevgeny Yevtushenko, 'Heirs of Stalin', *Early Poems*, Calder & Boyars, 1957. Reprinted by permission of Marion Boyars Ltd

I must also add very deep thanks to my editors, Gail Pirkis and Roger Hudson, without whose patient skills the book would have been more shapeless and yards longer; to Douglas Matthews who, as always, has done me a splendid index; to my close friend Margot Walmsley for, once again, invaluable help with the proofs; and to Terry Jordan, for courageously grappling with my handwriting.

Index